EVERYBODY WANTS YOUR MONEY

EVERYBODY WANTS YOUR MONEY

The Straight-Talking Guide to Protecting
(and Growing)
the Wealth You Worked So Hard to Earn

DAVID W. LATKO

Collins

An Imprint of HarperCollinsPublishers

EVERYBODY WANTS YOUR MONEY. Copyright © 2006 by David W. Latko. All rights reserved. Printed in the United States of America. No part of this book may be used or reproduced in any manner whatsoever without written permission except in the case of brief quotations embodied in critical articles and reviews. For information, address HarperCollins Publishers, 10 East 53rd Street, New York, NY 10022.

HarperCollins books may be purchased for educational, business, or sales promotional use. For information, please write: Special Markets Department, HarperCollins Publishers, 10 East 53rd Street, New York, NY 10022.

FIRST EDITION

Designed by Joseph Rutt

Library of Congress Cataloging-in-Publication Data has been applied for.

ISBN-13: 978-0-06-085115-6
ISBN-10: 0-06-085115-5

06 07 08 09 10 DIX/RRD 10 9 8 7 6 5 4 3 2 1

For my wife, Jan, who is the beacon of my life, and my two children: Tiffany, who I know will always choose to dance; and David Jr., whose sensitivity and insights never fail to amaze me.

CONTENTS

ACKNOWLEDGMENTS

Not only do I enjoy a splendid private life, but I think I just may have the most fascinating career in the world. No, not presidential important or movie-star exciting, just plain interesting.

On a daily basis, people trust me implicitly with their hard-earned assets earned over a lifetime to secure their financial futures. Not only do they trust me with their personal financial world, but in most cases the decisions I make will affect their family's fortune for years, sometimes for generations, to come.

To me, it sure beats trying to sway a jury with theatrical rhetoric or being the proverbial yes-man in some corporate hierarchy. Fortunately for me, I learned a couple of decades ago that I don't take orders very well—a fact supported by several past employers who abruptly asked me to take my career and move on down the road.

Today, if time starts to drag, I have the luxury of throwing back the doors to my radio studio and taping a segment of my nationally broadcast radio show, *David Latko's Money & More.*

On the show, my cohost, Earl Merkel, and I talk and share views with some of the most fascinating and powerful people in the world. How many people can say they spent time today with Steve Forbes, Newt Gingrich, Neil Cavuto, Richard Kiyosaki, Lis Wiehl, Brian Kilmeade and other household names too numerous to mention? Better yet, many of these same people I now have the pleasure of calling "friend."

And then there are my books, of which this is the second in what I envision to be a long list of titles to help the everyday investor better understand and master the pitfalls of the financial world that surrounds him or her. All seen not from some theoretical perspective, but instead from someone who has been in the trenches and dug his way out.

Or maybe on this day I will be the guest on someone else's radio show, maybe a television interview awaits, or I may have the pleasure of speaking in front of hundreds of people in a crowded lecture hall. Few people will ever have this privilege to express in print, over the airwaves, or as a guest speaker the sum total of what they have learned in life.

But even though I love the old Frank Sinatra song "My Way" and have built my career and fortune in similar fashion, this book would not be in your hands today without assistance.

Help from my wife, Jan, without whose love, support, and encouragement I would not be the individual I am today. Also my two children, Tiffany and David Jr., whose happiness, well-being, and future have been my greatest enjoyment and motivation since their births.

But I also owe a special thanks to Herb Schaffner, senior editor at HarperCollins, an individual with whom I instantly felt a special bond, from the moment he came down the elevator to shake my hand and welcome me to the HarperCollins family. I trust in him and believe his expertise will undoubtedly take my final effort to a new plateau.

I must also thank Marion Maneker, who, with Herb Schaffner and all the great people behind the scenes at HarperCollins, made me feel right at home from day one and helped make this book what it is today.

A gigantic thank-you goes to writer and author Earl Merkel, great friend, radio-show cohost, and sometime personal psychological guru who never lets me believe that the glass is anything but half-full. Through his perseverance, dedication, persistence, and humor this book is now complete.

But also, this book could not have been written without the help of my dedicated staff, which was always there to pick up the slack so I could spend the time writing just one more page.

Kudos to Gary Russell; even though we live hundreds of miles apart, our daily telephone visits and genuine interest in each other's life have allowed us to chuckle at all of life's struggles. His laughter, encouragement, and camaraderie could not be replaced with a mountain of gold. Well, on second thought . . . maybe it could.

I also must thank my agent, Sharlene Martin, for her tireless days, fierce loyalty, and her constant struggle for perfection in all I do. I no longer call her my agent; she is now my friend.

Of course I thank my clients, without whose life stories over the last quarter century this book would have little meaning. I only hope in their eyes, through our friendship, I have given as much as they have shared.

And thank you to my father, John J. Latko, and my late mother, Violet, for instilling in me the values, tools, and discipline to allow me not to shoot just for the stars, but far beyond. Although the years we have left together may be few, I will feel your love for eternity. Thanks also to my late stepmother, Genevieve, for her concern and daily prayers.

To my only brother, John Latko, I feel blessed that I have the exceptional privilege to see you in my office day after day to discuss, and resolve, all the world's problems. Although you are frequently wrong, I love you, and you will always be my big brother.

A very special thank-you to Dr. Tim Harlow, head pastor of Parkview Church, for helping me rekindle my relationship with God, a flame that I am ashamed to say at times seemed in danger of becoming extinguished.

Finally, to God, for the plan He has for me, and for holding my hand through life.

—David W. Latko
January 2006

IT'S TRUE. EVERYBODY *DOES* WANT YOUR MONEY.

If I had consciously set out to come up with a philosophic manifesto that would echo the ravings of a street-corner schizophrenic, I could not have done better than the title of this book.

I *love* it. *Everybody Wants Your Money*—doesn't that say it *all*?

Still, even after months of laboring over the pages you are about to read, I look at the title and imagine myself standing on a soapbox in what my fellow Chicago-area natives still affectionately call "Bughouse Square," alternating between incoherent muttering and impassioned outcries, detailing dark conspiracies and heinous plots.

But, as one of my clients told me not so long ago, "It ain't paranoia if they're really out to get you."

And "they" are, my friend; they *really* are.

In today's world, there's no shortage of charlatans and con artists lying in wait for the innocent or the unwary. Pick up any newspaper, tune in to any TV news program (local or network national), and the evidence is clear: we are as far from a utopian society as humankind ever was.

To paraphrase Blanche DuBois, late of the still-soggy wasteland that was once New Orleans, we've all come to depend on the kindness of strangers—a level of naïveté not dissimilar to that of the wildebeest calf who saunters toward the water hole, assuming that those lurking shapes awash near the shoreline are merely harmless logs.

The result: today's crocodiles are sleek and well fed, both those found in nature and their two-legged brethren alike.

And that's why I wrote this book: it is my humble attempt to pry apart the links of the food chain that bind prey to predator, economically speaking.

An honored adage in an earlier Wild West stated simply: "God made all men. But Samuel Colt made all men *equal.*" Used effectively, the information I present in these pages can serve the same purpose that the Colt Peacemaker did on the American frontier. Knowledge is power, and power is the great equalizer for all of us.

But do not think that I target only the faceless predators out there who consciously seek to do us harm.

In my career as a financial advisor and counselor, I've regularly been taken aback by the damage I've observed inflicted on the financial well-being by members of the victim's own family—often, with the best of intentions.

A parent dies, for instance, and well-meaning adult children gather to provide vital emotional support for the surviving partner—and then, because "don't we have to do *something* now?," well-meaning kids assume the mantle of decision makers in matters of which they are clueless. When those decisions involve the surviving parent's money, the result can be horrific—both from a financial viewpoint and in terms of the emotional toll inflicted on all involved.

So I deal with that situation in this book, too—along with other examples of how to protect your finances from the people you love . . .

. . . or, conversely, from those persons who no longer love *you*.

Divorce is a fact of life in today's world, and the adverse impact it can have when one life is severed into two has become almost a cliché. A cold analysis of divorce statistics presents a clear picture: in virtually every instance, the so-called equitable division of marital assets results in near-term financial disaster for the female partner.

"Who-gets-what-and-for-how-long-sign-here-please" is the rule rather than the exception in American divorces. It's a shameful situation, and one the American legal system appears incapable of resolving.

But in this book I propose a new initiative, a fresh system of projecting precisely how "equitable" any proposed divorce settlement will ultimately be. In that way, both parties—as well as the legal system that oversees the divorce process—can clearly understand the long-term impact of the decisions they are making . . . and as a result, retain the money, property, and security that is rightfully theirs.

Other chapters deal with real estate, investments, identity theft, estate planning, the secrets of buying cars without being cheated— even the ever-expanding varieties of con games and scams that target all of us today. If you consider this book a survival guide for modern times, you won't be exaggerating its scope or intention.

Everybody Wants Your Money is not a textbook, however—far from it, in fact. I've used the human stories of my friends and clients to populate each chapter with real-life illustrations and examples. The names have been changed, and where it was necessary I've done what I could to preserve the privacy of the individuals concerned—but I hope the flesh-and-blood qualities of those whose experiences I use here still comes through clearly.

Who is "David Latko," and why should you accept what I will present in this book?

I was raised in a lower-middle-class family in northwest Indiana not far outside Chicago, famous today as the "buckle of the rust belt." I grew up hearing my father say that education was the only way up (which to us meant "out"). His words had weight with me, in large part because I knew that he had to drop out of high school in the 1930s, taking a job to help out financially at home.

And as is often the case with those who have little, there was always someone trying to ensure that we had even less.

Willie Sutton famously proclaimed that he robbed banks because "that's where the money is." But not all crime focuses on the single "big score"; stealing the widow's mite—from a *lot* of widows—is a long-practiced approach of the despicable bottom-feeders who prey on the impoverished.

For that reason, much of my early education was aimed at making me what today pop sociologists would call street-smart.

I learned early in life how to penetrate the smoke screen of half-truths and lies that surround every scheme. I learned what questions to ask, and (even more important) what answers I should expect. I learned to double-check any so-called fact I encountered, and to examine all so-called conventional wisdom through the microscope of common sense.

But I didn't ignore the "book larn'ing," either.

I started college, and did rather well, while still attending high school at age sixteen. At my graduation, I was young, energetic, good-looking (I also had plenty of modesty, you'll note), and the proud possessor of not one, but *two* master's degrees.

I've worked in the legal system as a court administrator and served in other functions on the government payroll. After several odd attempts in the private sector (a few of them *very* odd indeed), I landed a position with E. F. Hutton, one of the biggest firms on Wall Street. I was elated; I had finally found my niche. I would be *around* a great deal of money, even if it was not my own.

From there I was lured to another major brokerage house, and then another—a managerial position with the biggest name on Wall Street.

Quickly, I only learned that as a boss, I now merely reported to an even more important boss. Worse, my new company managed strictly "by the book" (*their* book) and discouraged what they scornfully termed "independent thinking."

I still remember my last day. As I carried my boxes to the car, the executive to whom I had reported followed in lockstep, scornfully telling me what a mistake I had made; *I would never succeed on my own.*

I'll fast-forward past the next sixteen years. But if you listen closely, you'll hear that they have their own sound track. It's one of my favorite songs: "My Way" by Frank Sinatra.

These lyrics became my mantra. "Mistakes, I made a few . . . but too few to mention . . . but this, much more than this: I did it my way."

I've built a company that manages more than $100 million in assets entrusted to my supervision; I've become a self-made multi-millionaire; I've written books, appeared on national network television programs, written columns for newspapers, and hosted my own nationally broadcast radio program, where I've interviewed such luminaries as Jack Welch, Steven Forbes, House Speaker Dennis Hastert, Fox News' Neil Cavuto, Brian Kilmeade, Oliver North, and too many other fascinating people to list here.

Throughout this time and these experiences, there has been only one constant: by the grace of God and because of the upbringing I was given, I never forgot to *learn*.

In recent years, as an author and host of talk radio's *David Latko's Money & More,* I've been given the rare opportunity to share much of what I've gleaned throughout my life with people who had a crying need for such knowledge.

Because you're reading *Everybody Wants Your Money,* the odds are good that you have such a need, too. I hope that this book provides everything that you require.

Again, knowledge is power. As you acquire the former, I'm confident that you will feel the latter grow within yourself.

Savor it: it's the feeling of freedom—of knowing you can protect yourself. Few experiences equal the satisfaction you will experience.

I envy you this voyage of discovery.

—David W. Latko
January 2006

HOW BROKERS, ADVISORS, AND OTHER "PROFESSIONALS" GET THEIR HANDS INTO YOUR POCKETS— AND HOW TO BEAT THEM AT THEIR OWN GAME

ONE

THE NAME OF THE GAME . . .

If life were truly straightforward, you could discover much of what I write about in this book on your own—simply by tapping a key on a computer.

Do you want honest information about an investment in which you're considering placing your hard-earned money? *Tap!* Do you need to calculate the mix of risk versus reward—in professional circles, we call this "asset allocation"—that is right for your age, income, family situation, and so on? *Tap!* Do you feel an urgent desire to separate the scams from the genuine opportunities? *Tap!*

Alas, despite the proliferation of ever-more-powerful computers and access to ever-more-voluminous data offered by today's Information Age, it seems that about all one taps into is an ever-increasing level of maddening confusion, personal frustration, overly complicated efforts at elucidation—and outright misinformation.

Not coincidentally, this is precisely what most of us have come to expect when dealing with actual human "professionals."

There's a reason for this. And as with so much of what passes for "reason" in the world of personal finance, it's not good news for most common folks.

Consider: Do you *really* need a financial advisor to invest your money? Of course not; with the proper access to accurate information, you could calculate your financial requirements, track performance records, determine a risk tolerance acceptable to you, and come up with a pretty good financial plan for yourself.

But the fact is that most people wouldn't. They've been convinced by a barrage of TV commercials that they are incapable of it. They are terrified at the prospect of navigating these dark waters without an "expert" hand on the tiller. And as a result, many of us throw open our doors to often-affable strangers—"experts" whose concern for *our* prosperity comes in a distant second to their own and that of the companies they represent.

The sad fact is that in today's world, there are relatively few real experts in finance (or law, health care, or any of the purported "professional" disciplines)—but certainly, there are vastly more expert *salespersons* than most people realize. Consider it the victory of style over content, of hyperbolic sizzle over the authentic flavor of a fine steak.

Over the next few pages, I'll show you how slick salesmanship, not professional competence, allows many so-called professionals to get their hands on your money—often leaving you without the slightest clue of how it happened, or that it even happened at all.

———————

Let's start with the person you most need to trust: your personal-finance hired gun, the financial advisor.

It's not hard to find a financial advisor these days; in fact, it's hard to avoid 'em. Stand on virtually any street corner in the United States and throw a brick in any direction. Odds are good you'll incapacitate at least one so-called financial advisor and wing several more.

According to the National Association of Security Dealers (NASD), today there are more than 650,000 "registered representatives" toiling away approximately at 100,000 branch offices, representing over 5,000 member firms.

What they all have in common is that each office is filled with people who understand without reservation that they must produce or perish. It's a savagely Darwinian existence for them; an apt analogy is that of a pack of hungry dogs snarling and slashing and snapping at the prospect of any fresh meat that happens their way.

Guess who is cast in *that* singularly unappetizing role?

Nonetheless, the atmosphere at most brokerages, wire houses, or financial-advisor offices (with minor exceptions, these are inter-changeable terms) is carefully designed to camouflage their intrinsic carnality. In fact, *au contraire;* in most of them, you'd swear that you had transported to a land populated by particularly benevolent Rotarians.

If you've been escorted to an office (you may not be: see below), you'll likely find the desk festooned with pictures straight out of Norman Rockwell; an attractive spouse and adoring children beam at the random visitor from every frame.

Some of these pictures are, I'm sure, even real. Nonetheless, back in my own days at a major brokerage office, I knew of several bro-kers who acquired their "family" pictures secondhand. One knot of brokers even traded their desk pictures back and forth in a regular rotation—in their own way, perhaps, spicing up their fictionally monogamous worklives.

More likely, particularly if you are a "walk-in" to the brokerage—that is, one who has not been prescreened to determine how much money you represent—you may not even be sitting in an office. In-stead, you're walked to one of several open cubicles known to the initiated as the "bull pen."

If so, this is a sure sign that the broker smiling warmly at you is either a raw rookie or a snakebitten veteran who has had an ex-tended streak of miserable luck; either way, the branch manager has a chart that lists your prospective broker's name lower than the for-tunate few assigned a *real* office.

That's right; neither age nor seniority nor union rules holds sway here. Produce income—for the firm, that is—and a broker moves into an office (or into a nicer one, if she's a *real* moneymaker). Have an off year, and she's back among the Dilberts on the main floor. Ironically, brokers are themselves commodities: fungible assets, cogs in a machine that relentlessly reconstitutes itself with ease. Every month, brokerage firms receive thousands of applications from new-bie salespersons, each hoping to sign on and cash in.

The stakes are indeed high: produce a paltry $200,000 in annual commissions for the firm, and the hapless broker will feel the bull's-eye on his back. Make it half a million, and he probably will be al-lowed to keep his desk . . . at least for another year. Losers are not tolerated, but a top producer can earn a seven-figure income. All he has to do is keep selling, keep moving the product—*and keep earning more money for the firm.*

Note the emphasis: the focus is on the company whose name is above the door—the Morgan Stanleys, the Merrill Lynches. It's not on the client—that is, *you*—and that fact alone illustrates the peril faced by the average investor who seeks professional advice.

The reality is a far cry from the image that brought you there in the first place: that of the deeply involved financial advisor, a personal friend—so close that he can make the keynote speech at your daughter's wedding. *(NOTE: My personal favorite of the genre comes courtesy of Charles Schwab Corporation, the mammoth discount brokerage firm; in it, an earnest voice-over warmly invites you to "call Chuck" for a consultation—blithely finessing the fact that the Chuck in question is founder Charles R. Schawb. With a current personal net worth estimated by* Forbes *at $2.6 billion and in place at the head of a firm with millions of accounts and billions in assets managed, one wonders just how many callers get through to Chuck unscreened.)*

Campaigns abound with such images on TV, radio, and the print media. Mass seminars—often promoted through costly direct mailing campaigns, frequently held at such costly venues as country clubs, and known generically as the "swordfish dinner" circuit—add to the price of promoting the services offered. Major brokerages spend a staggering tally of advertising dollars annually—all of it aimed merely to motivate you to drop into an office and talk about the sackful of money Aunt Mabel left you. The major houses do all this just to *become your friend*—more accurately, to convince you that your new best buddy is the smiling person with the steely eyes who now sits across the table from you.

Know this: with any brokerage, you are at a disadvantage. You are up against a finely tuned machine, designed to extract every last dollar they can from your pocket. They will do this legally (in most cases), and invest your money in assets that actually exist (in most cases). But in *virtually every case* they will do it in a way designed primarily to profit themselves, and to benefit you only secondarily.

So what is one to do?

Well, many financial advice books will simply tell you to do it yourself, and proceed to outline their version of how to do that. I consider this advice akin to suggestions on how to swim amid hungry sharks: it may be well-intentioned counsel, but it is clearly fraught with peril . . . and certainly, one could find fault in the underlying wisdom of the act itself.

The truth is there are millions of people with trillions of dollars who simply don't *want* to handle their financial affairs—certainly not by themselves, alone. They have neither the time to spend acquiring the knowledge nor the luxury of being secure enough financially to survive their inevitable mistakes.

Throughout my career, I've met thousands of people who feel this way. They may be widows, or retirees, or business owners, or . . . well, I've found that they may be just about *anybody.* Their common denominator is that they have money to invest—literally, in the aggregate, trillions of dollars. That makes them, as a group, a significant factor in our economy. It also makes them an attractive target for the unscrupulous among us.

A good example of what can happen comes in the form of Willa and Tony, a retired couple who became my clients after a horrific experience with their first advisor. A working-class couple and lifelong residents of Chicago's South Side, they had never experienced significant financial prosperity—until a 401(k) plan to which Tony had diligently contributed over the years came into their life.

"We had never had any kind of financial advisor," Tony confided in one of our early meetings. "Why should we have? Heck, we never had any money before."

That changed, to the tune of slightly more than $450,000—an impressive windfall for them and an important factor in their retirement-life security, and certainly more useful than the gold-plated watch that Tony's former employer also bestowed.

"We were scared silly," Willa admitted. "We had done all our own bill paying, banking, and so on for almost forty-five years. But all this money! We knew we didn't have a clue about what to do."

So they solicited some advice from other retired friends. One of them had received a postcard in the mail a week before, and he passed it along to Tony and Willa. It gave the name and number of a financial advisor who worked in a branch office of a major brokerage.

"I knew the company's name from TV," Tony said drily. "They were the people with the big bull." He grimaced. "They sure fed me a lot of bull, at least."

In short order, their new advisor "handled" their prosperity problem. He put them into a range of investments that Willa and Tony did not clearly understand. Then, after a month or so of frenetic activity, he stopped calling—or returning *their* calls.

After a period of growing frustration, during which time they mentioned their problem to a person who happened to be a client of mine, one bright morning they arrived at my office without an appointment. Fortunately, I had a light schedule that day—and after all, they were friends of a client.

It didn't take long to diagnose the problem. Their broker had locked them into investments that carried staggeringly large up-front commissions; others carried long-term (and expensive) surrender charges.

"We were taken," Tony summarized, his voice glum, as I explained the situation.

I felt awful; there was little I could do to salvage the situation. The couple was tied into investments that could not be changed without taking a significant financial hit—in Tony's case, the tab would have come to more than $26,000. The best I could offer was to help them restructure some of the smaller items in their account. Somehow, the broker had overlooked a bit of Tony and Willa's money in his campaign to hike his commissions; this amount we moved into more suitable vehicles—none of which had *any* surrender charges or up-front commissions. On everything else, they were stuck.

Tony and Willa are not unique.

In this section of my book, I provide a window into the workings of the so-called professionals who forage in the field of personal finance. Knowing how they tick—what motivates them, how they earn their salaries, and more—will give you invaluable insights as to what they want from *you*.

To help you cull the chaff from the wheat (more accurately, the venial from the wise), I list ten questions you must ask *any* prospective broker/financial advisor *before* you sign on the dotted line. But even more valuable are the answers to these questions, which I provide—answers that you should expect to hear from the advisors you interview. As a bonus, I've provided a guide that helps you understand why the scoring for each question is important to you. With these answers, you will be armed with the knowledge you need to separate the charlatan from the true expert resource.

Knowledge is power. So accompany me as we examine how the financial game is rigged . . . against *you*.

TWO

FINANCIAL ADVISORS: TALES FROM THE DARK SIDE

The tale is told of a busload of brokers, money managers, and financial advisors who took the wrong turn in the backcountry region of the Ozarks. The driver lost control and crashed the vehicle into a ditch. A farmer happened by and, finding the occupants of the bus lying in the road, buried them.

The state police arrived on the scene just as he finished tamping the dirt down over the last one.

"You buried *all* of them?" asked the police officer. "You sure they were all dead?"

"Well, some of 'em *said* they wasn't," answered the farmer, "but you know how them kind of people lie."

And so it goes. There's an odd sort of inconsistency that, over my quarter century in the financial field, I've noted time and again.

Virtually everyone who has ever dealt with a "financial professional" has done so despite a definite skepticism, if not a sense of downright paranoia—after all, we "know how them kind of people lie." Nonetheless, the vast majority of us turn over our money (and our hope for long-term security) to complete strangers, about whose record or background we know little, and about whose trustworthiness we know even less.

Even the savviest of hard-bitten business executives fall prey to this puzzling paradox. At work—or in any endeavor that they understand and in which they feel competent—none of them would dream of handing over their hard-earned nest egg to anyone whose bona fides they had not checked with a level of thoroughness not unlike that of an Interpol investigator.

So what's the story? Why do so many otherwise capable, intelligent adults drop the ball here?

There are two possible reasons—one of which I simply find hard to believe. Let's start with that one, just to get it behind us.

1. Laziness.

Instead of doing your own search for the financial advisor who is right for you, it's simply easier to take the recommendation of your friends, your accountant, or even your lawyer. If you follow the advice of others, consider it only as the starting point . . . not the finish line.

Sadly, word of mouth is by far the usual way we find a new doctor, lawyer, or financial advisor. Humans are social animals; we like the comfort of the herd—of knowing, if only subconsciously, that even if we've made a mistake, at least we're not alone in doing so.

It's obvious why the lazy person's approach to financial expertise is foolhardy: What does your friend *actually know* about the advisor he uses? Did he make the recommendation because his advisor is a charming guy with a six handicap who drives a flashy Porsche Turbo? Did your friend do *his* homework, researching all the areas that determine demonstrated competence, a proven record of performance, and a history of trustworthiness?

Does your friend even know the right questions to ask?

Aha! Now we're getting somewhere—because this is where I believe most people stumble, surrendering their common sense and walking single file up the ramp to the slaughterhouse floor. Rather than laziness, I believe our problem is the result of . . .

2. Lack of knowledge of *how* to find a good financial advisor.

The sad fact is that—in more than twenty-five years of interviewing thousands of potential clients in my office—inevitably, *I am the one who asks the questions!* Let me repeat: over a quarter century, *not one person* who has entered my office seeking advice has come armed with a list of questions to ask me about my business, background, clients, financial strategies, or the like.

The fact is that most people don't understand the complex and often-illogical machine that is the financial world. They're baffled by the stock market, not understanding the fickle forces that drive it up or down; they read the financial pages of their newspapers, studying articles written by "experts" (never suspecting that these experts are, all too often, themselves totally ignorant of the processes on which they report). They suspect the financial markets are part of a "fixed game" (and sometimes we find it is, but not often); as a result, they seek as an advisor anyone who has the slick confidence to talk a "good game" (even if that talk is often febrile nonsense).

When we don't understand how something works, we tend to look for an expert. If the problem is automotive, all we look for is a good mechanic; but if it is financial, for a number of deep (and dark) psychological reasons, many of us look for a magician.

It seldom works. There's a right way and a wrong way to seek financial help; the right way works and the wrong doesn't.

So let's let Laura illustrate the difference between these two paths. Along the way, her story will also help you understand precisely how to find the right financial advisor for *you*.

———————

My mother used to tell me, "There's no sense in closing the barn door after the horses are already gone"—a statement that, since we were too poor to own horses, I figured had to be metaphoric. So it was with Laura; in her case, just substitute the words *financial advisor* for *barn door* and *money* for the horses.

By the time I met her, Laura had already run afoul of my Prime Axiom of Financial Health: get all your financial ducks in order *before* you need them.

She had divorced her husband almost six years before, when she discovered that he had set up house with a twenty-year-younger woman who was a client of his law firm. Prior to this revelation (and the subsequent legal proceedings), Laura's ex-husband had handled everything that dealt with the couple's finances. Every time Laura asked a question—and, she reluctantly admitted to me, that wasn't nearly often enough—her husband, Ben, would express contempt at her concerns.

When the dust settled from the divorce, Laura took the advice of a friend. She made an appointment with a financial advisor at one of those name-brand brokerage houses one sees advertised each day on TV. She had a mid-six-figure settlement (as it turned out, even that amount was inequitable; see Chapter 14, which deals specifically with divorce matters). Still shell-shocked by the exhausting divorce proceedings, she was grateful to find a financial advisor so quickly and effortlessly.

"He certainly was charming," Laura recalled. "He *sounded* as if he knew what he was doing."

"What did you ask him about his qualifications, or his record?" I inquired, trying to sound neutral.

"Not much . . . actually, not anything."

"Did he ever discuss investment strategy?" I asked. "Or talk about how he was going to invest your funds?"

"No, not really." Her tone was wary now.

"I don't want to make you feel pressured, Laura," I said. "But you were trying to decide whether to give him just about every dollar you had. Exactly what *did* he tell you?"

She was silent for a moment, then shook her head.

"That he was going to take good care of me; that I should trust him."

I grinned to take away the sting of my next words.

"Sound familiar?"

"It was exactly what my ex-husband would say." She shrugged, ruefully. "Okay—so I figured that if he was good enough for my friend, he was good enough for me. I turned all my financial problems over to him."

And with that, Laura had signed the papers, handing over a check for slightly more than $400,000 to a virtual stranger.

It's humorous, in a way: people talk about their former financial advisor much like many erstwhile sailors talk about boats. You know the story: boat owners are happiest on two days—the day they *buy* the boat and the day they *sell* it.

This was certainly the case for Laura. She recalled feeling as if a massive weight had lifted from her that day she signed with her friend's advisor. But as the months passed by, her account became stuck in neutral, despite an ongoing series of buy-and-sell trades. Then the net worth of her account began to slip—slowly at first, but steadily.

" 'Think long-term,' he'd say," Laura told me. "That is, when I could reach him. He always seemed to be in a meeting, or out to lunch."

The end came one autumn afternoon when she opened her mailed statement and saw that her account had fallen below $300,000—more than a 25 percent drop. No phone call would suffice; she drove to the brokerage office immediately and confronted her advisor.

"He said that if I was that unhappy, I could move my account somewhere else," Laura said. "I couldn't believe how little he cared."

I could. It's an old trick among unscrupulous brokers, used when they have squeezed every last dollar in commissions out of your account. You're no longer an asset to them, and they want you out of their hair.

I studied her statement, already guessing what I would see.

"Your account is stuffed with the kind of loaded mutual funds where all the commissions are paid up front," I said. "That means your broker already took his commission; there's no advantage for him anymore. And look here—all your mutual funds are from the same family of funds. They're all issued by the brokerage house where your advisor works."

She frowned. "And that's bad?"

"Currently, there are more than eighty-five different families of mutual funds where you could invest," I said. "The idea is to pick the best funds available in the market, and it's absolutely ludicrous to believe that any *one* family has *all* the best funds sold. What your broker did was invest your money so that it stayed with his brokerage."

I pointed to another item on her statement.

"And see here?" I said. "He even put you into a couple of their own variable annuities where you're locked into an eight-year surrender charge. To any financially trained eye, that's a *huge* red flag. If you move out of them now, it will cost you another twelve thousand dollars in surrender charges."

Laura was devastated. If she wanted to cash out now, she would have lost almost one-third of her capital—the money she had counted on to support herself.

But there was more to come. Laura had never considered herself overly religious, but with her divorce and the loss of money weighing heavily on her, she started noticing the many programs her church had set up for its congregants.

"I was relieved," Laura admitted. "Finally, I found people who were going through the same problems as I."

Laura began attending a Tuesday-night program for people going through divorce.

"Ninety percent of the members are female," she said—and that was fine with her. In fact, she was so embittered that by this time she was overly suspicious of the four men in the class. "I figured that they were probably there just to meet women," she said, her voice wry.

One Sunday, the topic of the pastor's sermon was church finances—and a sudden revelation came to Laura.

"I had never thought about asking my pastor for advice about money," she said. "He referred me to one of the elders of the church who handled his personal account. I didn't know the man personally, but I had seen his face in several church bulletins." That, Laura told herself, was a good sign.

She approached him after the services.

"He said he'd be glad to help and gave me his card," she said. A quick look at his card revealed another one of those household-word firms.

"We met and he reviewed my statements. His conclusion: start all over with a clean sheet." She shrugged. "It made sense—until I saw my next few statements. With all the selling, buying, and penalties paid, my account was down tens of thousands of dollars."

"I can't believe I fell into the same trap. He did exactly the same thing to me as the first broker—just with different names on the funds."

She slumped, despair written on her features.

"What happened to me?" she said, her eyes brimming.

What I told her is something every investor must know.

First, understand that most brokers are salesmen. They are spurred on by their office managers to push products that benefit their firm, and not necessarily their clients.

Here's how the system works. When Laura put up her $400,000 with the first broker, he "earned" about $24,000 in up-front commissions on Laura's money. Not bad for a few hours' work. However, he only got to keep about 35 percent of that money—$8,400—for himself.

The rest went to the well-known brokerage firm that employed him. That is why the firm *is* well known; the cut received by the firm pays for advertising, as well as other overhead. It also pays millions of dollars to the layers of executives and other upper-echelon staff who are based in the firm's East Coast headquarters.

Financial advisors can be compensated in a number of ways—for instance, an asset-manager type of broker who does *not* work on a commission basis will usually charge an annual fee of between one-half of 1 percent and 1 percent or more of the assets under management. In Laura's case, this would have resulted in a charge of somewhere between $2,000 and $4,000 per year in fees; of this, the broker would have earned between $600 and $1,200. (Not to mention the haircut the brokerage firm would take on its share.)

Let's think about it: Does a broker want to make $1,200, or $8,400?

That didn't take long, did it?

The same was true with the second broker, differing only in that he was dealing with a lower initial figure. It didn't surprise me. This is how most of the new clients I see have had their accounts set up—solely to benefit the broker and brokerage firm.

It shouldn't be this way; certainly, it doesn't have to be, for *you*.

Laura had selected both of her financial advisors on the basis of a single referral from what she believed to be reliable sources. Given what we now know about how Laura's accounts were handled, is there any reason to think her friend or her pastor is doing any better? Probably not—yet that did not deter them from recommending their advisors to Laura. And why not? Unless you have a way to know what makes a person a good financial advisor, isn't one just as good as any other?

For the same reason, many people select an advisor with *no referral at all*—unless, that is, you count the postcard, bulk-addressed envelope or glossy brochure that arrived one afternoon in their mailbox.

If you have purchased any big-ticket merchandise over the last couple of years (or if you are simply lucky enough to live in a "prestigious" zip code), such envelopes arrive in your mailbox with regularity. Sometimes they look like a wedding invitation; others are simple postcards. Some look like checks. Still others are touted in local newspapers or flyers left on your car's windshield while you shop at the mall. Some promise financial freedom, others tout investment returns; a few even claim they have "nothing to sell you," instead offering instant prosperity as a "free" gift.

Regardless of the medium or message, their goal is to take money from your pocket and put it in theirs.

A client of mine, Janet, had attended one of these "educational" seminars—this one held at a prestigious country club, where Janet had the swordfish for her "free" dinner—and fell easy prey to the lure of the pitch.

"I knew it sounded too good to be true," Janet admitted, when she finally brought the problem to me, after three years. "They said that I couldn't lose money. Worst case, I would get all of my investment back, no matter what."

A few minutes of reading through the papers was all it took for me to discover Janet's real problems.

"You have invested a hundred thousand dollars in an S&P 500 index annuity," I said, and the expression on her face told me she had no idea of what that was. Not many people do.

The concept is not wholly bad. An insurance company guarantees you can never get back *less* than you invest; if the stock market rises, you earn a profit. That's a major 'if," given how some contracts are written, but it's not the primary problem. At this point in the pitch, either the broker stopped talking or Janet stopped listening; she didn't remember anyone telling her that she had to leave the money in the investment *for seventeen years* or pay significant penalties. The penalty: *17 percent of her original investment!*

"That's seventeen thousand dollars!" she cried. "That's highway robbery."

Indeed it is, but it is also perfectly legal. So, too, was the compensation taken by the bright young man who sold her this product: he made $15,000 in commissions—up front.

And that, my friends, will pay for an awful lot of swordfish dinners.

In Florida, seminar nights have become the norm for senior citizens. Seniors peruse the papers during the day, pick out the seminar giving the best dinner, and round up their friends for an evening of dining pleasure. But inevitably—just as in the jungle—every night one, two, or more gazelles are going to be cut from the herd.

Seminars, mailings, ads in newspapers or on radio—no matter the method of ensnaring fresh meat, all have one element in common: they count on a basic human weakness in their potential prey.

Let's get real here. Just who do you think is ultimately going to pay for that fancy dinner?

THREE

THE GREATEST STOCK CON OF ALL

Harry Houdini was the most famed illusionist of his day. But it is a little-known fact that he was fiercely skeptical about his own craft, taking pains to expose those charlatans who attempted to convince the gullible that magic was real.

It's a good object lesson to remember: if psychics and fortune-tellers do exist (and I have my suspicious about Warren Buffett), it's unlikely that we mere mortals will have access to their insights.

Case in point: a true story that came to me from one of my clients, an otherwise sensible man we'll call Harold.

Harold was a relatively successful businessman, who several years ago had a modest account with one of the major brokerage houses. Like many people, he was entranced by the stock market; as with most ordinary people, he secretly admitted that he did not understand its mystical workings.

"I knew there are always winners and losers," he told me, not long after the incident described below. "I figured that insiders had information that the rest of us didn't have, and got rich because of it." He shook his head sadly. "When I started getting those letters, I thought maybe I was going to be one of them."

And so began Harold's flirtation with what some call the "greatest stock scam of all"—a scam employed by a small but energetic ring of "financial advisors" that is never legal, usually costly, and always an embarrassing experience to the "marks" it targets. It's also effective, because most of those who fall prey to it never know they were conned in the first place.

Mail lists are a staple of direct marketing today. Using them has become a sophisticated science: you can target virtually any demographic, any locale, any income segment. It was inevitable that certain unscrupulous persons would find a way to use such lists for their own gain.

Here's how it works: a broker buys a list of 5,000 names, specifying a demographic that is conducive to investment activities. He divides these names into Group A and Group B. He will then pick a stock—for our purposes let's call it Silicon Techtronics. But it could be *any* stock, because the name really doesn't matter.

And then it's time to work the marks.

He mails a politely worded letter to everyone in Group A. He introduces himself as a "proven financial expert"—but emphasizes that you should not trust him without demonstrable proof.

"Send me no money now . . . I want to *earn* your trust," he writes. "I'll do so by giving you the same recommendation I'm providing to my other clients—on a confidential basis, of course."

He advises them to watch the price of Silicon Techtronics closely— "because, due to new-product development not yet announced to the public, this stock is *definitely* going up over the next few weeks."

A brazen ploy, and a risky one at that—right?

Wrong.

He immediately sends the same letter to everyone in Group B, telling them to watch Silicon Techtronics—"because it is *definitely* going down."

As with the proverbial broken clock, our unscrupulous broker knows he has to be right with *one* of the groups.

In this case, let's say the stock does indeed see a price rise. Farewell to Group B, which goes into the trash. But the 2,500 names in Group A, who were told the stock was going up, are about to get another letter in their mail.

From Group A comes two new groups of 1,250 names each. The broker again picks a stock; let's say it's called Omega Bankcorp. He sends the first 1,250 a new letter reminding them of his Silicon Techtronics recommendation; he may even sympathize over the profits they missed out on—even providing verifiable information on how much a $10,000 investment would have made.

"But it's not too late," he writes, "because now Omega Bankcorp is poised to take off in the marketplace!"

Of course, you've seen his ploy: the other 1,250 individuals are told Omega Bankcorp's stock is headed down.

He may repeat this process several times, patient as an angler reeling in his quarry. But at a certain point—that is, when his marks are convinced that he truly possesses second sight—even the most skeptical prospect is inclined to jump in and open an account. At, say, $20,000 to $50,000 per account, the cost of a mailing list and several rounds of first-class stamps is a minor expense for our wily broker.

There are but three possible outcomes here:

- First, and least painful, is that you will find out soon that your new broker is neither better nor worse than his slightly more scrupulous brethren. You'll pay plenty in commissions—if he's gone to the trouble to land you, he's doubtlessly calculated his profit structure—but relatively speaking, it could have been worse.

- Second, you may find you've been hooked by a predatory boiler-room operation; not satisfied with reeling you in, they're prepared to scale, gut, and panfry you. For instance, your new broker now explains that the Big Board stocks like Silicon Techtronics and Omega Bankcorp are not profitable enough. "We need to put you into some of these lesser-known stocks to get a better yield." This should be a vivid red flag for you: it's typically a scam where your advisor buys small-priced stocks for your account at huge-spread prices.

    Very likely, his firm already owns the stocks (bought for several cents a share) and daisy-chains the share price upward many hundred times over—that is, pushing the price higher simply by having its brokers peddle it to clients. You won't be able to sell it on the way up; the broker will never return your call. When this operation sells out of stock, the price plummets to the few cents a share it was worth in the first place—and you lose, big-time.

- Finally, you may simply have been hooked by out-and-out crooks. While your money is supposedly "clearing the banking system for deposit into your account," the scammers are busy clearing out their desks and moving the con to another state— they hope, one step in front of the law.

In any event, Harold lost more than $20,000—most of it through high-commission purchases of very risky penny stocks that a reputable broker wouldn't have gone near. Worse, as is the case with many investors, the money Harold tapped to invest in the scheme came from a bank account he had paid into for years . . . that had been earmarked for his daughter Julie's college costs.

"I didn't think of it as a risk at all," Harold berated himself later as he tried to rationalize his actions to me. "I was convinced that, with the guy's track performance so good, I could afford to send Julie to Stanford after I was done."

So long, Stanford; hello, community college. And Julie's tuition is being paid *there* on the installment plan.

It was a painful experience, but—as Harold recently admitted— "the cheapest tuition I could have paid for the lesson *I* learned."

Moral: *never* send money to anyone you don't know; even if you check them out thoroughly with the proper government agencies, the potential for fraud is simply too high.

FOUR

IT'S ALL ABOUT THE BENJAMINS (UH . . . I MEAN, "THE COMMISSIONS")

Fact: brokerage firms are not staffed by disciples of Mother Teresa. They exist for one purpose only: *to make money for themselves.* They do this by using *your* money, enticing you to let them "manage" it with the premise that their superior financial expertise will earn you more return than if you tried to manage it yourself.

In a nutshell, that's the deal. But note the priorities I cite.

As a client, you come in second—sometimes a distant second. If you make a few dollars along the way—well, that's nice, and the word of mouth may bring in other business for the brokerage. But it's not the main objective (for them, at least).

Don't misunderstand me: in twenty-five-plus years in this business, I have never known a single broker who has *intentionally* run a client's account into the ground. But it is hard for any broker to focus on the altruistic when his manager is in 24/7 whip-flailing mode, striving to focus the troops on maximizing profit to the firm.

The name of the game is "commissions earned." Moreover, if the brokers can collect those commissions in advance—the term here is *up front,* which (given the unspoken disadvantages to the investor) they definitely aren't—so much the better.

Of course, this creates an inherent conflict of interest. For instance, let's say the markets really look dismal—unemployment is running rampant, inflation is flaring, and terrorist attacks in our country are a distinct possibility. For the foreseeable future, there seems no feasible way to make a decent return on an investment.

In a logical world, what would you do with your money? If you are like many folks, you'd sit on the sidelines with your money held tight in your hand, waiting until the picture cleared.

Okay for you—after all, you have your money already. But the poor brokerage firm is in a pretty fix: unless they buy and sell constantly, there's no revenue ("commissions") coming in.

Can you imagine a financial company sitting on the sidelines until the storm passes in—say—six months or so?

No commissions for six months?! That means no dividend checks for the shareholders of the brokerage. No dividend checks means that the president of the company is . . . well, toast. Fired.

But he won't go out alone: branch managers (the ramrods who push the brokers to sell more, earn more) also are . . . replaced. But before *they* go, they fire the "underperforming" brokers. Chaos reigns: bearing torches and pitchforks, out-of-work brokers and financial advisors riot in the streets . . . nations fall . . . civilization collapses . . .

A horrific picture, to be sure—and one that no respectable broker could in good conscience allow (that is, if the aforementioned broker actually *has* a conscience). Hence, regardless of the financial prospects—and however much it may cost you, the investor—the brokerages must soldier on and collect those commissions.

Remember this the next time you see one of those TV commercials proclaiming how hard the brokerage houses work for *you.*

But despite their professed best intentions, brokerages still admit to the occasional—albeit minor—misstep.

"Minor" is, of course, relative. Some of us may remember, a year or two ago, a minor bit of embarrassment that touched some of the biggest names on Wall Street. By *minor,* I mean the loss of hundreds of millions of dollars of clients' funds; by *embarrassment,* I mean "malfeasance and fraud."

What happened was this: Merrill Lynch (and subsequently, several other major brokerages) was caught with its corporate hand in the cookie jar.

Here's how it works (or, at least, is *supposed* to): let's say that a company needs a hundred million dollars or so to expand. It approaches a financial company like Merrill Lynch, seeking to sell new issues of its stock, thereby obtaining the capital it needs.

Merrill Lynch then does its homework on the company. If the company's prospects are economically viable, Merrill Lynch will have its brokers attempt to sell *you*—in legal terms, the "client"—shares in the company.

Merrill's reward? Let's be conservative; call it $5 million or so (plus other commissions and fees) for placing the stock with their huge 14,000-broker army, which is spurred on to sell the stock.

Sound fair so far? When it works properly, it is.

But issuing new shares dilutes the per-share ownership in a company, which can have an adverse impact on both existing shareholders and those who purchase the new issue. Or it could be that the company is in an industry that's not projected to fare well in the near term—making buggy whips comes to mind here. But for whatever reason, the circumstances indicate that an issue of new stock is not always a great deal for investors; as an advisor to individual investors, Merrill Lynch is supposed to wave its clients away from less-than-advantageous stock purchases.

In the real-life version of our example, investigators soon found that Merrill Lynch was releasing glowing reports on the public offering, aggressively urging clients to buy the new issue.

The problem: Merrill Lynch already knew the stock was a dog; confidential internal memos among Merrill's officials said, in effect, an investor would have to be crazy to invest *any* money in the security. Meanwhile Merrill Lynch was pushing it hard, eagerly pocketing commissions both from the issuing company *and* from clients its brokers convinced to invest in it. When the stock tanked—which it did, emphatically—a lot of individuals lost a lot of money.

Sadly, this was not a unique case. In fact, it's been standard operating procedure for a very long time.

Years ago, when I was a manager at a major Wall Street brokerage house, I attended a meeting at one of our larger offices. Before the meeting began, I watched the local manager of that office hand a slip of paper to each of his brokers.

"What's this all about?" I asked.

"New public offering coming up," he said, then winked. "Everybody's got to move their share. I'm letting 'em know how many shares each of them has to sell."

"And if a broker doesn't sell them all?" I pressed.

The manager looked at me as if I had questioned the facts of life—which, in a way, I guess I had. After all, I knew that every manager's bonus was partly based on the amount of new issue stock and bond sales his brokers made during the year.

"Then *he* owns it—for his *own* account."

As I said, that was a long time ago, but you can bet that brokers are still incentivized in one way or another to move these stocks—it puts an added contemporary emphasis to the ever-useful term *caveat emptor.* Free advice is not always free. For the unwary, it can be expensive indeed.

In mid-2002, Merrill Lynch bought its way out of the case by firing a few employees and paying what to the financial giant was a relatively minor fine—in fact, to a company the size of Merrill, a light slap on the wrist: $100 million, none of which went to the Merrill clients who had been conned by the company. Instead, it went to the government's coffers as a penalty.

In return, Merrill Lynch was allowed to settle without admitting or denying its guilt. Uh-huh. A hundred-million-dollar fine—why would *any* company pony up if it was innocent of the charges?

Lest you think I'm being too hard on my former employer, rest assured that Merrill Lynch is not alone in this dubious practice. In December 2002, several other Wall Street firms were accused of markedly similar acts in pressuring their own investment-banking arms to create good reports for brokers on its new deals. In each case, they, too, bought a "get-out-of-jail-free card" with a sizable fine.

The list includes some of the most prestigious firms on Wall Street. Morgan Stanley (fine: $125 million); Salomon Smith Barney (fine: $400 million); Lehman Brothers (fine: $80 million); Goldman Sachs (fine: $110 million).

Will it ever change? I doubt it—at least, not until a few dozen bigwigs find themselves taking extended vacations at government-owned correctional facilities. It's far too profitable—and the penalties are far too mild.

So that's how the system works, from a macro point of view. Let's zoom into closer focus to see how it impacts you, as an individual. This is where we get into the real nitty-gritty of how commissions are earned and split.

Flash back to the very beginning of this story, where you found yourself in the chair across the desk from your newfound best friend . . . your prospective broker. You've been provided with a cup of coffee, traded a few witticisms (of course, he laughed at each of *your* jokes), and by now you feel comfortable telling him your life story, including all your financial secrets.

As you talk, he is sizing you up. Will you be a difficult client to handle? Will you follow his recommendations without too much debate? Will you panic at every fluctuation in the market? These are important matters to him; time is money, and wasting it on a reluctant client means less time available to spend more profitably on the easily led.

But even more important, there is now a dollar sign placed on your forehead that only he can see. His questions may sound casual, but his intent is anything but.

How much do you bring to the party? Five thousand? *Peanuts.* Ten, twenty, thirty thousand? *Better, but still minor league.* There must be more, he coaxes; and you find yourself wanting to . . . well, to *qualify.*

How about transferable 401(k) accounts, or self-directed pension funds? What's already in your stock portfolio? He shakes his head, almost sadly: you'll be far better off divesting those . . . well, he doesn't come out and call them "dogs," but the implication is clear. Of course, he'll receive a commission on any buys and sells you "need" to make.

Are we into the six-figure level yet? The higher the total, the more attention you (and your money) will get.

Here's a fact that may surprise you: *almost certainly, he already knows what investments he is going to recommend to you—no matter what you may have to say.*

In many languages, words are read from right to left on the written page; not by coincidence, that's exactly the way most brokers read when fresh meat is seated in the chair across from them.

That's because they're looking at a list of available investments the brokerage has compiled. The left column provides details about the investment, which is of secondary importance to any broker.

But it's the right-hand column that is important to him, because that lists the commissions he will earn—*if* his new client takes the hook.

Quick quiz here: given a choice between several possible investments—each paying him a different percentage in commission—is he more likely to recommend:

- one that pays him 1 percent?

- one that pays him 5 percent or more?

Time's up; pass your papers to the front, please.

Another criterion is even more important to your prospective broker (or more accurately, to his commission). This is the fact that most investments are sold with several ways of paying for them.

For instance, some investment vehicles pay brokers commission annually, as long as the money stays on their books. Others pay on a basis the industry calls "front-loaded," that is, the commission is paid to the broker immediately upon sale. Typically, the trade-off comes in a longer surrender-charge period: if you want to sell the investment before the end of that period, you pay a penalty—often, a significant amount.

The reason, of course, is that the up-front commission—designed to motivate the broker to sell the investment to you, since he gets a larger immediate payment—has to come from somebody's pocket. Since the issuing company has carefully calculated what it can earn from the money you invested—and how long it will take to make a profit—it protects itself at your expense by the longer surrender-charge period.

As a rule of thumb, always assume that there is a less expensive way to buy any investment than what your broker initially suggests; also assume that he will never tell you *unless you ask,* because it would reduce his up-front commission.

And the commissions he "earns" are sometimes absurd.

Here's an example: you are contemplating retiring and have, say, $300,000 in your 401(k) plan at work. You want to roll it over into an individual IRA account—not at all unusual in today's world. The broker suggests a couple of mutual funds, maybe a variable annuity, and voilà! You have a portfolio. And it took only two hours, more or less—and that includes filling out the paperwork.

Let me offer congratulations—but to your broker, not to you.

Your broker will earn about 5 percent commissions on the mutual funds if they are "load" funds (which they usually are) and about another 7 percent on the money going into the variable annuity.

Grand total for two hours of work and signing a few documents: about $18,000 in commissions. Wait a minute—*that's $9,000 an hour!*

It gets worse. Almost inevitably, you are usually stuck in those investments for years. Remember what I said about long surrender charges? Your new variable annuity will list a predetermined set of surrender charges, one for each year you own it. It may look something like this:

Year 1: 8%	Year 2: 8%	Year 3: 8%
Year 4: 8%	Year 5: 7%	Year 6: 6%
Year 7: 5%	Year 8: 4%	Year 9: 0%

This means that if you need to withdraw all (or even part of) your money over the next eight years, you'll pay dearly for it. There will be an "early withdrawal" sort of penalty, similar to that applied to a long-term CD.

Stated another way: if you took all your money out after the first year, your penalty on the $150,000 variable annuity you bought would be *about $12,000.*

Why so much? Most people don't know this, since it's an industry secret: it's because the *annuity company paid the broker $10,500, up front*—simply for selling you the investment. If you leave the money with the company for the full eight years, they will have earned enough in annual fees (from you) to offset this up-front cost.

But if you change your mind and want out, the annuity company cannot legally go back to your broker and get the commission back. Someone has to pay, and the only one left is *you*.

Odd, isn't it, that the broker "forgot" to explain all this in full detail when you signed on the dotted line.

There's a question I invariably get at my seminars, and when I do radio and television interviews: "David, my broker used to call me almost every day before I opened an account with him. Now he never returns my calls, even after I invested *all* my money with him. What's up?"

Well, what's up is the game. It's over, but you don't know it yet.

Once you went "all in"—a poker term that indicates you've ante'd up every penny you have—your value as a client plummeted. Aside from some minor sell-a-little/buy-a-little chump change, your account has been milked of any potential commissions.

The broker knows that you are unlikely to make major changes in your investments in the foreseeable future—so why bother with you? You have become the albatross around his neck. There's no incentive to spend valuable time answering *your* questions when he could be busy snaring another investor—fresh blood that will pump more money to his (and his firm's) bottom line. That, or he'd have to shell out a few bucks to hire staff to deal with inquisitive pests like you.

Over time, you'll probably threaten to move your account. Fine with him—by now, he's earned all the commissions. If someone else is left holding the bag—i.e., "servicing your account"—that's no problem for him, and it's usually a boon to your new broker.

Why? You are once again fresh meat. Your new broker sympathizes with you over how you were treated—and then declares your existing portfolio to contain more dogs than the American Kennel Club.

She makes an enthusiastic case for selling out all your positions now: "you have to bite the bullet and eat the penalties before it's too late!" And of course, she has her own program of investments for you to buy into—and her own commissions to collect.

In most cases such as this, you'd be hard-pressed to find anything but a predator seeking your business. In such circumstances, an honest broker would decline to handle your account. He would tell you the sad truth: he cannot legitimately earn any fees from you. If he took on everybody in your situation, he would bankrupt himself.

––––––––––––

Remember that $18,000—the money that it took your broker two hours to "earn"? Ever wonder how the commission is divided at the average Wall Street retail brokerage house?

It depends on a host of factors, including:

- how long the broker has been in business (the longer he's been in it the more is expected out of him in annual commissions)

- his total commissions earned to date in the current year (the more he earns, the more he gets to keep)

- any contest that may have been running at the time, *and*

- the type of investment you bought

With minor variations among the different brokerage houses, a broker will usually get from 25 percent to 50 percent of the total commission earned for his efforts.

The balance goes to the brokerage house. It's what pays for all the local-office expenses; the expensive local, regional, and national advertising campaigns that draw new business; and all those multimillion-dollar salaries in the New York corporate headquarters. Oh, yes—some of it goes into dividend checks to the brokerage's own shareholders. (Independent brokers keep even more—up to 90 percent—but have to pay their own expenses from it.)

All in all, there are a *lot* of people who have their hands in your personal-finance pocket.

Much of what I've discussed in this chapter paints a bleak portrait indeed; it's a jungle out there, and heaven help the unwary.

Remember my client Laura, who found herself victimized by staggering brokerage commissions—this, from the financial advisor who had been recommended by a friend?

In Laura's case, compounding the problem was Laura herself—not in being lazy, but in being uninformed. Never having had experience in financial matters herself, she simply did not recognize a legal scam when she was snared by one. Worse, she did not make a dedicated effort to find out before she threw herself on the mercy of a shark.

There is an answer, of course. As in all matters of personal growth and decision, it requires you to obtain the information you need to know—and that means asking the right questions.

For Laura, and for all of you who are reading this book, the following ten questions give you all you need in order to screen the wheat from the chaff in your search for good financial advice. We'll walk through each of them in detail so you'll see why each question is relevant. Even more important, I'll tell you what answers are good, and what answers should make you run for the hills.

The only question you can't expect any prospective financial advisor to answer is what everybody *really* wants to know. By law, financial advisors are not permitted to discuss the individual holdings, amounts, or returns earned on any client's account to any third party. This is just as well: Would they not tell you only about their successes and leave out the failures?

———————————

Fortune favors the prepared person. Don't worry—in the next chapter, I will show you a list of all the questions you ever need to ask a prospective broker. You need not be victimized—and if you have been already, it need never happen to you again.

Ready? Then let's begin.

FIVE

PICKING THE *RIGHT* FINANCIAL ADVISOR: TEN QUESTIONS TO ASK . . . AND HOW TO SCORE THEIR ANSWERS

1. "What types of financial licenses do you hold? Is my account with you insured? What other licenses or ratings do you have?"

Right off the bat, we give you a bonus: three questions—let's call them 1A, 1B, and 1C—all for the price of one! There's a reason for this; it will be clear by the end of this section, but until then, you'll simply have to trust me.

1A. The answer to question 1A is a "Series 7 registration." This is the license a person is required to possess by all state and federal regulatory agencies to sell stocks and bonds legally to individuals just like you.

Today, anyone can hang out a shingle and call themselves a financial advisor. This tends to annoy those in the field who have spent decades learning how to help their clients prosper; nonetheless, there's no law against the guy at the gas station touting a mutual fund when you try to pay for your gas if he is properly licensed.

So it's up to you to filter out the static.

Simply stated, do not even *consider* dealing with anyone without a Series 7 license. Only a Series 7 producer is legally authorized to discuss in detail all types of investments—stocks, bonds, mutual funds, limited partnerships, and so on.

Repeat after me: Series 7. This is an important term.

For instance, you may already be hooked up with a really great guy—call him Al—who handles all your insurance needs. Al does a good job on your car, home, and life-insurance policies.

But for his company—we'll call it Allied United National Mutual Insurance Corp, a financial services conglomerate based in, say, Delaware—that's not enough. The firm doesn't want to miss out on a single dollar in potential income.

So they may have helped Al get a Series 6 license—impressive-sounding, but essentially only a simple permit that allows him to *sell* mutual funds. You walk in his door next time with a question on your auto policy and you walk out invested in Allied United's new company-run mutual fund that the broker is pushing that day.

Fine—that is, until that fund runs into difficulty and you need to decide whether to dump the investment (or if you should even consider it; remember Laura and the surrender-fee problem?). You want someone who can explain *all* your financial options, not just the ones he can sell—and that makes 7 infinitely better than 6.

Also ask your potential advisor if she has a Series 8 or Series 24 license under her belt. This is known as the Securities Principal License. The holder of this one has the power to supervise other advisors' activities—but more to the point, it hopefully means he knows better than to make foolish suggestions with your account.

Finally, *always* ask if he has a Series 65 license. Most states require a Series 65 to legally qualify as an investment advisor. Why? Because, among other things, a Series 65 license makes a person a Registered Investment Advisor and allows him to charge you fees *by the hour* rather than on a commission basis. Do not accept such answers as "I'm registered under my firm as an investment advisor"; this is definitely not the same as having a Series 65 license of his or her own. Most major wire houses prohibit their advisors from even setting up such a fee arrangement.

1B. Next question: Is he covered by SIPC (Securities Investor Protection Corporation) insurance?

This is the same general type of insurance that banks provide through FDIC insurance. If the entity holding your securities goes broke, the insurance will pay you up to $500,000 per account; $100,000 of this can be in cash. Remember, this is insurance only against the firm going broke, not you going belly-up in your personal account.

SIPC is nice, unless your account is valued at upward of $500,001. As a result, *most* advisors carry extra insurance that will bring total protection to $10 million or more.

But not all do carry this insurance, which is why you must ask. If your potential financial advisor is not covered for at least $10 million or more, it's a deal breaker. Get up and walk out the door, immediately.

1C. Ah, the alphabet soup of today's complex world! Hardly anybody is anybody these days without a string of capitalized, if cryptic, letters attached to his or her name.

In the world of financial advice, you'll find CFP, CRPC, CDFA, and dozens more. It's enough to make one regret learning his ABC's. Anyone could get confused, and after all—what do those letters have to do with investing your money wisely?

A lot, as it happens. Generally, such letters indicate the additional licenses or expertise ratings that the broker has earned. They usually indicate that he or she has passed some type of qualifying exam that demonstrates a proficiency in a certain field of financial planning.

For example, some of the most popular licenses quality a person as a Certified or Charter Financial Planner (CFP), Certified Retirement Specialist (CRPC), or Certified Divorce Analyst (CDFA); the list goes on and on. Ask about them even if (rather, *especially* if) these descriptives are printed on your prospective advisor's business card. They indicate that she or he has gone the extra mile to learn more about the business.

That's good, because in today's rapidly changing environment, continuing education is essential just to keep up with current regulations and conditions. Give your prospective advisor an extra point for effort for each designation next to her name . . . subtract two points if there are none.

(NOTE: award no points simply because she or he is a "vice president," a "senior managing director," or holds any other intentionally impressive-sounding title; most firms hand these titles out like party favors—and not infrequently for activities not particularly in the client's interest.

For instance, many firms base such "promotions" on sales performance: all they mean is that he has sold more than the next guy at the firm, not that he has made more money for the client. And the latter is what should concern you.

Besides, in what universe does it make sense for a twenty-six-year-old to be a senior vice president of anything except a college fraternity house?)

This first set of inquiries alone will put you far ahead of the pack. It helps you know whether you are dealing with a true professional or just a salesman out to help himself. If you don't like the responses you receive . . . don't continue with this person, or if you are already involved, move your account immediately to someone who can pass all ten questions of this test.

Now let's look at how to score the responses you receive.

SCORING QUESTION #1

No Series 7 license	**Stop the interview process immediately.** Politely excuse yourself and search for a true financial advisor to interrogate. *NO EXCEPTIONS*
No SIPC insurance	**Stop the process.** You will not do business here.
Series 7 license	4 points
Each additional designation earned	1 point for each designation (maximum 2 extra points)

Has Securities Principal license (Series 8 or 24)	2 points
Has Individual Investment Advisor license (Series 65)	2 points
No additional earned designations	Subtract 2 points
Willing to come to your house to talk	Subtract 2 points

(No true professional has the time . . . unless you have several million dollars in your account.)

Total Points Question #1 _____ (maximum 10 points)

2. "How long have you been a Series 7–registered broker?"

Here you are looking for someone marked with the battle scars of financial combat. Experience counts; you want your advisor scarred from battling the S&P 500 Index or from dueling with hundreds of tax-law changes. If she has worked under the reign of more than one chairman of the Federal Reserve, so much the better.

For those reasons, the *absolute minimum* qualification here is five years. As in so much of life, more is better.

The sad fact is that more than 70 percent of all people who are licensed as financial advisors will end up out of the business within three years; the statistic varies little for both independents and major brokerage-house employees. Thus, few rookies ever have the opportunity to experience the peaks and valleys that, over the years, inevitably batter the various investment markets. People learn through mistakes; get an advisor whose previous clients have *already* paid for his education.

A great example was the financial devastation that occurred shortly after September 11, 2001. I encountered an avalanche of prospective new clients on my doorstep, all in a tizzy. These individuals were watching their financial futures plunge daily in a crash-and-burn state right before their very eyes.

Most had their money managed by some bright young advisors with a great smile and a lot of charm who had never envisioned that the stock market could dive as well as rise. In their short careers, it had always gone up. They only knew what their managers told them to tell you to think . . . "long-term."

Bottom line here: the longer the person has been in the business, the better. However, *too* long can be just as bad; dinosaurs tend to be set in their ways and sometimes don't keep up with the latest trends.

Here's how to score Question 2:

SCORING QUESTION #2

0–5 years experience	**Stop the process.** Tell him to call you when he grows up.
6–10 years experience	3 points
11–15 years experience	6 points
16–20 years experience	8 points
20-years-plus experience	10 points
40-years-plus experience	Subtract 2 points

Total Points Question #2 _____ (maximum 10 points)

3. "What is the *minimum*-size investment account you accept?"

The dollar amount here will vary—but the higher the number, the better for you. A high minimum requirement tends to indicate an advisor is doing rather well and doesn't need to snare every walk-in simply to make the month's rent. But certainly beware of any advisor who has a low-dollar minimum (or worse, *no* minimum requirement at all).

Generally speaking, a minimum of $100,000 or more is best. Don't worry, though, if your investment funds don't total in the six figures; many people don't come to financial advisors with that much to invest.

A good financial advisor will sometimes make an exception if you ask (but get a commitment that an exception won't mean a lower level of service). Others won't—but one way around a high minimum is to hire an advisor who is licensed to charge a by-the-hour fee. Be sure to check, because most advisors are not so licensed. If the advisor you *really* want won't budge on the minimum, ask about an hourly consultation arrangement.

SCORING QUESTION #3

Minimum-size investment accepted

If he says, "If the check clears, you're in"	**Stop the process.** Tell him you forgot to shut the oven off at home. Leave immediately.
$50,000 plus	2 points
$100,000 plus	5 points
$250,000 plus	7 points
$500,000 plus (but makes exceptions)	10 points
Everyone seems to be an exception	Subtract 5 points

Total Points Question #3 _____ (maximum 10 points)

4. "How many *current active households* do you have as clients?"

Ideally, the answer to this question is between 200 and 400 households. Note: I said "households," and not "accounts."

There's a semantics game some advisors like to play. One client could have a personal account, a joint husband/wife account, an IRA account, a pension-plan account, a—well, you get the idea. Specifying "households" minimizes the opportunity for a prospective advisor to fudge this information.

Fewer than 200 households indicates a practice that is either new or probably not too successful; more than 400 means you could easily get lost in the crowd. There are exceptions (for instance, 50 *very* large accounts could indicate a successful, established practice; a practice with a *very* large staff might indicate an ability to manage more than 400 accounts well). But as a general rule, my numbers apply.

Also, *always* ask to meet and talk to the potential advisor's personal staff. Do not assume that just because you see movement in the office, these people are going to move for *you*. It is not unusual to see one assistant for every four or five financial advisors.

SCORING QUESTION #4

0–50 households under management	**Stop the process.** Look elsewhere, let him make his mistakes with someone else's money.
51–100 households under management	3 points
101–150 households under management	5 points
151–200 households under management	7 points
200–400 households under management	10 points
Each full-time assistant dedicated to advisor	1 point each (maximum 3 points)
No full-time assistant dedicated to advisor	Subtract 3 points

Over 400 households under management (without additional support staff for help)	Subtract 3 points

Total Points Question #4 _____ (maximum 10 points)

5. "How many clients have closed or moved their accounts with you over the last three years?"

Be wary of any advisor who quickly answers this question with an emphatic "none—my clients all love me." Unless your prospective advisor is Lassie, universal love is rare; even rarer is an advisor who has never had a semipsychotic client-from-hell who walks out on him or her.

Lost clients can obviously be chalked up to bad investment advice; but as in any relationship, there are times when the personalities of the individuals involved just don't mesh.

Also be extremely leery of the advisor who tells you he doesn't keep such records. I even keep track of the number of times the front door of our office opens in a day.

The answer you should be looking for here is *five or fewer lost clients over any three-year period*. More than this is a definite red flag; you'll want details to know for sure, but it is usually a bad sign.

Here's a bonus tip for you on this one. When answering this question, did your prospective advisor mention any clients he or she *asked* to leave?

Sometimes, clients are "fired" by advisors simply because the client doesn't want to follow the advisor's advice. Sometimes, the advisor believes the relationship is no longer in the best interests of either party.

All advisors have clients they wish they didn't have on their client list. Find an advisor who admits he had the guts to jettison clients even though it may have affected her bottom line. It will speak volumes about her integrity—and it will go a long way in proving the advisor doesn't deal with anyone who has a pulse.

It's curious: survey after survey indicates that few clients leave an advisor because of poor *performance;* they realize that financial markets gyrate in ways that nobody can control. Rather, most clients leave because of poor *service.*

Finally, as you ask these questions, closely watch the demeanor and body language of your prospective advisor; these may well tell you more than any verbal answer.

SCORING QUESTION #5

10+ accounts closed or transferred within 3 years	**Stop the process.** Even his mother may have moved her account—look elsewhere
0–5 accounts closed or transferred within 3 years	10 points
6–7 accounts closed or transferred within 3 years	5 points
8–9 accounts closed or transferred within 3 years	2 points
Advisor asked 5 or more accounts to move within 3 years (told you without asking)	3 points

Total Points Question #5 _____ (maximum 10 points)

6. "Have you, or your practice, ever had a written complaint filed against you?"

Ideally, the answer you want to hear is a strong *no.*

But in the real world, even good advisors can have a complaint on file with one or another of the agencies that regulate them. If your prospective advisor has had complaints filed, ask for the specifics of each circumstance. Also ask about the specific outcome or resolution of each complaint. Certainly, though, if the number is more than three over the past ten years and the advisor can't provide understandable, believable, and overwhelming evidence that the fault is not hers—well, politely excuse yourself and keep looking.

SCORING QUESTION #6

4 or more complaints filed over the last 10 years	**Stop the process.** Where there is smoke there is likely to be fire. This is inexcusable.
No written complaints filed over the last 10 years	10 points
1–3 written complaints filed over the last 10 years	5 points

Total Points Question #6 _____ (maximum 10 points)

7. "Precisely what services can I expect from you and your staff? Will I deal with you directly, or will I be passed off to a member of your team? How will we communicate, and how often?"

What you are essentially asking here is what *quality of service* to expect for your money.

Is he a true wealth advisor in all relevant areas? For instance, does your prospective advisor provide tax or legal services through his own sources? If you already have a lawyer or CPA you like, your financial advisor should have no problem working with them; if the advisor balks, it's a bad sign.

But if you don't have these services already, it may be valuable to you to have the access to (or a reference for) legal and accounting services through your financial advisor. Certainly, done correctly, this saves you time; it is also far better than flipping through the Yellow Pages playing "eenie, meenie, miney, moe." But don't neglect to check the credentials and other references of any lawyer or accountant, just as you would check your financial advisor's.

Similarly, you want to know what to expect when you call your financial advisor—is your inquiry going to be bounced to a junior staff member rather than answered by your advisor? More precisely, if this happens, would it be satisfactory to you?

(NOTE: If size is important to you, ask: Does he even have a staff or does he share assistants with other advisors? Some very good advisors run one-person shops, and others are part of a "pool" that time-shares staff and office resources. But so do some fly-by-night operations and you will do well to find out about this area before you place your assets with such an advisor.)

And definitely, you want to know how often you will get statements (at least quarterly, and ideally on a monthly basis) and how often (and under what circumstances) your advisor will review your overall financial picture.

This should be done at least once each year and you should feel comfortable that you can call his office anytime with questions. Larger accounts should request semiannual in-person, detailed reviews. *(NOTE: Always ask how the advisor defines a "larger account." If you don't qualify—and feel you should—now is the time to know.)*

Ask about other communications: for instance, many advisors publish a regular newsletter to keep clients up-to-date; others regularly contact clients by telephone to check in, or alert them to opportunities or potential concerns. Still others prefer to conduct quarterly or semiannual seminars to bring their clients up to speed on the ever-changing financial environment and new investment ideas.

Warning: stay clear of advisors who don't offer some type of continuing-education/seminar process for existing clients. Ideally, see if you can attend one of these functions before you sign. These allow you to mingle informally with your prospective peer group. It's a golden opportunity to chat with other clients about how they view the advisor.

If a prospective advisor doesn't offer client seminars, it may indicate serious problems ahead. Perhaps she doesn't place a high emphasis on keeping the client informed; perhaps she's just cheap. More ominously, perhaps she doesn't want you talking to anyone.

By the way, don't expect to get a list of any other clients. There are serious confidentiality issues involved here; I wouldn't want my name bandied about and neither should you. Besides, do you really think the advisor would give you the name of someone with whom he is having trouble?

SCORING QUESTION #7

Offers regular seminars for clients	3 points
Handles ALL *financial questions himself*	4 points
Has backup support for questions when out of the office	3 points
Has dedicated staff to handle nonfinancial concerns	2 points
Sends out regular monthly communications	2 points
Doesn't offer regular client seminars	Subtract 5 points
Doesn't have at least 2 full-time staff members working just for him	Subtract 3 points

Total Points Question #7 _____ (maximum 10 points)

8. "Exactly how will you earn your money from me—commissions, percentage of my account balance, or hourly fee?"

Ah, the age-old issue of compensation: it's the nitty-gritty of most fledgling advisor–client relationships.

Different people need different services from a financial advisor; one-size-fits-all is as potentially uncomfortable here as it is in lingerie.

There are three basic ways for advisors to charge for their services; two are good, and one is a deal breaker.

First, most brokers still charge up-front commissions on the products they sell. Such commissions can vary widely. With financial vehicles called "A shares" or the equivalent, 5 percent is a fair average; most mutual funds fall into this category.

An extremely good question to ask here: "Do you charge up-front commissions? Why, or why not? How would either option be good for *me*?" Usually, you'll find out the honest answer to the latter question is, "it's not good for you." Instead, it is very good for the *broker.*

Without doubt, the number one question I hear at seminars or talk about on TV and radio shows goes something like this: "David, I put all my money up with my broker six months ago; now I can never get him to call back. He used to call me all the time before I became a client. What gives?"

My answer: "You do—or rather, you did."

When a person gives her broker, say, $250,000, that broker likely earned $15,000 or so in up-front commissions depending on the product mix. If you have no new money on which he can earn additional commissions, what is his incentive to return your calls? More to the point, what is his reason to keep you as a client?

Many brokers like to hide their up-front commissions behind a smoke screen called "B shares." These products still pay the broker huge commissions up front but have *five- to seventeen-year* surrender charges attached to them.

Clients are amazed to learn that an 8 percent up-front commission on some variable annuities is the current going rate. But for some S&P 500 index annuities I've seen offered, the commission comes to a whopping 15 percent . . . *all up front!*

These charges are patently obscene. Worse, they encourage a situation where the broker gets his money and runs.

People grumble over long surrender-charge periods, but not a single investor out of over 10,000 I've encountered over the last twenty-five years has ever been able to accurately explain why these surrender charges exist. Small wonder: it's considered top secret by the financial industry.

But I'll reveal the answer now: one way or another, the investment company must earn back that up-front commission it paid the broker those long years before—either by retaining and charging daily fees on the money you placed with it, or—if you pull out—through the hefty surrender penalties you must pay.

Always ask your advisor if the same investment is offered with a shorter or no-surrender-charge option (most are). If she admits that yes, it is, politely excuse yourself and go elsewhere. If she isn't being straight with you about all your options now, at the start, she probably never will be.

Aside from the "straight commission" basis we've discussed, the second way to pay your broker is called the "pay-as-you-go" fee schedule. This is done either through quarterly fees or through a method called "C shares."

The broker's fee is based upon the size of the account and the effort involved in preparing annual reviews, arranging seminars, variety of services provided, and so on. The customary annual rate ranges between one-half of 1 percent to 1 percent or more of the account value. Should you need your money released to you, there is usually no surrender charge, or if there is, it is seldom more than 1 percent, and then only in the first year.

Finally, a growing number of brokers use neither the commission nor the pay-as-you-go method. Instead, they have instituted either per-hour charge or an annual charge that prepurchases a block of their time. Depending on what you want from your advisor, this can be a perfectly acceptable arrangement. If, however, you tend toward being overly thrifty, you may unwisely skimp on paying for reviews and advisory sessions.

In virtually every case, an investor is well advised to avoid any plan that pays a broker up front. Pay-as-you-go and the hourly/annual fee methods are far more advantageous to the investor. There are two major reasons for this.

First, you can vote with your feet; if you're not satisfied, you move your account elsewhere . . . anytime.

Second—and probably more important, in the long run—the financial advisor who charges either pay-as-you-go or a percentage of the account will usually have your interest in the forefront. If your account rises in value, because he earns a preset percentage of that value, he makes money when you make money. If you lose, the advisor loses, too.

That is the kind of behavior you want to encourage. Nonetheless—and shockingly—more than 95 percent of all the prospective clients I see each year pay their advisors using the up-front commission process. Even more sad is the fact they had no idea what or how their advisors were paid.

SCORING QUESTION #8

Advisor charges by using up-front commissions	**Stop the process.** Find a financial advisor—not a salesman.
Advisor charges an annual fee based on the size of the account	10 points
Advisor who charges by the hour	10 points

Total Points Question #8 _____ (maximum 10 points)

9. "Who is your real boss? Are you somebody's middleman?"

We're nearing the home stretch. Up until now, we've focused only on the potential advisor who is sitting across the desk from you. But let's examine who the advisor works for and how that larger picture can affect you and your money.

The fact is that some companies that purport to offer "financial advisory services" don't—at least, not the kind of services that work in the interests of the customers.

Insurance Company. These people may know a lot about life, health, or your auto policy, but they're seldom a sound alternative to hiring a true financial advisor. With an insurance company, the best you can hope for is a few good mutual-fund recommendations (but most often, from mutual funds that they hold an interest in themselves—beware). Insurance companies exist to sell insurance. For that reason, don't use them as financial managers or advisors.

Bank. See above advice regarding insurance companies; ditto here. Banks exist to make money on your money, giving you, say, 3 percent on your deposits while loaning it out at 7 percent. That's why there is a bank on every corner. Adding a broker to the bank's staff is a relatively new self-defensive move; they're trying to retain the deposits (or better said, the commissions you pay to invest those funds).

The quality of most in-bank brokers is seldom high. In the real world, the best advisors can make a seven-figure income in this country. Few local bank presidents crack the $250,000 salary line. Fewer banks would allow a thirty-five-year-old broker to outearn (by a factor of three or four) the bank's president. Bottom line: don't bother looking for financial advice in small banks.

Accountant's Office. Most accountants know numbers; they know where to place them on a 1040 tax form. Surveys indicate that most people trust their accountant. So it would seem a natural to turn to your accountant for financial advice, right?

Presumably, you trust your doctor, too; most likely, you also trust your priest, rabbi, or minister—and if you don't trust your own mother, shame on you.

My point is this: it is very rare to find someone who can master two complicated trades at the same time, be it accounting, medicine, theology, or motherhood.

But like banks, most accountants love to build on that trust relationship and have gotten some of the licenses to sell some or all financial products to help bolster their bottom lines.

Unless you deal with a large firm—one that provides full-time financial advisors of proven ability—you'll probably do well to avoid using an accountant to manage your money. If you do consider it, at least make certain that your candidate scores highly on the other nine questions on this exam. If so, she could be a diamond in the rough.

Wire Houses/Brokerage Firms. These are the financial companies that come to the minds of most people when positioning their funds. You know them—they spend tens of millions of dollars annually in advertising to make sure you do. They deal with investments every day. Who better to turn to for financial advice?

How about "anybody else"? It's a flippant answer, I admit; but I spent many years working in their system, so listen carefully to what I say.

Most of the time these companies are more concerned about *themselves*—their own salaries, and the returns provided to their shareholders—than they are about you or your portfolio. They exist to earn the maximum they can (on you) so they can pay a fat dividend to their shareholders. This creates a fertile environment for all the games brokers play with your money—games like pushing the product-of-the-month; in turn, this wins the contests that net the free trips and inflated titles.

Okay. To be fair, I'm sure that you can still find some very good brokers with the right intentions at these firms. *I* don't know any— but in an infinite universe, quantum physics, chaos theory, and post-Euclidean logic all posit that there must be *some*.

Good luck finding them, at least on this side of the cosmos.

Independents. These are your true entrepreneurs. They pay their own bills, pay their own rent, hire their own staff, and are responsible for their own destinies. Many have to earn certain licenses and meet minimum standards before they are allowed to hang out their own shingle. As a result, this is where the cream of the crop of advisors usually lands. But beware, milk does sour also.

Bottom line: I believe your best chance of finding your financial soul mate rests among the ranks of the independent financial advisors—but only *if* he or she passes the grade on my other nine questions.

SCORING QUESTION #9

He works for an insurance company	Forget him, unless you need insurance
He works for a bank	Don't even think about this one

He is an accountant	3 points (10 points if he passes the other 9 questions with flying colors)
He works for a wire house	3 points (10 points only if he passes the other 9 questions with high scores)
He works as an independent advisor	5 points (10 points if he makes the grade on other 9 questions)

Total Points Question #9 _____ (maximum 10 points)

10. "What makes me an ideal client for you? What don't you like about me?"

Taken together, these are good catchall questions with which to end the interview. In many cases, they elicit the answers that either clinch the deal or give everybody a last chance to politely walk away from it.

Listen closely to the answers, apply the judgment you have gained from your life experiences. Be wary of the prospective advisor who has only good things to say about you or your financial situation. Stay away from advisors who pressure you to sign with them—*right now!*—without giving you a chance to consider your decision. A good advisor knows this is an important decision that may require time to make; she would rather have you take the time you need rather than encounter problems down the road.

Hopefully, the advisor will provide answers that fit your circumstances. If you are divorced, expect him to tell you how many divorced individuals he has as clients. If you have indicated that you are an intense player in the stock market, expect to hear that he is a stock jockey. If he hasn't clearly communicated his investment philosophy, now is the time you should expect answers.

If you don't hear what you expect, ask—in terms as specific as you can. Is she the tortoise or the hare? You need a financial advisor who is an expert in the problems you have and the goals you have set. This is the time you want to hire a specialist, not a general practitioner.

Remember, you are considering a professional relationship that, in many ways, is similar to a financial marriage. A little honesty now—from both of the parties involved—goes a long way to helping ensure a trusting, mutually beneficial relationship with a long future.

SCORING QUESTION #10

Answers the question to your satisfaction	5 points
Brings the question up without you asking	5 points
Answers, "I love everything about you"	Subtract 5 points

Total Points Question #10 _____ (maximum 10 points)

Total Points all 10 Questions _____ maximum 100 points)

SCOREBOARD TOTALS

50 points or below	Get out the business section and start flipping a coin. You will probably do better yourself.
51–60 points	Not much value here. The guy you sit next to on the bus may have a leg up on these advisors.
61–70 points	No cream here . . . just sour milk.
71–80 points	May be worth saving the name for future use, when he grows up. But you can do better today.
81–85 points	This is the minimum acceptable grade. But would you hire a brain

	surgeon who barely passed the test?
86–90 points	Recheck your scores. Time to go with your gut feelings: Who makes you feel comfortable?
91–95 points	This may be as good as you will ever find. Should make others you are interviewing look dismal by comparison.
96–100 points	Hey, I'd hire this guy myself.

There you have it: ten simple questions *and* the answers. This is an invaluable tool for those looking for a new advisor or those who question their current financial arrangement. For those with an existing financial advisor, go ahead and give her the test. I will venture to say that over 90 percent will not get a grade of 91 or better. If not, don't keep them around . . . shop around.

HOW TO INVEST IN REAL ESTATE WITHOUT GETTING TAKEN EVERY TIME

SIX

REAL ESTATE: AN INTRODUCTION

For most of us, the idea of wealth—indeed, of ownership itself—centers around the tangible. People being people, we like to be able to touch our possessions, to hold them in our hands, if only to convince ourselves that they really exist. As a species, we're most comfortable believing that when we deposit our paychecks, the proper number of greenbacks is immediately placed in a secure, Scrooge McDuck–type vault in the bank's subterranean stronghold.

It's a primordial instinct, and only in relatively modern times has the concept of intangible wealth—stocks, bonds, e-accounts, etc.—been accepted even to a modest extent.

This is probably why so many people truly like real estate as both the pathway to, and the reward of, personal wealth. Everything about it proclaims security, permanence, safety. For instance, we talk about real estate "holdings"; the term itself promises that, unlike "ethereal" financial vehicles that exist only as charged electrons in computer's data-storage system, "real" estate is . . . well, *real*.

And just as real is real estate's potential for profit—that is, if one approaches it *without illusions or distractions.*

Over my lifetime, I have made more money in real estate than in any other investment. I've owned houses, commercial buildings, condos, vacant commercial land—even a 600-acre farm. They have all been attractive properties, and some of the homes have been spectacular.

But that's not why I made money on them; in fact, the emotional appeal of any given piece of real estate can be an obstacle to achieving its full profit potential. Far too many investors are seduced by the siren song of a striking architectural design or a breathtaking view.

No. I made a profit on my holdings because I approached each buy-and-sell with one purpose in mind: *to make the most money on each deal.*

And in a nutshell, that's the secret.

In real estate, the first step toward ruin is to fall in love with any particular property. To become enthralled by a scenic vista framed by floor-to-ceiling picture windows, overwhelmed by walk-in closets, or dazzled by a fully equipped, state-of-the-art kitchen—these are *emotional* responses. And in financial matters of any kind, it's usually best to keep affairs of the heart strictly out of the picture.

Certainly, I can appreciate beauty and well-planned functionality. But as a practical matter, it is far more important that I understand the potential impact of the property's aesthetics on the next person in the ownership chain—that is, the guy I sell it to, ideally for substantially more than I paid.

There is great truth in the adage "Buy land; they aren't making any more of it." But the real talent lies in knowing *what* land to buy, *when* to buy it, and *how* to ensure a profit from it. As a result, emotional attachment is a liability; it clouds your judgment and slows your trigger finger.

I'm only human; I confess that I've not always been able to follow my own advice here. But when I have (and that's been more often than not), I've been able to follow the classic rule of the successful investor: buy low and sell high.

This rule has allowed me to steer clear of real-estate speculators and investment advisors whose practice is to buy high . . . in the hope of selling higher. Real estate is rife with people whose livelihood is based on "flipping" their holdings as rapidly as possible, counting on the fast profit to allow them to buy into another speculative real-estate "opportunity." Sadly (at least, for *them*) I've often ended up bidding on their holdings at bankruptcy auctions or capitalizing on their desperation by offering them a fire-sale price. It's the nature of the business.

And a cutthroat business it can be, too; in virtually every real-estate deal there is a winner and at least one loser. The only way to avoid ending up holding the sticky end of the lollipop is to understand that everyone wants your money . . . and to know how to use that knowledge to your advantage.

Ready? Then let's begin.

SEVEN

FOUR REAL-ESTATE MYTHS

To Buy or Not to Buy: *That* Is the Question . . .

With apologies to Shakespeare, this is the logical place to start. Home ownership is the American dream, and a solid majority of home owners sincerely believe that buying their own abode is the best investment they ever made.

Unfortunately, they are dead wrong. Were I a less charitable person, I might state flatly, with outrage in my soul, that these home owners are the victims of a cynically deceptive device employed by real-estate salespeople, bank loan officers, and seminar *banditos* alike.

But in kinder terms, I'll just say that they have a misplaced belief in one of the myths that revolve around real estate in general, and home ownership in particular. Let's look at what I call the Four Great Real-Estate Myths . . .

Myth Number 1: "Owning Your Home Is a *Great* Investment."

Let's define our terms here. As I mentioned earlier, an investment is properly defined as something you put money *in* that pays you something *back*. When was the last time *you* got a check paid to you by the people who live in your house?

Never, unless you're renting the place out while you circumnavigate the globe (or have one dickens of a sweet deal with your spouse and kids). *You* pay the bank every month; by definition, your residence is an investment by and for the bank, not you. They loan you their money, which you "rent" by paying it back with interest. The red ink on your so-called investment adds up quickly, since it includes the monthly stipends you pay to the utility company, Ma Bell, Joe the Plumber, and Tony the lawn maintenance guy (and let's not even think about those ever-increasing property-tax bills, twice a year).

Already, I can hear your screams of outrage. Don't worry: I hear the same from my clients all the time. "But, David," they tell me, "I only paid two hundred and twenty-five thousand for the place fifteen years ago. Now the guy down the street is asking four-oh-nine for his house and it's not *nearly* as nice as mine."

For the sake of discussion, I'll stipulate that:

1. Yes, you have a very nice house (okay, okay—I'm sure that it's the nicest on your block).

2. Unless you have had *incredibly* bad luck (i.e., you discovered too late your place was built over an abandoned hazardous-waste dump, atop an earthquake fault line, or amid an ancient burial ground of a politically connected ethnic group lacking a sense of either humor or irony), your house is worth more today than it was when you bought it.

But the sad (and startling) fact is that, historically, homes in the United States have appreciated at *only about 1 percent a year over inflation*. This is compared to, for instance, the stock market, with its seventy-year-plus average return of somewhat more than 10 percent.

For a fairly recent example of what this means, let's visit with two of my clients; we'll call them Jerry and Susan.

A little background on Jerry and Susan is in order. At the time they came in to see me, Jerry was sixty-four and Susan was sixty-two. Jerry was blue-collar, having worked all his life in one or another of the steel plants outside Chicago. Susan worked in an office part-time to bring in a little extra money.

As a couple, they are about as all-American as they come. They are well liked and active in their community—PTA when their children were in school, members of their Neighborhood Watch; when his work schedule permitted, Jerry enjoyed helping out as a youth league assistant basketball coach for a few months each year. Neither was a college graduate. However, they made sure both of their kids were—even though, as Jerry said, "It cut us a little tight for a few years."

Those days were past now, and the couple had settled into a comfortable lifestyle, living in a house they had purchased for $225,000 fifteen years before. Jerry had recently made his last mortgage payment, and—as with so many people—the joy of retiring that debt sparked ideas of another type of retirement. For that reason, I wasn't surprised when Jerry called my office to schedule an appointment.

I had a pretty good idea of what to expect. Earlier, he and Susan had asked my advice about selling their current house and moving into something less expensive. "We'd like a little more freedom," Susan had said. "Maybe do a little traveling, now that the kids are on their own."

Before the meeting, Jerry did a bit of research. He calculated that $409,000 would be a good asking price for his home, figuring that after haggling, he would sell at $400,000. (This was, by the way, pretty ordinary. It amounted to slightly more than a 4 percent gain for each year they had lived in their house. Since the annual inflation rate had been approximately 3 percent a year, that put them right at the historical average gain of 1 percent annually for home prices.)

"I think I'm ready to cash in on the place, David," Jerry said, and grinned. "Susan and I have plans for the money."

Jerry was happy and excited; I hated to be the one to burst his private real-estate bubble.

"Before you cash the check," I said, smiling to take the sting from my words, "let's look a little closer at the numbers."

I jotted some words and figures on the notepad I keep on my desk.

"Okay, let's start with the realtor. Figuring the sales commission at six percent, there goes twenty-four thousand from your profit." I said. "That leaves three hundred and seventy-six thousand—still a pretty nice sum. But then there are the closing costs. These include lawyer's fees, title insurance, that sort of cost."

Jerry's lips twisted sourly; then he shrugged.

I nodded in sympathy. "Now, by law you have to disclose any known problems with the property—leaky roof, wet basement, and so on. Anything like that to worry about?"

Jerry and Susan looked at each other knowingly. I took their silence for an answer.

"So let's figure that it's going to cost you a few thousand dollars to fix those problems," I said. "So with closing costs and fix-ups, let's say it will cost you about six thousand." I made the calculations and penciled in a figure: $370,000.

Surprised? Jerry was, but we shouldn't be. Almost everybody overestimates the worth of their home, usually for one of two reasons:

1. They let their emotions get in the way and overestimate the cold facts of the marketplace (those pencil marks on the closet wall, indicating the various heights of our children over the years, may have value to *us*, but seldom have an impact on the sales price).

or, as Jerry did;

2. They don't take into account the various charges associated with real estate (including what I call "terminal maintenance"— that is, the cost of fixing all those cracks, leaks, and upkeep items that *we* may have learned to live with, but that a new seller will demand be resolved before the sale).

Still: a gain of $145,000 on a $225,000 investment, realized at the end of fifteen years.

Not bad—or is it? Let's see by looking at Myth Number 2.

Myth Number 2: "Your Home Is a *Great* Tax Write-off for You."

I hear it constantly from my clients: "How about all the great write-offs for my interest and taxes?"

Yeah, how about 'em?

Or rather, "When do I *get* them?"—because most of us don't. Sadly, most people don't understand that if they file the short form for their federal income taxes, they are not allowed to write off any deductions.

Under current law, the federal government generously allows every couple filing a joint return the so-called standard deduction. In 2004, it came to about $9,700 per year; while the amount varies from year to year, the good news is that you get it simply for breathing.·

It allows a taxpayer to opt out of the more precise method of listing actual deductible expenses, and is used either because the standard deduction is the higher figure or because the taxpayer can't be bothered to save all the receipts and records needed to document the actual deductions he claims.

For that reason, only taxpayers who decide to itemize their deductions get the opportunity to write off the *actual* interest and other deductible costs associated with home ownership. For those who go with the standard deduction, home ownership provides *no tax breaks at all.*

Here are a few details. Let's say you are in year ten of a mortgage loan (let's call it 7 percent for $175,000, with a fifteen-year term); you pay $18,875.40 each year. Of that, $12,823.39 goes toward the principal (not tax deductible) versus an interest cost of $6,052.01 (deductible).

For the sake of argument, let's assume that you're paying $3,500 a year in taxes, (which are also deductible) and your total of deductible home-related expenses comes to just under $10,000. Unless you have a lot of deductible expenses in other areas (for instance, medical costs not reimbursed to you from insurance), you may well decide simply to take the standard deduction and save yourself the paperwork hassle of itemizing your expenses. It's simple common sense.

But there is no free lunch either. In the situation I cite, each and every dollar you paid in interest means absolutely nothing: There is no write-off.

Even if we double your mortgage interest and taxes amount to roughly $20,000 a year (roughly, two times the $9,700 standard deduction), it's hardly reason to break out the champagne for a celebration. If you're paying that much, you are likely in the 25 percent federal tax bracket; your state will demand another 5 percent or so. Itemizing expenses means you will get a tax deduction of about 30 percent of the "extra" $10,000. That's about $3,000.

Let's see; you spend $20,000 and get $3,000 back . . . well, it's better than nothing, but hardly what you were led to expect when the realtor first showed you around the house.

But I want to be fair, because not every part of Myth 2 is uninformed bunkum. Home ownership is a lousy tax shelter—except, in most circumstances, when you sell your home.

Under current IRS rules, if you and your spouse have lived in your home at least two of the last five years, for a married couple, the first $500,000 is totally federal-tax-free. (For a single home owner, it's $250,000.) You make out like a bandit, though only on the back side of the sale.

Myth Number 3: "Buying Is Better Than Renting."

Not surprisingly, given what most people believe about Myths 1 and 2, expressing any doubt about the preferability of buying over renting is akin to voicing heresy inside the Vatican.

But let's put it to the test: What if you rented a house similar to the one you own, and *invested the rest elsewhere*—say, in the stock market? To see the ramifications, let's use the example of a modest, $225,000 home purchased with a $40,000 down payment and a fifteen-year mortgage at 6 percent.

Here's the approximate breakdown:

- $40,000 in cash (the down payment). Rather than amortize this figure, we'll simply call it money that is no longer available as an investment asset

- Monthly payments of $1,561 a month

- Taxes of $333 a month

- $500 a month for home repairs. These would include air-conditioning and furnace repairs and replacement, roof repairs, driveway, landscaping, appliances, painting, and a whole lot more. When one rents, these are typically paid by the land-lord . . . at *his* expense;

We'll also use a realistic figure for the tax advantages that accrue from home ownership; in this case, let's say a generous average of $300 a month in real tax savings over the fifteen-year time period. When we subtract this from the approximate $2,400 a month in actual cash outlay, our bottom line is a monthly outlay of almost $2,100. In a few moments, we'll also factor in the profit, if any, from selling the place.

But for now, let's look at the rental side. Because housing markets vary so drastically in any given locale, we'll use a hypothetical, medium-size town in the midwestern United States as our basis; in fact, we'll use Jack and Susan's house, because I'm going to make an important point in a few paragraphs.

In any event, everybody needs to live somewhere. In our hypothetical example, that someplace is a $225,000 house, originally purchased about fifteen years ago. Way back then, the rent on a house of that type might have been only about $800 a month.

We'll tack on a 3 percent rent increase every year, add it up, and average it out over fifteen years: about $1,100 a month. As renters, then, that would leave us with approximately $1,000 extra dollars to invest each month. We'll invest it in the stock market, along with the original $40,000 we didn't use as a down payment to buy a house.

Our $40,000 is earning us a return of about 8 percent (a reasonable figure: remember, the stock market historically has returned a little over 10 percent a year for the last eighty years). To that, we'll add $1,000 every month. At each year's end, we'll pay approximately 30 percent in taxes on our gains.

Push the button on your calculator, and over the course of fifteen years we have a grand total of $376,699.

Hmm . . . that's about $6,000 *more* than the check Jerry and Susan will walk out with if they should decide to sell their house and downsize after retirement—and remember, we used a very reasonable 8 percent annual return, well below the historical average (which, to repeat, is about 10 percent).

It gets worse. If we had made the same investment in a tax-deferred annuity (where you pay taxes on the money only when you pull it out), our decision to rent would have earned us (or Jack and Susan, since it's their house anyway) a grand total of *$466,665!*

Now, I won't mislead you. If Jack and Susan cashed out all of their gains at one time, some depressing issues of taxation would arise, both with Uncle Sam and all his nieces and nephews at the state level. By the time the government took its bites from the pie, only $360,332 would remain.

But to repeat: that is only if Jack and Susan took out all their money at once. And in more than twenty-five years of advising clients, I have not had anyone who has ever cashed in all her money at one time. Instead, my clients usually draw gradually against that lump sum to live comfortably (which allows them to earn additional interest on the amount that hasn't been withdrawn yet).

But what about an environment where house prices are skyrocketing?

I can almost hear what some of you are saying as you read this.

"David, I just bought my house three years ago and they are already selling new ones just like it for twenty-five percent more. I'd be crazy to rent instead of riding the wave upward."

Certainly, if house prices continue at an 8-percent-a-year gain over the next twelve years, you'll be right. But the odds against that occurring are high indeed; over the past hundred years, it's never even come close to happening.

Typically, what has happened in the wake of housing-market boom times is a subsequent period where prices may not plummet, but instead simply stagnate.

The value of the house does not appreciate, and the owner cannot recover his or her equity by selling—possibly for years to come. To compound the problem, because the money is tied up in the house, it's not available for more profitable investment. Home ownership becomes a classic lose/lose situation.

This is a secret long known by the wealthy among us. They understand that as the price of property skyrockets, the better off one is who rents, investing the difference. They know that the rent the market will bear for such a place never covers the outflow it takes to own it. Other factors may intrude (particularly the emotional one that psychologists call ego, which is a primary reason why *nouveau riche* rap stars and professional athletes build those ridiculous mega-mansions), but the smart money knows how to live well—and still prosper financially.

Let's take a real quick look at a $2 million home; to make it even easier to follow, let's stipulate that the buyer avoids any interest charges by paying cash. A reasonable assumption is that the taxes will be about $40,000 a year, with maintenance another $45,000.

If the initial $2 million plus the additional $85,000 in annual upkeep costs had been invested for an 8 percent annual yield, over a ten-year period the value of the property would have to go to $5,601,879—*just to equal what the investment return would have earned by putting that money into a tax deferred annuity!*

Okay, so even the rich have to live someplace (and most likely, someplace nice; that's one of the reasons people want to *be* rich, isn't it?). A reasonable rent for a $2 million residence, factoring in periodic increases over a ten-year period, would average to about $10,000 per month. Do the math. Financially, you would still be better off paying that rent and investing the difference.

Bottom line: I am not saying that owning your own home over many years is a bad investment—but it's not the one real-estate agents would have you believe.

Myth Number 4: "Real Estate Will Always Appreciate in Value, 'Cause They're Not Making Any More of It . . ."

You may live in one of the real-estate hot spots around the country that have seen 40, 50 or 60 percent gains over the last several years. If so, you're probably feeling pretty smart (or, if you're exceptionally honest with yourself, very lucky) about the real-estate purchase decisions you made in years past. You may even be looking with anticipation toward the future, when the appreciation in your home's value will make even today's figures look paltry . . .

. . . because isn't real estate the best, safest and most prosperous investment ever? And won't it always continue to be?

In your mind's eye, you should be seeing Robby the Robot waving his mechanical arms wildly; inside your head, a tinny voice should be intoning: "Danger, Will Robinson! Danger!"

If the comments you're hearing about how the real-estate boom will never end sound familiar to you—well, they should. Certainly, I heard the same kind of comments about the stock market in 1999 and 2000—before the big crash. In fact, one of the main factors driving home values upward over the last few years is all the money that fled the stock market and found refuge in the open arms of real estate. Inevitably, that trend will one day reverse itself.

Newtonian physics says it best: what goes up, must come down. Despite periods in which home prices have soared, there has been no shortage of times when prices stalled, stagnated, and in particularly overheated markets (for instance, in California, New York, or Florida) even *fell*. Historical averages remain the best indicators of real-estate appreciation, if for no other reason than that they continue to prove themselves accurate.

Sure, there are always a fortunate few who (by dint of insight or plain dumb luck) are able to time their entry and exit from the real-estate market. They make out like bandits, but they are the exception. For the rest of us—as with the gambler who bets heavily against the casino because of an emotional "gut feeling"—we must either cut our losses or go bust . . . or wait out the drought before we reap our rewards.

An illustration: during Chicago's condo-conversion craze back in the early eighties, I saw an opportunity to purchase a number of condominiums in the tony section of downtown Chicago known as the Gold Coast.

I wasn't alone. Along with dozens of other potential investors, I found myself standing in line to get a number; if my number was drawn, I'd have the right to purchase one or more units in a fifty-two-story rental building that was turning condo.

Because of the demand for what all of us saw as a once-in-a-lifetime opportunity—after all, this was a prime location close to the pulsating core of the city, and there weren't a lot of locations like that left—the sellers decided they could dictate the terms.

They didn't let us inspect the units, for instance: if we wanted to bid, it was going to be on a sight-unseen basis, with only the basic floor plans on which to make our decision. Worse, given the rental rates the Chicago market could bear at the time, even if I succeeded in finding a tenant, I'd end up with a horrible negative cash flow.

I remember how hard I worked to convince myself that all this was still a good idea; after all, it was real estate—and they weren't making any more of it, right? If everybody else wanted in, I did, too.

But basically, I think I knew the truth. I was waiting in line to lose money.

Which I did, for years and years. It took over *fifteen years* before the Chicago real-estate market improved and I could sell the condos for what I paid for them.

I recently sold off every condo I owned in downtown Chicago. The market picked up and allowed me to make a 300 percent profit. Still, fifteen years is a long time to wait for the drought to break, and I still wince when I think of what I might have been able to do with the money I had tied up in the properties.

I learned a lot about real estate during that time, and most of it reinforced what I instinctively felt while I stood in line twenty-some years before, jostling amid a crowd of people clamoring to buy into a money-losing proposition. The main lesson I learned is this:

Real estate is like most other investments. When everybody can't get enough of something, sell 'em all you have. When nobody wants it, buy all you can.

———————

Okay—we've examined all the reasons why *buying* a home may not be the most advantageous move.

But I don't expect that I've convinced many of you on the subject; after all, we're talking about the American Dream here. So in the next chapter, let's take a look at the cautionary side you should know about when you buy your next home.

A little clue here, everybody. Being financially successful is about far more than owning a big house. Being financially successful is owning a huge home, not working, and having your investments paying all the bills. Your biggest concern should be whether to take the Bentley or the Ferrari to the club when you play golf for the day.

EIGHT

IF YOU'RE THINKING ABOUT BUYING A <u>NEW</u> HOME . . . DON'T

I know, I know—even if you agree that the previous chapter made a good case for the advantages of renting rather than buying, in reality I realize that I made very few converts. The lure of ownership is still too strong for most of us to resist.

I understand completely; you see, I live in a house that I own.

Of course, I should also mention that my home is *the* worst investment I have ever made. I bought it in the late eighties at a great price—at a foreclosure sale, to boot. It's a lovely place: a 6,000-square-foot house on a wooded acre lot, overlooking a private, eighteen-hole golf course.

Yet today, almost twenty years later, it would be tough for me to get back all the money I have sunk into that pit over the years. Add in almost twenty years of outrageous taxes and you can remove all doubts.

Surprised? Shocked? I would have been, too, if you had tried to warn me about it back when I was preparing to buy the place. But it wouldn't have been such a shock if I had known then what I know now.

So before we move on and find out the best way for you to ignore my advice and buy your own residential money pit, let's work the numbers on my house.

Over the years I have replaced the windows, kitchen, bathrooms, roof; I've had work done on the plumbing, wiring, and replaced all the HAC (heating and air-conditioning, for the rookies among us); I've moved walls, added a three-car garage, and ante'd up for a few other improvements that contributed to what I consider my quality of life.

The total cost of these improvements: approximately $400,000. (In case you're wondering, I've calculated that if I never put an unessential dime in the house—that is, limiting my efforts to repairing and replacing only what actually needed repairing and replacing—the results would have differed by only $100,000 or so over all these years. Simply stated, upkeep on a house is, unavoidably, very expensive.)

But while I live in what most people consider an excellent community, like so many others around the country, it is one that has largely been bypassed by the hyperappreciation of real estate that has run rampant in other Chicago suburbs and select parts of the country. If I could pick up my house and plunk it down on a similar lot, say, forty miles north and a touch west, it would be worth as much as three times its current in-situ real market value. Move it to Naples, Florida, or Malibu and it would probably rival the gross national product of some third-world countries.

At block parties and other get-togethers over the years, most of my neighbors have agreed that none of us would make a substantial profit if we sold our homes. Some still live in dream world, believing what they read in the paper. Without exception, all of us agree that we live in a great place to raise our children—but as a real-estate market, it's an awful place to raise your net worth.

If I didn't have so many other real-estate holdings in other locations (farm, condos, vacant land, commercial real estate) that have done very well, I would have probably moved long ago, despite the pleas of my wife and kids to stay.

So don't think everybody is making a killing in the real-estate market just because they've made the transition to "owners." They're not, and you may not either.

And since you're going to do it anyway, allow me to let you in on a few tips that can make home ownership more advantageous—and at the same time help you understand why most people don't become rich in real estate.

———————

Never ever buy brand-new. The popularity of *Extreme Makeover, This Old House,* and other fix-'em-up TV shows aside, relatively few people want to buy old homes. The effort and expense of tearing out antiquated kitchens, renovating lime-green bathrooms, and steaming off a half century of stained wallpaper loses its appeal quickly in real life, particularly if you're already faced with the other challenges of job and family.

For that reason, given the choice, most people will opt for new construction when they shop for a home.

(And that's too bad, because, from a purely financial point of view, old is where the best values usually are found. Sweat equity invested into a sound older structure is one of the most certain ways to build value into any property.)

But there's a reason it's called a "dream house," and practicality has little to do with the ultimate decision. When the urge hits, otherwise sane prospective home owners spend each weekend visiting countless model homes in search of their fantasy. When they find it, they don't let a minor detail like price deter them.

To illustrate this, let me introduce Barry and Megan, two of my younger clients. They are an attractive, up-and-coming couple. My association with them came through Megan's parents, who had been clients of mine for almost twenty years and had referred the young couple to me for financial counseling.

Barry and Megan were young and full of love for each other. Like most people embarking on a life together, their list of wants was long. About two years after I started managing their meager finances as a favor to Megan's parents, I saw the signs: at every review session, one or the other (eventually, both) would talk about the "inconveniences of apartment living."

Finally, Barry was unable to hold it in. "David, we simply *have* to get out of that apartment," he said, and Megan nodded solemnly. "There's just no sense paying rent and having nothing to show for it but canceled checks."

Well, there can be something (please see "Buying Is Better Than Renting" in the previous chapter), but neither Barry nor Megan wanted to hear of it. They admitted they had become weekend bingers—spending every Sunday morning scanning the "houses for sale" ads and the rest of the day driving to various open houses. By the time they admitted their malady to me, they had already narrowed their search down to three houses.

To their credit, they had done their homework. They had contacted several financial institutions, filled out the forms, and had been preapproved for the maximum amount of money their bank calculated that they could afford to borrow—in their case, $350,000.

(Big mistake, by the way. Why buy a nonproductive asset that costs the maximum amount for which you can qualify? If your bank says that you can afford a $350,000 home, why not buy a $275,000 home and get another loan for the extra $75,000 to buy a parcel of investment real estate? Answer: ego. A young couple [or maybe I should say most *any* couple, regardless of age] wants the most lavish house they can afford because they believe it shows the world that they are financially successful. It's an expensive conceit, but sadly commonplace.)

All three homes Barry and Megan were considering were brand-new, all priced at around that $350,000 maximum loan amount for which they qualified.

"Nice," I said, nodding, as I flipped through the listings they showed me. "But are you considering an older home or maybe just a less expensive new one?"

They looked at me as if I were speaking Esperanto. Neither thought had ever even entered their minds.

And that's too bad. With a previously owned home, several factors can be used to your advantage that are not usually available to the new-home buyer. We'll look at them in more detail in a moment, but first let's take a look at how the cost of new construction has an impact at every level of home ownership.

Simplified, here's the process: one day, a farmer who grows corn and soybeans on his 240-acre spread finds in his mailbox a letter. It's from a real-estate agent who notes that farmland that once sold for $4,000 an acre may now be worth $21,000 an acre to a local developer.

"Any interest?" the letter asks. "I'm always ready to help."

Farming is backbreaking work. Sooner or later, it occurs to even the most traditional-minded farmer that taking $5 million and retiring to Palm Springs beats getting up at 4 A.M. for a sixteen-hour day while he hopes corn will get up to $2.70 a bushel.

In our hypothetical case, the farmer gets his $5 million from a developer, who then proceeds to get the land rezoned for single-family residences. If it's not already inside the boundaries of a nearby town or city, most likely he'll also work to get the parcel annexed in order to obtain access to city utilities and support services. This process can take months or even years, with the developer dangling the increased tax base in exchange for the city's increased cost of expanding its infrastructure (roads, water, and sewers, etc.).

If all goes well, at some point the development is ready for home building. If he's not a builder himself, the developer will then sell the individual lots he created to various home builders for, say, $50,000 a lot. Typically, there are two to three lots per acre created by the new land plan.

At this point, the developer is getting up to $150,000 an acre for land he paid only $21,000 an acre to buy just a year or two before.

Sound like a bundle? Well, it is—but to be fair, getting a property zoned and annexed is very costly. Doing surveys, hiring land planners, building streets, digging sewers, running water lines, the interest on the $5 million he paid the farmer—these cost the developer big bucks . . . and all up front. And of course, there's always the risk that when he is finally done, the economy could have changed and there are few or no buyers for his newly platted lots.

But if all goes well, the developer stands to make millions of dollars on the deal.

Of course, he's making it from the builders. On each lot, the builder will erect a house on which he typically plans to make a profit of about 25 percent; the first lots he will sell to the home buyer for $75,000 . . . an immediate $25,000 profit.

In total, the simple new 2,500-square-foot house he will sell for $350,000 costs him about $250,000 to build—that is, a $75,000 profit on building the house and another $25,000 on the lot. Total potential profit to him: approximately $100,000 on that $350,000 house you bought. (This, by the way, does not include any of the "extras"—say, high-end appliances or environmental systems, a fireplace in the master bedroom, or an extra garage to house all the junk one accumulates over a lifetime—that a buyer may order him to install. Such items are great additional profit centers for the builder.)

But the builder also has costs and risks that will cut into that gain. Someone has to pay the taxes on the property until it is sold, cover any cost overruns, and pay the interest on money he borrows to finance the construction costs. At the same time, there's always the possibility that no one will buy the spec house before this financial house of cards collapses.

At the end of this chain comes you, the purchaser of your own dream house. So in keeping with the title of this book, *Everybody Wants Your Money,* this means that *you* are paying the profits for the farmer, the developer, and the builder.

I explained all this to Barry and Megan, trying hard not to notice the hint of exasperation I saw behind their eyes.

"I'm telling you all of this for a reason," I implored. "For instance, what happens if you need to get out from under the burden of debt represented by your personal dream? For instance, what if one of you loses your job or gets transferred? God forbid, but what if a major health problem comes up, or you incur some other major expense that makes your 'new' house unaffordable?"

Neither offered a response, unless you count the look Barry gave Megan.

But I knew the answer anyway: to put it plainly, they'd be screwed.

Why? Well, first of all, they're going to incur all the costs of selling any house.

For instance, real-estate brokers charge about 6 percent in commissions. If they have to sell their $350,000 house in the first year, Barry and Megan will need to receive $372,000 just to break even.

Second, they are at a marketplace disadvantage. As with a new car, a new house usually *loses* market value the moment it is sold to the first buyer (unless it is a builder closeout that he wants to dump at somewhere around his costs in order to move on to his next project). In effect, their house is a "used" product that is competing against other brand-new houses.

If a spanking-new home down the street is selling for $350,000 to $360,000, why would anyone buy Barry and Megan's "used" home for tens of thousands of dollars *more*?

The answer, of course, is that nobody would.

So then, for Barry and Megan, the question becomes: "How low must they go to just to sell the damn house?" If the need is great enough, the answer could be catastrophic for their financial future.

And they can't expect the builder to bail them out by constantly raising prices. If a builder detects a slowdown in housing demand (or if he is close to closing out the project anyway), he may well decide to drop the price he charges for new houses. The asking price may even dip well below the $350,000 Barry and Megan paid. Remember, his actual land and construction costs were only about $250,000; he has a lot more wiggle room than Megan and Barry have.

Just to show how dire their situation is, let's say that they find a prospective buyer who offers to buy their almost-new house for $330,000. Where does this leave Barry and Megan?

Unless they're able to do a "sell by owner" deal, they will still have to pay about $20,000 in real-estate commissions; closing costs and legal fees will run about $3,000 more. Bottom line: the house that Barry and Megan happily paid $350,000 to buy only a year before will net them just $307,000—a *loss of $43,000!*

In summation, in most circumstances, it usually takes several years of house-price appreciation just to break even on any new home.

Compare that painful reality to the other choice that Barry and Megan could make: buying an existing home. It may be one that needs minor renovation work; it may be a distress sale, or a foreclosure that has come on the market. Such variables can have a significant impact on the asking price, and certainly will influence what Barry and Megan would offer.

As it turned out, I put Barry and Megan in touch with a friend who lived for over twenty years in a house not far from one of the developments they were considering. A widower, he was in the process of preparing himself for retirement in Arizona; as a result, he was motivated to sell.

My friend had paid $148,000 for his home over two decades earlier—in a lovely location on a quiet street lined with century-old oaks and majestic elms. Did I mention it was just a few blocks from the train? With a few minor repairs and updates, coupled with a good real-estate market, it should now have brought around $350,000.

But because the seller was anxious to get on with his life and the fact that he would save almost $20,000 bypassing the real-estate commission, he was willing to accept an offer of around $275,000.

Caught up in my own enthusiasm, I outlined a feasible plan of action: Barry and Megan could sink $25,000 into new carpeting, drapes, painting, and a few new appliances. Total investment: approximately $300,000 for a home they could, if necessary, place on the market for $350,000.

Compare that with the original scenario: Barry and Megan need to sell the home on a crash basis. After they make all the home improvements, let's say they have to negotiate down to a sale price of $340,000. After paying a real-estate commission of about $20,000 and that inevitable $3,000 in closing and legal fees, they will still get a check for $317,000—and a profit of $17,000.

"A few fix-ups, a little effort spent on cosmetic repairs," I told Barry and Megan. "That's all it'll take to bring the worth of that house to three hundred fifty thousand."

I saw the look Barry shot Megan; it was dubious, but it was obvious his interest had been sparked.

"The owner's anxious to move on," I said. "I know you could get him to sell the property as is for two seventy-five."

That did the trick.

"We'll look at it," Megan said, and Barry nodded.

I wish I could give you a storybook ending here: I wish I could tell you how the couple bought the house, turned it into a showplace—and, of course, by doing so maximized the value of their home and their total net worth.

But, alas, I can't. A couple of weeks later, I ran into Megan at a local event. She was beaming and couldn't wait to give me the news.

"We did it," she said, her voice excited. "Barry and I are home owners now! You've got to come out and see it—it's beautiful, and everything is brand-new!"

Win some, lose some.

NINE

SECOND-GUESSING SECOND HOMES: A RADICAL NEW APPROACH

Not so many years ago, if a father put a roof over his family's head, he was considered a success. Today, in addition to the roof, it takes a pool, sundeck, and access to the beachfront.

And that's just the vacation home.

There comes a time in a successful life when all the *i*'s are dotted, all the *t*'s crossed. For many, it comes when the kids are out of college, the mortgage is paid off, and the portfolio is puttering along nicely, building security for the long term. Life is good.

Inevitably, that's when what I call "the Urge" rears its ugly head.

It's the time when many of my clients visit me bearing dozens of glossy brochures—each resplendent with full-color floor plans and packed with exquisite photos of suntanned couples playing tennis and hiking through lush mountain meadows or simply lounging on the boardwalk as a crimson sun sets over the endless sea.

Every conversation begins the same way: "David, we've been thinking about investing in a second home—a *vacation* home . . ."

Indeed.

Now, I am anything but the kind of soulless, number-crunching drudge that populates most stories involving money managers and financial advisors; I believe that enjoying life—and the fruits that come from years of hard work (or an inheritance)—is an excellent way to . . . well, *live*. Clearly, a vacation home can be a satisfying way to spend one's hard-earned money.

But are vacation homes a good deal, financially? Here, the answer is anything but clear.

Today, the kind of getaway home that people want—and are buying—doesn't even remotely resemble their father's dream of the A-frame cabin down on good ol' Bass Lake.

Instead, this dream has been supplanted by the high-rise condominium overlooking the Gulf of Mexico or the capacious home along the fairway in Arizona (preferably, with a country-club membership included). These days, it's not unusual for my clients to be considering vacation homes that are larger, more lavish, and considerably more expensive than the family's primary residence.

And why not? Leisure has become a major industry throughout the world. In a day when a night's stay with an ocean view at a leading resort can easily approach the four-figure range in season, a private lodge in the mountains or a quality beachfront condo can seem like a sensible bargain.

Certainly, it did to Betty and Dan, a couple who have been great clients of mine for more than eight years.

Partners in work as well as in life, through hard work and a great deal of business savvy and common sense they built the business they founded into a prosperous operation. From its genesis as a mom-and-pop venture (literally: as infants, their two children had learned to sleep in a crib only a few feet from the production floor), Betty and Dan oversee a company that now employs over fifty people.

Along the way, they learned to play hard as well as work hard. After years of short (or no) vacations, a cadre of managers they recruited and trained now permits them to take real vacations. As a result, they are making up for lost time—taking three- or even four-day weekends every chance they get. They have become journeymen black-diamond skiers, low-handicap golfers, and have even mastered the art of guilt-free relaxation on sun-drenched beaches.

Now they were ready to take the next step: the Urge was upon them, and they were not hesitant to spend whatever it would take to buy the right vacation home.

"I'm kind of tired of hearing my friends brag about all the money they're making on their vacation homes," Dan said, chuckling. "I want in on that action—bad."

Betty shook her head, a smile on her face. "I just want out of the hotel rat race, David," she told me. "Checking in, trying for room upgrades, and all the other hassles—and I've had it with the last-minute surprises that come with every checkout."

I nodded in sympathy. Like Dan and Betty, I had two kids—and as every parent knows, if you want a minimum-stress vacation, expect to take along each kid's current best friend. That means reserving two (or more) hotel rooms (adjoining, if humanly possible). It also means stratospheric hotel bills and a restaurant tab that rivals the GNP of a small country.

"Thousands of dollars for a seven-day vacation"—Dan shrugged— "and nothing to show for it afterward. That's obscene."

This year, they showed up for their annual financial review wearing ear-to-ear smiles—and carrying a shoulder bag filled to bursting with brochures. They lasted about two minutes before they couldn't hold it in any longer. Betty took the lead.

"David, are we doing okay? Financially, I mean."

I nodded.

"Anything we need to change?"

"Just a couple of minor things." I smiled. "Nothing unusual."

"Good," Dan said, and took a deep breath. "So now we can talk about something we'd like to do." He nodded at Betty, who placed the heavy shoulder bag on my desk. "We want to buy a vacation home."

They were like kids pulling candy from their Easter baskets, handing brochure after brochure across the desk and talking excitedly about the benefits of each. I could see that Dan and Betty were captivated: they had visions of romantic nights strolling on the beach, of enticing their now-college-age children to relive happy vacations past, of introducing future grandkids to the joys of multigenerational vacation togetherness—all that, plus visions of huge profits as property values appreciated over the years.

"I've run the numbers on the computer every night for a month, David," Dan said. "Okay—I know it'll be a *little* expensive—"

"That depends on what you expect from your vacation home," I broke in, but I doubt either of them heard me speak.

"—but with about twenty percent down, I think we can handle buying a vacation home somewhere around a million dollars."

If that sounds like a huge number—well, it is. But for a couple in the financial condition Dan and Betty were in, it's not unreasonable. In fact, current studies indicate that the average price paid for prime vacation homes today is around $600,000—not infrequently, a figure that exceeds the value of the buyer's primary residence.

But no matter the amount, anyone who considers the purchase of a vacation home is venturing into a potential minefield. Contrary to conventional wisdom, buying a vacation/second home most often turns into a disastrous investment for all concerned—*except* the real-estate agent, the bank, and—sometimes, though not always—the person selling the home.

There are a number of reasons, most of them the result of the intoxication that comes with the thought of owning "a piece of paradise." I am often dumbfounded at how people who've spent months to find and buy their primary residence will sign a legally binding contract for a vacation home during the course of a three-day weekend getaway.

You've heard the expression "Buy low and sell high"? With vacation property, most people buy at the height of the market (for instance, in established markets *after* the property development has been completed) in areas that, as a result, are both overbuilt and overpriced. To pay for these properties, the new owners must often give up virtually every other recreational activity. Just as bad, they usually tire of their new purchase in short order—if only because they now feel they *must* vacation in the same place all the time.

With Dan and Betty, I could see that any attempt to dissuade them would have been akin to trying to catch a falling knife. I had but one question for them.

"Did you look at any of the alternatives to purchasing a vacation home?"

Dan frowned. "You mean like those time-share things? Absolutely not. I don't want to—"

"I know exactly what you mean," I said. "When I went shopping for my 'dream vacation home,' I felt the same way you do. But I did find an alternative, both to time-shares and to buying a second house." I smiled. "I joined the club."

That got their attention. "What club?"

Before I tell you what I told Betty and Dan, let's look at the situation today.

First, they were right to scorn the idea of purchasing a timeshare. Nothing has caused some of my clients (not to mention tens of thousands of other families) more regret than buying into this hoary scheme.

If you have traveled to any desirable location in the last twenty years, you undoubtedly know the scene. Prospective buyers are lured into a sales-pitch session with the promise of gifts (typically, cheap trash), tickets for "free" golf, discounted car rentals, or some other inducement; sometimes they're offered cash simply for sitting through a session. In return, they get a marathon sales presentation and a "fabulous offer of a lifetime—if you just sign up *today*!"

On its face, the time-share concept is simple. You buy a block of time—usually a specific set of dates—which you "own" each year. Most time-share schemes promise you reciprocity: that is, you can "trade" your locale and dates on the beach to someone who owns another time-share—say, in the mountains. It theory, it sounds great.

But in practice, you usually end up locked into vacation at the *same* place—on the *same* dates—every year. This, in return for a onetime purchase price that the salesperson may start at, say, $25,000 for each week you "buy"—a price that not infrequently can fall by $5,000, $10,000, or even $15,000, if it can get you to pick up that pen, *right now*!

Welcome to the carnival. All that's missing is the sound of honkytonk music from the hoochie-coochie tent and the slick patter from the barker selling snake-oil cure-all at the next booth over. It's designed to short-circuit that part of your brain that might question how the pricing can be so flexible, or to keep you from asking about those ever-escalating monthly fees and assessments mentioned only in the small-print codicil.

Nonetheless, the approach works on a surprisingly large number of people, if only because they are swept up in the sheer euphoria of participating in what is little more than a carefully scripted version of rip-off-the-rube.

Suffice it to say that usually the only winner here is the

salesman—that is, unless you count the paid shill planted in the audience. He's the enthusiastic fellow who nods eagerly at every pitch point and appears to be literally salivating at the chance to write out a fat check; a tip-off is to look for the first guy to raise his hand and shout "I'll *buy* it!"

My advice is to let him do so, and pass on time-shares yourself.

Nonetheless, if you absolutely *must* buy a time-share, at least don't do it at the carnival. Instead, check out the tens of thousands of resale offers that are available from the original owners—the vast majority of whom

a) finally realized they'd made a ghastly mistake

or

b) have simply tired of trying to find someone with the same locked-in vacation days who is willing to trade hellholes with them this year.

By seeking out secondhand time-shares, you can at least cut out all the middlemen and buy in for a fraction of the costs the original sales team is asking. You'll also be more likely to look at the deal with a clear eye, and be more susceptible to such commonsense steps as getting your lawyer involved *before* you sign anything.

But if time-shares are usually bad deals, there is a newer option available in today's vacation-property marketplace. These are the so-called fractional ownership operations, sometimes referred to as "residence clubs."

At present, residence clubs typically are associated with some of the most prestigious names in the travel industry—operations that generally evoke thought of luxury and quality (such as Ritz-Carlton and the Four Seasons, to name two of the most prominent).

As the name implies, in fractional-ownership programs, you actually share ownership of property with other people, as opposed to owning only a specified block of time in a time-share. Most clubs of this sort deal in condos, town houses, or even houses at a variety of locales—beachfront, ski resort, and so on—at which members book reservations at times that are convenient to them.

That is, *if* those times are available. For example, in a ski resort you might buy a total of three weeks; generally, this is two weeks of prime time and one week in the off-season. Guess when most people want to visit the ski slopes?

For that reason, these reserved weeks usually change every year to give each fractional owner a chance at high-demand seasonal dates and holidays. If you cannot fit your schedule into the window assigned to you, the options are limited: you either try to exchange with someone else, vacation at another of the club's resorts (in many clubs, there may be only three or four), rent "your" time to someone else (if your membership contract even allows this; many don't)—or lose your slot altogether.

As it happens, I know a great deal about these operations. I should, because in my own search for the perfect vacation/second home, I researched them in detail.

"The good news: fractional-ownership clubs are generally a better deal than time-shares," I told Dan and Betty.

Dan's lips twisted sourly. "And the bad news?"

"I still advise against getting involved with the majority of them," I said, and shook my head ruefully. "A few years ago, I put down a ten-thousand-dollar deposit on a residence-club unit. At the last minute, they tried to change the units to be sold—in my view, it was a classic bait-and-switch tactic. I cut and ran, then and there.

"One of the biggest drawbacks," I continued, "is that the name-brand companies running the program could sell out at any time to fly-by-night partners, who in turn could then milk as much as possible (and as quickly as possible) from the unwary."

There were other problems, too: for instance, simply getting *out* of the program seemed excessively complicated and costly. The question of trust aside, the drawbacks had come to outweigh the positives—a fatal flaw at any time, but particularly in an investment that usually costs between $150,000 and $400,000.

"But there is a new movement," I told Dan and Betty. "It's one that I believe could make ownership of your own vacation home an outdated concept. It's called the 'destination club' movement. I like it—in fact, so much that I decided to buy into it myself."

Destination clubs are relatively new to the marketplace, having emerged in the past few years. At the time I write this, more than twenty-five new entries have now joined such established players as Tanner and Haley Private Retreats and Distinctive Retreats (formerly known as Abercrombie and Kent) and Exclusive Resorts.

The biggest appeal of the destination-club concept is that it removes the two biggest drawbacks of time-shares, fractional-ownership plans, and even outright purchase of your own private vacation home: the lack of variety in locale and the absence of flexibility in scheduling.

Says Rob McGrath, who heads Tanner and Haley's destination clubs, "We free our members from having to choose one location because they feel financially obligated to go there every time they travel. Nobody wants to feel trapped. Destination clubs are designed to put members in some of the finest homes in over thirty of the best locations and destinations the world offers."

Most clubs offer a surprising variety to their members. Depending on the club you choose (i.e., the amount of money you pony up), you can expect to stay in two- to five-bedroom residences at many of the most desirable places in the world.

These include beach locations in Cabo San Lucas; Costa Rica; Bermuda; Naples, Florida; and St. Thomas. Skiers can have access to the slopes at Beaver Creek, Whistler, Telluride, Zermatt, Lake Tahoe, and Aspen. For golfers, there are residences in Scottsdale, Maui, Kiawah Island, Palm Desert, and even Scotland.

For those who prefer the urban landscape, most club operations offer city residences, town houses, penthouses, and suites in New York, San Francisco, Las Vegas, Miami, London, Paris, Tokyo, and Rome. The nautical-minded can select clubs that offer fifty-foot sailboats and catamarans in the Caribbean; one destination club even offers two-bedroom staterooms on a luxurious cruise ship that features stopovers in major ports worldwide.

You say that a million-dollar home isn't quite enough? If you want to try something a bit more elaborate, you can check out clubs like Quintess, which focuses on houses valued at $4 million and higher. Quintess's promotional materials also proclaim that, for any question asked by a club member, the only answer is yes.

A newer entry just coming into the market is a superluxury outfit called the Emperor's Club. Here, you will have the choice of

$5-million-plus residences around the world—complete with maid, butler, and chef services, and a Hummer, Land Rover, or Ferrari in the garage for your personal use. The Emperor's Club also promises hundred-foot luxury yachts docked in the Mediterranean, the Indian Ocean, Hawaii, and Fiji. These, too, will come equipped with private chefs, butlers, and a full crew to cater to your every whim—all included in your annual fee.

Perhaps the pinnacle of destination-club luxury (at least, at present) is the Montana-based Yellowstone Club; as I write, this newly formed club has just begun to accept members who are lining up to pay an initial membership fee in the $10 million range.

In return, they will vacation in European castles, have free use of two yachts (each half the length of a football field), and fly at whim from beach to golf course to ski slope on the club's private jets.

Most upscale destination clubs typically purchase homes *adjacent* to beaches or golf courses. Not so the Yellowstone Club. Tim Blixseth—the timber tycoon who owns the club—plans to *buy* each of the beaches, ski slopes, and golf courses on which his superrich members will frolic.

Most upper-end clubs now offer as standard equipment other advantages—among them, online flight reservations, concierge service, refrigerator and pantry prestocking, dinner reservations, hard-to-get tickets for sold-out shows, babysitters, tee times. A private chef can even be called in to prepare the ultimate romantic dinner for two (one of whom is not, presumably, the chef).

Can't be bothered with airports or long lines, or have that very special someone, business or personal, to impress? Many clubs can arrange for a private jet to pick you up at your airport of choice and at the time *you* want to go.

You can literally ski in Aspen one day, play golf in Scottsdale the next, and run your toes through the sand on the beach in the Cayman Islands the next. Everything can be arranged with the same call. Some of the newest clubs coming online specialize in wine-country homes, golf, or boating.

Try doing *that* with any time-share, fractional ownership, or single-home ownership.

"And how much does this cost?" Dan asked, his voice skeptical.

"For most, less than the down payment you're considering for your vacation house," I said. "And as an investment, there's usually less downside risk. In fact, I believe you're likely to find more money in your pocket years down the road than you would if you own a second home. By investing what you would have spent—"

"Whoa, David!" Dan interrupted as I began to warm to my subject. "We've already thought about the expense involved. Fact is, Betty and I have talked about renting out any place we'd buy, if only to pay for the upkeep when we're not there."

"Many people experiment with putting their vacation home on the rental market, Dan," I said. "Who can blame them? Owning *any* house is outrageously expensive, and everybody wants to recoup some of the costs involved."

"Darn right," Dan said, only slightly mollified.

"Except there's the nightmare that comes whenever you open your doors to strangers," I said. "People can be hard on houses they rent; if so, good luck chasing them down for the rent or damages to your property."

"We'd hire a property manager—" Dan began, and it was my turn to interrupt.

"And you'll lose at least one-third of your rental income to his fees," I said, and kept myself from adding, "And don't forget that little under-the-table stipend you'll have to pay simply to get your manager to put your property at the top of the houses-available list." In my considerable experience, without such additional "consideration," other owners' properties invariably get rented first.

"Based on the brochures you have, I see you're only considering warm-weather locales," I noted. "I guess you've given up on your winter ski jaunts?"

There was a moment of awkward silence; it was obvious that I had hit on a sore point here. That wasn't surprising; it's not even uncommon.

"Of course, if you're serious about renting out your new house, that may not be a problem," I said. "After all, you've already taken into account when you can get the most rent and the highest demand, right?"

Wrong—at least if the expressions on Betty and Dan's faces were any indication. In seasonal-dependent markets, the highest demand is precisely when *you* want to use your place yourself. Thus, you find yourself vacationing in the Florida Keys in July or visiting your Colorado ski chalet during that particularly soggy month immediately following the spring thaw.

For Dan and Betty, this was one of many points they needed to consider—and one that, like most people swept up by the Urge, they clearly had not considered.

Let's take a closer look at the numbers in what is already a $2 billion industry—and currently growing at a 100 percent clip annually. We'll do it from my personal perspective, because about four years ago I joined my first destination club.

Before I proceed, though, let me emphasize this: aside from my own membership experiences, I have *no* personal financial interest in the destination-club industry as a whole, or in *any* of the other clubs I mention here.

In fact, should any club-industry executives read the rest of this chapter—in particular, my list of questions to ask the representative of any potential club you may consider—they would most likely want to paint a bull's-eye squarely on my back. (Which, as a side note, might make for an interesting specialty club—though few taxidermists are up to the challenge of stuffing and mounting bullet-riddled financial authors . . .)

With that said, let's run the numbers.

The initial cost for my first club was an up-front, onetime initiation fee of $159,000. I also had to commit to $6,500 a year in membership dues; these offset the costs of managing and maintaining the club properties and paid property taxes on the residences—a significant expense, since the average value of each residence was $1 million. I also agreed to pay a flat fee of $150 for every night I stayed at any of the club's resort locations.

By contract, the club was limited to an annual per-night fee increase that equals the cost of living—currently about 3 percent a year.

Let's look at how these costs compare with the cost of owning a vacation/second home outright.

First of all, paying the $159,000 initiation fee meant that I no longer had that money available to provide me with an investment return. Over time, even choosing conservative investments, I felt I could earn 6 percent on that money—that is to say, had I not joined the club, my erstwhile initiation fee could have earned $9,540 a year ($159,000 × 6 percent).

Next, there's the $6,500 in annual dues. That now totals an annual "expenditure" of $16,040 (the $9,540 I didn't earn plus $6,500).

I must now add to this the $150 for each day I stayed at any of the club's thirty residences. Sadly, I don't get a great deal of vacation time; happily, my spouse often does. So let's say my wife and I (or, occasionally, my wife with a group of her friends; or even less often, me and an associate traveling on business) averaged an annual usage of twenty-eight days. *(NOTE: studies indicate that people who own a second home average about twenty-five-days-a-year in residence; by happy coincidence, this permits me to compare apples to apples.)*

Twenty-eight days at $150 per day equals another $4,200. We add that sum to the $16,040 for a grand total of $20,240 per year. This is the true out-of-pocket annual cost to me for the club program.

Divide $20,240 by the twenty-eight days a year we use the program: I pay about $723 per day.

If this sounds expensive—and at first blush it does, even to *me*— in a moment we'll see how it compares to what I'd spend if I owned a comparable second million-dollar house.

Here's a fact that is as interesting as it is ironic: the more days that I use the club, the more my cost per day *goes down*. If I could spend 300 days a year on vacation, my daily cost would drop to about $203 per day—slightly below what most people pay for a night at a beachfront room (though non-ocean-view) at a Holiday Inn. The difference is that I would be staying in million-dollar homes, with concierge service and a long list of other (free) amenities.

Moreover, I'd also avoid those irritating 13 percent to 18 percent room taxes, staggering room-service tabs, and pay-per-view-movie charges, and the random double-digit valet-parking fees that make hotel checkouts such a thrilling experience for most of us.

Let's say that you are an avid golfer or love those downhill ski runs. Put *this* in your calculator and smoke it: my initial membership included *free* greens fees for two (for every day of my stay) or *free* lift passes at the ski resorts (also each day of my stay).

Unfortunately, I don't golf well, and I ski even worse. Still, these freebies could easily have reduced my annual costs by *thousands of dollars* each year.

And don't forget, the price of that hotel room will probably double over the next ten years; depending on your contract, that can't happen with most destination clubs. You are locking in your prices today; most clubs are able to increase your dues only by the amount the CPI (Consumer Price Index) goes up each year.

Now let's compare all this with the million-dollar vacation home that Dan and Betty were contemplating. (And we'll eliminate the mistake made by most second-home buyers: we'll include the sometimes-hefty sum needed to furnish the home. This is wise, unless you plan to retire each night to a pair of sleeping bags in an otherwise empty house.)

Purchase Price of the Home	$1,000,000	$159,000
Cost to Furnish the Home	$150,000	$0
(Total Outlay)	$1,150,000	$159,000
Down Payment Amount	$250,000	$159,000
Bank Loan	$900,000	$0
Lost Investment Income/ Mortgage Interest Paid at 6 Percent	$69,000	$9,540
Maintenance Costs Per Year (Taxes, Insurance, Utilities etc.)	$50,000	$6,500
Cost Per Day at 28 Days (28 days at $150 per day)	$0	$4,200
Total Annual Costs	$119,000	$20,240
Average Daily Cost at 28 Days Per Year	$4,250	$723

If anyone who owns a million-dollar second home knew that it was actually costing her more than $4,000 a night to stay in her retreat—well, I doubt that she would sleep much at all. Tell her that she could have spent $723 for that same night in a similar million-dollar home next door—well, *nobody* in her neighborhood would get much sleep, what with the hammering of all the "Vacation House for Sale" signs going up along the street.

But that's not the whole story; for that, we need to look at all the numbers much more closely.

Let's assume that, with a down payment of $250,000, you could get a loan on the balance ($900,000) at a 6 percent rate. That comes to $15,000 a year in *lost income* on your $250,000 down payment and another $54,000 a year lost in interest payments (6 percent on the $900,000 loan balance).

According to Tanner & Haley's McGrath, home owners pay about 5 percent of their house value in annual maintenance costs—that is, property taxes, repairs and upkeep, insurance, heat, air-conditioning, telephone, electric bills, swimming pools, money for capital reserves, and so on. On a million-dollar home, 5 percent comes to $50,000 a year.

Total so far for Dan and Betty's private vacation house: *$119,000 per year.* Remember, it doesn't matter whether you made a $250,000 down payment, made no down payment, or even paid cash for the home; what's important is to figure in the 6 percent annual return that you could have earned on the money now tied up in your second house.

For Dan and Betty, our example does not include any principal paid down against the mortgage. There is no need to include this: every dollar they put against the mortgage could be put into another investment and earn a similar return.

In fact, to make this equation easy to understand, let's assume that they sign up for one of today's superpopular (but potentially catastrophic) interest-only loans for the entire amount.

To keep everything equal, we'll also assume Dan and Betty use their second home a total of twenty-eight days each year. As a result, *their* daily cost of ownership jumps to $4,250 per day—with all twenty-eight of those days spent at the same vacation home.

There are also a few of those little surprises that plague all home owners. For instance, there's the roughly 3 percent in transfer tax ($30,000, in this case) that many communities charge purchasers of real estate. The interest Dan and Betty will lose on this money alone comes out to another $64.29 a day.

This raises the daily costs for twenty-eight days to $4,314.29.

And we're not done yet: legal fees and other closing costs will easily bring the daily cost for each of the twenty-eight days of use to more than *$4,500 per day*!

I can already hear you saying, "But, David—what about the tax advantages and appreciation of the property?"

This is a good question that the real-estate and lending industries have schooled us all to ask. But sadly, the answer doesn't help Dan and Betty nearly as much as the real-estate agents and bankers would lead us to believe.

Under current tax provisions, property taxes are definitely tax deductible; interest on the loan *may* be—but is not always.

Under provisions of a little-discussed law, you can deduct only interest paid on loans of $1 million or less—a total that combines outstanding balances on both your primary home *and* your vacation home. Dan and Betty still owe over $400,000 on their main home—thus the second-home purchase would put them a full $300,000 over the limit. They will receive no deduction on that $300,000.

But, for our example, let's make the home-buying comparison look as good as possible. We'll allow Dan and Betty to write off *all* the interest and taxes on their vacation home (and assume that the IRS isn't reading this chapter).

We already know that Betty and Dan would pay $54,000 in interest; let's figure property taxes at 1.5 percent annually, based on the value of the home. Thus, the total tax would be $15,000. (In fact, in some communities it is significantly less, since many communities use lower tax rates to attract outside investment. The downside for Dan and Betty is that this means they would get a smaller tax write-off.)

So that's $69,000 in interest and tax deductions.

In today's environment, $69,000 would provide a real-dollar tax decrease of $22,770 (assuming a combined 33 percent federal and state tax rate). We credit this income against the $119,000 in Dan and Betty's vacation-home-ownership expenses.

That gives us a real out-of-pocket cost of $96,300 annually to *own* that million-dollar home—compared with my $20,240 expenditure as a member of my club (or any similar-type destination-club program).

In short, even by cooking the books in favor of second-home ownership, there's still an after-tax difference of $76,060 a year—in favor of *me*, the destination-club member.

But we still have to look at appreciation.

I stand with most other financial gurus in that I do not subscribe to the belief that real estate, especially vacation real estate, only *rises* in value indefinitely.

Obviously, some properties will do better than others; some may not change in value; others may even fall in value. (Some of my readers on both coasts know this all too well: if you bought certain real estate in California and New York in the late 1980s, there is a good chance you spent most of the nineties waiting for property values to rebound enough to equal your initial purchase price.)

However, it is a fact that historically—depending on location and the economy—you will see your vacation home's value rise about 1 percent over inflation—about 4 percent per year, currently.

Of course, all bets are off if another massive terrorist attack occurs or if the federal government radically changes the tax laws (especially those relating to capital gains or the deductibility of interest payments or property taxes). And if your house is on the coast, the recent hurricane seasons show how precarious life—and property values—can be.

With that said, let's assume a *compounded* 4 percent increase in the price of that million-dollar condo or home Dan and Betty are considering. Remember, we can't count the furniture as an *appreciating* asset: after ten years it will likely be deemed worthless, creating a $150,000 *loss*.

The numbers will look something like this after ten years.

End of Year 1	1,040,000
End of Year 2	1,081,600

End of Year 3	1,124,864
End of Year 4	1,169,859
End of Year 5	1,216,653
End of Year 6	1,265,319
End of Year 7	1,315,932
End of Year 8	1,368,569
End of Year 9	1,423,312
End of Year 10	1,480,244

Not bad: a price gain of $480,244 over the ten-year period. (Don't complain if you don't see similar results. Remember, this is only an example: some of you will fare better, while others will lag behind the average. The price of your property could actually go down, depending on where in the real-estate cycle you bought.)

But if Dan and Betty sell their vacation home using a real-estate agent (as most people do) with these numbers, this is what will happen:

- First, Dan and Betty will pay the real-estate agent 6 percent in commissions: that's a cool $88,815 off the top of that impressive $480,244 gain. Add another $5,000 for closing costs and legal fees; don't forget that $30,000 in transfer taxes Dan and Betty had to pay when they bought the property. Total so far: $123,815 to be subtracted, leaving them with $356,429 in appreciation.

- Under the *current* long-term tax law (among the lowest in tax history), Uncle Sam will take 15 percent of the remaining $356,429: so subtract another $53,464. Carve out approximately another 5 percent of the gain for taxes to Uncle Sam's nieces and nephews at the state and local level: that's another $15,148. Suddenly that $480,244 gain is reduced by $192,427.

That provides an appreciation of $287,817—not what Dan and Betty expected, but still very respectable.

Interestingly, the average time a person holds his second home in this country is just three and a half years. If you factor in these statistically correct numbers, after fees and taxes many second-home owners are lucky to get even their original investment back—a dismal picture indeed.

With all these numbers in mind, let's look at how the numbers play out under different scenarios. To keep things equal, again all of the following are based on a 6 percent interest rate, being able to earn 6 percent a year on investments, and using your vacation home twenty-eight days a year.

And while I'm using the million-dollar home in this example, it works the same way for second/vacation homes at virtually *any* level. We could do the same comparisons—and get essentially the same results or better—for a $500,000 vacation home versus one of the many destination clubs that specializes in less expensive destination properties around that $500,000 mark. Or we could even move the bar up to the many new destination clubs that compete in the $5-million-plus home category or higher as I noted earlier.

So let's put them both in the blender and see how they fare.

The central question: Should I (or would you) recommend that Dan and Betty join a destination club or buy the million-dollar house they are so excited about?

For my recommendation, we'll employ the method by which destination clubs typically operate today.

Liquidity

The club's directors guarantee me in writing, backed by the club's assets, that upon my leaving the club, they will buy back my membership and hand me a check for 100 percent of my investment. (Beware any club that doesn't.) The only hang-up is that it could take as little as one week or as long as a maximum of twelve months to get my money. This maximum twelve-month rule is actually a safeguard for all members of the club. If the club should receive a large number of resignations all at one time, it can sell off assets to meet its requirements in an orderly fashion . . . not at fire-sale prices. (Be leery of any club that wants to stretch this time frame beyond a year.)

Club rules will require, for example, that for every four new members who buy into the club, one old member will be allowed to resign with check in hand. Thus, someone else is buying the resigning member's membership. There are no closing fees, appraisals, real-estate-agent costs or legal fees, moving costs, no storage of furniture, not to mention all those annoying showings of your property to prospective buyers. Also, try selling *any* home if mortgage rates go back up to 10 percent and everybody tries to get out the door at the same time. Sure, fewer folks will be joining the club at that point, too, but that should only mean it will take a little longer to get my money back. If I don't want to sell, I don't have to. In fact, the membership can usually be passed down to the next generation free of charge.

Bottom line: Don't bother me with *any* of the details. Just send me a check. **Advantage to the club.**

Risk

Try this one. At closing, try asking the real-estate agent who sells you your vacation home to put in writing that your vacation home won't decrease in value when you want to sell it. It won't happen. But in theory, with my club I am guaranteed my original $159,000 initial investment back when I leave the club. In other words, by contract, I can't lose a single dollar.

Now, I am not naive, nor should you be. The value of my membership is based solely on the value of the property that the club holds. In case of a major disaster, severe recession, or significant tax-law change—that is, if everyone tries to sell vacation properties at the same time, the quick sale of many properties could lead to a significant loss that any club will not be able to cover.

But let's say all vacation property goes down by a third in value because of some unknown disaster or tax-law change. I would stand to lose one-third (that is, $53,000) of my membership initiation fee. But if the prices of all vacation homes are declining, this means the owner of that million-dollar second home stands to lose the same one-third (or about $333,000) on her investment—and the absolute first items put on the block in bad financial or uncertain times are those sleek little Italian sports cars . . . and second homes.

In my destination club, even though I suffer the same 33 percent loses, I'll take a $53,000 loss over a $333,000 loss any day of the week. In fact, I am probably much more insulated against loss because my club has homes in over thirty different locations. What's the chance of all thirty going down the same amount at the same time?

Bottom line: A loss of $53,000 beats a loss of $333,000 every time. **Advantage to the club.**

Monthly Costs

I do not have to come up with the monthly mortgage, tax, and maintenance charges of almost $10,000 per month in my destination club. As stated earlier, I will get some of this money back at tax time, but $10,000 a month is still $10,000 a month. My monthly payments with the club are limited to approximately $1,687.

Bottom line: Paying less monthly is always a big plus. Paying six times less a month is a huge plus. **Advantage to the club.**

Flexibility

This one is impossible for home ownership to overcome. I call it frugal (but my friends call it cheap), but how could I ever think about vacationing somewhere other than where my personal vacation home is located? I couldn't sleep at night thinking about how much money I'm losing by spending money somewhere else while *my* vacation property sits empty. With the club, I can choose my vacations from over thirty of the best ski slopes in the world, world-class beaches, championship golf courses, or some of the greatest cities on the planet. And it's all-inclusive.

Bottom line: Thirty-plus vacation destinations to choose from beats one location every time. **Advantage to the club.**

Convenience

One telephone call and everything is done for me. Setting airplane reservations, stocking my refrigerator, dinner reservations, tee times, babysitters, private jets—you name it, my personal concierge handles it all. In fact, the club holds memberships to some of the best country clubs in the country, all free for my using when I am in residence. With my own home, I would have to do all the work myself and play the public courses unless I want to pony up another $50,000 to $350,000 up front for initiation fees plus about $10,000 more in annual dues for a private country-club membership.

Bottom line: Anytime you can delegate and get it for free . . . do it. **Advantage to the club.**

Financials

As you've seen above, with a 4 percent annual gain on your million-dollar property over the next ten years, you will exit this strategy after taxes and costs with approximately $287,817 in profits in your pocket.

Or will you? Let's look at this a couple of different ways.

Remember, I said that after tax deductions, that million-dollar house was costing you $76,060 more per year than my membership in my destination club. Because I did not have to pay that $76,060 extra each year for the vacation home, assume that I put that amount into a variable annuity that accumulated tax deferred and earned a net gain of 6 percent a year. Again, I feel quite confident in using a 6 percent annual return over a ten-year period. After all, over the last seventy-five years the stock market has averaged a little more than 10 percent a year.

Any idea what $76,060 invested every year becomes after ten years at 6 percent tax deferred? The answer: $1,062,683. Even if I pulled all that money out at one time and paid taxes at a combined federal and state rate of 36 percent on the $302,083 gain (remember I don't pay taxes on my ten yearly contributions equaling $760,600), I would receive a check free and clear for $953,933. (Note that any gains from a variable annuity pulled out before age fifty-nine and a half are subject to a 10 percent penalty on the gain from the IRS.)

So, after ten years, do I want a check for $953,933—or a

$287,817 after-tax profit that I made on the million-dollar home? *More than 330 percent more money!*

Here's a real mind-blower: Since you paid $76,060 every year in interest, taxes, and maintenance, it was not available to earn that $953,933 gain (after taxes) after ten years. Therefore, if you subtract the gain of $287,817 you made on the sale of your second-home investment, you've actually *lost a whopping $666,116 over ten years by owning the second home versus joining a club!*

Okay, I could go a little deeper and talk about some rental income each year—but that would easily be eaten up by the higher costs each year in taxes and operating expenses that I didn't even include with the home-ownership model.

Or you can do as I do (and often recommend to my clients): Simply study a certain real-estate market, buy *all* types of real estate cheap and sell it to the first buyer for a nice fat profit. Then, as with your shampoo, rinse and repeat, repeat, repeat.

Thus, invest in a club, travel to some of the most exotic places on earth, and take the money you would have invested in that vacation home and buy other real estate that you can hopefully flip for a profit down the road.

Here's one more advantage of some clubs. A couple of years ago I resigned my membership in my club to move to a (supposedly) more upscale club. Because I held one of the few issued as a "founding member," my membership included a special escalator clause. New memberships at the time I resigned cost approximately $100,000 more than I was originally charged; when I opted out, I received about 40 percent of that $100,000 gain.

Total: about $40,000 more than I paid; a tidy 25 percent profit.

Why did I resign my membership if I am so high on the club concept? I used the money to join *another* destination club—one in which the average home price was $2.5 million.

The new club cost me almost $400,000 to join, a sizable increase over my previous membership cost. But it's worth it, when you compare the membership advantages to outright ownership of a second home.

You see, there's leverage involved here. Simply stated, as the values of the houses rise, the financial advantages of joining a club compared to owning a second house of my own keep getting better.

Bottom line: It's not even close. In ten years, I could have $800,000 more in profits in my pocket. Now, *that*'s something to talk about at the next garden party. **Advantage to the club.**

Availability

This is the one area where the clubs, as far as I can see, have fallen short, and will continue to fall short, try though they may. The fact is, when you share access to any property, it's not always going to be available for your use.

Clubs generally work like this: on any given day, you call to see what's available and away you go. One club even states that if you follow the rules (you must call within certain time frames—usually three to six months before your vacation date) and your desired vacation location is not available, the club will rent comparable lodging in that location for you at their cost.

The exceptions are Christmas, spring break, and most other holidays. Everyone wants to go somewhere during these times. If you absolutely must have the family together for Christmas in Beaver Creek, make other arrangements. Destination clubs are not for you.

Also, most clubs have a maximum stay at any one location of between seven and twenty-one days. So don't join a club expecting to spend three months next winter in Naples.

If you like the idea of having your clothes and car waiting for you where you left them and guaranteed last-minute trips to your favorite destination, destination clubs fail miserably. This is something you must accept if you join any club.

Bottom line: It's nice not to have to get permission to visit your own place. **Advantage to home ownership.**

Who Can Go

Finally, clubs are available to members and their guests. That means you can invite anyone you want, but usually the member must also be in attendance.

So if you are accustomed to giving the vacation-home keys to a coworker or close friend (or even to your own kids) . . . well, club ownership is not going to be your avenue of choice.

Bottom line: If I can't go, no one goes. **Advantage to home ownership.**

So what did Dan and Betty learn? They learned they were on the verge of possibly making a big financial mistake, and they tossed their brochures in the garbage.

Why would anyone want to buy a private vacation home? The club experience requires less cash up front, less cash out of your pocket each month, less overall costs over the lifetime of ownership, and less overall risk—while at the same time providing greater liquidity when you want out, more flexibility in vacation alternatives, more hospitality service options, and probably more money in your pocket down the road.

If the club concept appeals to you, check them all out thoroughly. Crunch the numbers, using the experiences of Dan and Betty as your template; see if the logic works for your specific situation.

With over twenty-five clubs operating currently and certainly dozens more to come, make sure you know all the up-front costs, how fees can increase over the years, how and under what terms you can get your money back, and what really secures your investment.

And of course, do this *before* signing on to any club.

If you go online to Google "Destination Clubs," you will find a growing list of sites to visit. Narrow your selection to the three or four that interest you; then contact them and request their literature . . . *as well as a copy of the contract they expect you to sign!*

This latter request is so important to your well-being that some clubs will balk at complying. Don't let that deter you; insist, and if they won't cooperate—well, you're probably better off deleting them from your list.

Inspect the contract on a line-by-line basis. It's interesting how often little clauses show up that the salesperson neglected to mention; if you find anything involving signing over the right of first refusal to either your firstborn or your soul, it should, at the very least, raise a yellow flag; but be on the lookout for any other potential problems, too.

Every club will send you expensively printed, glossy brochures designed to catch your eye and inflame your desire. Such seduction methods are to be expected (and, to an extent, even enjoyed)—but also steel yourself to closely examine the pale underbelly of this low-slouching beast from a coldly dispassionate point of view. Compare and contrast.

You now know that a membership in most clubs should make better financial sense than owning a second home. Thus, don't let club salesmen waste your time on these details. Instead, concentrate on how their club differs from the other clubs on the market . . . something they don't like to discuss.

Finally, do not rush into consummating the relationship. Aside from the considerable financial issues involved, you are engaged in selecting the kinds and quality of leisure-time activities for yourself and your family: you're about to make a decision on that most rare of commodities, the time you spend with those you love.

Don't waste the opportunity.

In the following section, I've formulated a set of five basic issues to investigate when you're looking for a good destination club, with each issue supplemented by questions designed to ferret out the specific answers you need to know.

Use them well, and you won't be disappointed.

TEN

DESTINATION CLUBS: FIVE POINTS TO PONDER . . . *BEFORE* YOU SIGN ON THE DOTTED LINE

I have been involved with club membership for almost four years. Following are five important questions to ask before you join any club.

1. What is the *guaranteed* minimum price of each home acquired for the club's portfolio?

Does the club own multiple homes in each location? How many are currently in operation, and what is the club's guaranteed time frame for new acquisitions? A lack of available property will severely limit your chances of staying at a location and in a house at the top of your vacation list. The more homes the club owns or rents on your behalf, obviously the greater your flexibility will be.

Sure, most clubs will pretend they want you to have a good time—but make no mistake, that is not their primary goal. Their goal is to make themselves money. For that reason, some clubs will not hesitate to acquire inferior homes—that is, properties that do not meet the standard of price or opulence that their sales brochures claim. Sometimes a club will skirt the edges of their stated standards; less commonly (but often enough to raise red flags) their acquisition practices can venture into outright fraud.

Insist on taking a "complimentary" trip of three or four days to one of the club's locations that you chose. You want to see how the club operates—in person—before joining; this will provide you with a thumbnail sketch of what you can expect after you join the club. If a club will not honor this request, move on down the road.

2. How many days a year in advance are you *guaranteed,* and how many "space available" days can you use?

Depending on your contract terms, your annual dues usually guarantee you between fifteen and thirty days of usage; they best charge you a *daily* rate from the start—why pay in advance for days you may never use? The contract should also specify whether you can use more than this number of days and how much such space-available days will cost. Never join a club that limits your total usage, or charges an exorbitant rate for any days beyond your guaranteed minimum.

In a well-run destination club, there should be no more than six (or fewer) members for every property the club owns. This decreases the chance that competition for open slots will become savagely Darwinian.

But there are other numbers that are important, too. For instance, how many of the members have children? If the answer is more than one-third, you can forget about ever booking Christmas, Easter, or summer-vacation locations; everyone will be competing for these same periods when the children are out of school.

What is the geographic distribution of the membership? If too high a percentage of the membership is located in California, trips to Hawaii and Mexico will become virtually impossible to secure. Perversely, people tend to take the most *exotic* location that is *closest* to their homes.

Pick a club that lets you make reservations as far in advance as possible for a particular location or holiday—a year is ideal. A longer lead time usually allows you to get the best price on your airfares to that destination.

Ask how clubs treat last-minute cancellations; will you be unduly penalized because of health, personal, or family emergencies?

Also be wary of clubs that make you start and end reservations on a Saturday or limit stays to only seven days at a time. Does this really match your traveling needs or are you going to have to make major changes to meet club rules?

How and under what terms can the club change its rules? Procedures and bylaws that are in effect today may not fit the club's profit model tomorrow, leaving you on the wrong end of the membership stick.

Finally, how will communications be handled with *all* the members of the club? With all too many clubs, the motto seems to be "If you don't ask, no one is going to tell you." This form of communication might work for North Korea (or in any household wherein resides a teenager), but in a destination club it makes eventual dissatisfaction all but inevitable.

3. Perhaps most important, ask how your prospective club will make its money.

For most clubs, fiscal health depends on each member's payment of the initial membership fee and annual dues; as I noted, this can be a sizable amount. If you wish to resign several years after joining, the club will attempt to sell your membership for whatever is the current membership rate—presumably more than you paid. You get your original money back (or less), while the club pockets the "extra" amount.

Of course, logic cries out that this is counterproductive to *all* members. If the club will earn, say, $125,000 selling your membership when you *leave* it, why should it care about (or act upon) your opinions and/or complaints? This could turn out to be most clubs' Achilles' heel.

You'd also be well advised to ensure that the club can't simply keep refinancing its properties—in effect, cashing in on any increased value of a property and jeopardizing the underlying equity held by the membership. The best clubs will pay at least 75 percent in cash for any new purchase. Check to ensure the club is not allowed to borrow money to pay expenses or salaries.

Perhaps the most important question here comes not when you join but when you wish to exit the club. Some clubs even use this as their primary moneymaking activity.

In my experience, most clubs handle the return of your membership fee in three different ways: bad, worse, and awful.

The best, of course, is a guarantee that at the time of your exit, you will get 100 percent of your membership deposit back *and* some part of the monetary appreciation your membership has accrued. One club recently took out an insurance policy to guarantee the return of this initial membership fee to members. In general practice, this "semiequity" membership is limited to charter members of a club, if only because they are assuming the most risk.

Second best is a contract in which the club guarantees return of 80 percent of your original membership deposit, or 80 percent of what your membership sells for—whichever is *higher*. Long-term club members can actually turn a profit on this sort of deal, which is why such contracts are scarce in the marketplace.

Usually, a club offers an exit deal that's the worst option: a check for 80 percent of what you paid for your original membership. If you sign a contract on this basis—and I don't recommend it—at least insist that the contract incorporates a clause that returns 100 percent of your money if you leave the club within the first year. You should not be penalized for leaving in short order if the club's underperformance or mismanagement is the reason.

Before signing the contract to join an established club, it's also a good idea to ask how many members are on the waiting list to get *out* of the club; insist that this information be penciled into the contract, or you may be unpleasantly surprised at how that number can change *after* you are a member.

There will always be some members who for various reasons lose the financial ability to continue their memberships or find they simply don't use the club enough to justify the costs. But if you find more than a few resignations over a twelve-month period, alarm bells should start ringing. Happy members don't resign memberships.

And, of course, ask to talk to a few members who have either dropped out of the club or are on a waiting list to leave the club.

They will provide a wealth of information and often will eagerly tell you everything you really want to know. If the club balks at this request, at minimum insist on talking to no fewer than five persons who have been members of the club for at *least* a year, preferably drawn from a list you create asking for names from people in the states you choose.

4. Avoid favoritism: insist the club agree to a "best deal" contract clause when you join.

This provision should simply state that you are getting the best deal offered to anyone, and reiterates that no special rights are granted (or have been granted) to anybody in the past, nor will any be granted in the future without automatically being added to *your* contract. It also requires that every member will sign the same contract.

This should provide legal protection against any level of favoritism, but it probably won't: favoritism is a problem that can run rampant in any club.

Insist on full disclosure of all club practices, particularly those involving who can utilize club properties—this should be limited to members and their guests—and how reservations are booked— ideally, this should be done through a first-come, first-served online system.

I've heard of cases where "informal" usage policies have resulted in club facilities being booked solid with nonmember friends of the club's management, by club employees, even by nonmembers, whose rental payments conceivably could be pocketed under the table by unscrupulous club managers.

As for reservation practices, the potential for abuse here is just as clear. Let's say that at the last minute, you want a weekend in Las Vegas. You call the club only to hear that they will have to call you back. The return call sympathetically states, "Sorry—that property is already taken." Okay, but by whom? A club member? Or the club owner's best friend?

The wisest alternative is to pick a club that permits you to make online reservations. You see online what homes and locations are available and you book your reservation from your computer 24/7. Anything else will always be suspicious.

The technology exists, so if the club you are looking at doesn't offer online reservations, it is because it is either too cheap to install it or has something to hide—and neither possibility is an indicator of a well-run club.

Make certain that the membership contract clearly defines if *anyone* other than members can use the properties owned by the club. This no-use list should encompass the owner's best friends, employees of the club, family members of club members, and should specifically ban rental of club properties to any nonmember. Remember: *you* are paying for the upkeep of the properties; every day someone else uses it is one less day it is available for you and your family.

5. Always demand to see the club's financial statement.

You need to know how the club spends its money, and you certainly must ascertain in whose names the deeds for the property are filed.

Skip any club that even remotely skirts this issue. You have too much at stake to be soft on this issue. This is a totally unregulated industry at the moment—it's the Wild West, where only the strong and the careful survive.

———————

And there you have it: five cautionary notes that—if you follow them—can keep you on the right path (or at least stumbling in the right general direction).

But, as in any evolving area, change is really the only constant. You'd be well advised to keep your eyes—and your mind—wide open.

For instance, as new clubs come on the scene, *never* stop shopping for one that offers better properties, better home availability, and a better financial deal. Should your first club have been one that doesn't at least give you back 100 percent of your original membership when you resign, your options here will be severely limited.

But whatever club route you take—if you go the destination club route at all—be very cautious. As the club concept gains in popularity (and it continues to grow by leaps and bounds), it's inevitable that the scammers will begin to take notice. As I said, this is currently an unregulated industry, but expect that to change soon as complaints (and there will be plenty) hit the radar screens. Even clubs with the most honorable of intentions may become strapped for cash as the competition for new members inevitably heats up.

It may sound as if I am extremely negative on the club concept, but nothing could be further from the truth. As I've repeated here, I am voting "aye" in the most definitive manner possible: I've invested my own money to become a destination-club participant.

But that doesn't mean it is right for you.

As with all your financial decisions *always, always, always* consult your accountant, financial advisor, and lawyer *before* you sign anything.

If you exercise this level of diligence—and if you employ my list of five questions before shelling out your hard-earned cash—you can determine whether or not becoming an investment club member is suitable to your situation.

If it is, please remember to say hello if you pass me on the beach, in the mountains, on the slopes, docking my boat, or on the streets of Paris or Rome.

I'll be the guy with the big smile on his face.

ELEVEN

REAL-ESTATE AGENTS

It's a fact: of all the professionals out to get their hands in your pockets, real-estate agents are probably one of the least regulated of all the professional groups.

Sure, sure—they do have to take a test and obtain a license. But unlike financial advisors, lawyers, accountants, there are legions of part-time real-estate agents on the books. It's almost as if the word's been passed along on an Internet chat room: if you don't know what to do with your life, what the heck—get a real-estate license and try it for a while. According to the National Association of Realtors, there are now over 1.1 million people registered as real-estate agents in this country.

And it's not a bad gig, particularly for someone who may have only a minimum of employable skills but an overabundance of enthusiasm. Although it's hard to pinpoint, most sources place agents' median personal income at around $61,000, but some of the most successful are tallying earnings comparable to doctors and lawyers—simply because prices of homes have soared, dramatically boosting those 6 percent commissions. Currently 54 percent of all agents are women and 46 percent are men.

Real-estate agents have a stranglehold on the industry, handling more than 77 percent of all sales. That compares to 12 percent of transactions handled by the builder and only 9 percent direct from the previous owner. The remaining 2 percent are from other sources.

In fact, few professions can claim as great an increase in commission sales as real-estate agents. According to *Real Trends,* a real-estate-industry newsletter, more than $60 billion was paid in commissions last year—up a staggering 43 percent since 2000.

Throughout the years, the one constant in the real-estate marketplace has been the 6 percent commission paid to agents. Today, with many homes selling well into the six- and seven-figure range, is the seller getting value for the hefty commissions being paid?

In most cases, I assert, the answer is "absolutely not." In what universe does it make sense to pay tens of thousands of dollars for a few hours of work—and for the "privilege" of becoming a virtual commodity in a mass-marketed product lineup?

The real-estate industry gets away with charging a standard onerous commission largely because few customers have any knowledge about this intentionally obscured business. As a result, real-estate agents obtain money that otherwise would go to someone else—preferably *you.*

But real estate is not a mysterious dark art. It's like any other financial transaction: it's simply the process of putting buyer and seller together, agreeing on a price, and finalizing the deal. It's not rocket science, but it can be intimidating unless you understand how the system works.

To that end, let's demystify the process; after that, we'll look at whether you actually need a real-estate agent—and if so, whether you really need to pay as much as an agent will try to charge you.

Inevitably, when a real-estate agent encounters a prospective home buyer, one phrase flows from his lips over and over, not unlike the Dalai Lama chanting a sacred mantra: "Don't worry about the commission; the seller pays it, not you."

Doesn't that sound great? You get the services, insights, and guidance of a trained real-estate professional—*at no charge!* Even if you actually buy the house, you don't have to pay a penny extra!

We believe it because we want to—but of course, it's a lie. The $300,000 home you agreed to buy is actually worth $282,000. The difference between what you are paying and what the seller is receiving comes to $18,000—the 6 percent commission that goes to the agent.

Here are two points to consider:

- First, few sellers would object to passing a significant part of that $18,000 to *you* instead of giving it to the real-estate agent, if given a choice; buyer and seller sharing half a loaf is better than watching a salesperson eat the whole thing, right?

- Second, and logically, wouldn't a house worth $282,000 sell faster if it were priced at $282,000? Why, then, believe that you can get a better deal by going through a real-estate agent, whose "services" mean a $282,000 house must be priced at $300,000?

Real-estate deals bereft of an agent's involvement can be done, and with far less difficulty than the real-estate industry has led all of us to believe. I have purchased and sold many properties without the use of an agent. Each time I have realized thousands of dollars of savings.

For instance, if you're the seller, let's say you spend four hours a week for three months—total: forty-eight hours—showing your house to interested buyers. If you indeed sell the house for the same $300,000 asking price, you made $18,000—that's $375 an hour. Subtract for newspaper ads and other marketing costs and you will still probably end up with over $300 an hour. Do you make $300 an hour at your "real" job?

"Ah," the real-estate agents out there are saying, "many buyers don't read newspaper ads. They only look at property listed on various services like the MLS [Multiple Listing Service] or on real-estate-oriented Internet sites. That's why you *need* an agent!"

Baloney. For one thing, this is seldom true. But if you believe it's a problem, there are any number of discount real-estate firms that will, for approximately 1 or 2 percent of your home's sale price, handle all the marketing and multiple listing of your home; you simply do the showings. Compared with the 6 percent bite, that's a substantial savings.

Unless time is a critical factor, try marketing your property *sans* agent for at least sixty days, if only because there will always be people (like me) who prefer talking to the owner directly. We know we're more likely to find a win/win situation with the buyer, because we have at least a 6 percent cushion with which to work.

After two months, if you find the go-it-alone approach isn't working for you—well, you can always try the traditional 6 percent solution and list the property with an agent.

But there is a way to get the best of both worlds; I've used it many times, and it works. Here's the process:

- **Assign the property to an agent—but for a specific, limited time span.**

  Never, ever, ever sign a listing agreement for the sale of your house for more than three months.

  This is absolutely nonnegotiable. Why would you *ever* tie yourself up with a yearlong contract (which most agents will request) without any real idea if that agent is any good or will actively market your home? If the agent has a year to sell your house, whose property is going to get more attention? Yours, with twelve months to go; or a property that he listed ten months ago and is expiring in two months? If he is working his tail off and it shows, tell him you will have no problem relisting the property for another three months.

- **Protect your own sales efforts.**

  If you have tried selling your home on your own, you may have one or more hot prospects—they seem interested, but they just can't make up their mind.

  Unless you want to lose the fruit of your own efforts, ask the real-estate agent for an exclusion for these people.

  This means that if one of these people comes back and decides to buy the house after you've listed it with the real-estate agent, the agent is not entitled to any commission.

  It's only fair, and it's not unusual—but be sure to get it in writing.

- **Know how any commission will be divided between the sales agents involved.**

  So what is the best way to make your listing get sold quickly? Do you pay for a new paint job, new carpeting, a catchy advertisement?

  Nope. All you have to do is remember what a friend of mine

calls the Prime Axiom of Life: "People tend to act in their own self-interest."

In this case, you simply follow the money. That is, before you sign on the dotted line, it is imperative that you fully understand how the commission you agree to pay is actually divvied up after closing.

Here's why. Let's say your home sold for exactly $400,000, with the 6 percent commission totaling $24,000. The home was listed by an agent employed by Pay Too Much Realty Company, but was actually sold by another firm called Didn't Do Nuthin' Realty, Inc.

Typically, that $24,000 will be split four ways. The first $6,000 will go to the firm of Pay Too Much itself; the boss always gets his cut first. Then it's a $6,000 payday for the Pay Too Much agent who actually signed the sales agreement with you. But since an agent with Didn't Do Nuthin' saw the listing on the MLS computer and closed the deal with a couple she was representing, the remaining $12,000 is divided between her and her employer, Didn't Do Nuthin' Realty.

Now . . . of the four entities involved, which is the most important?

The Pay Too Much listing agent saw you as just another *schmuck* wanting to sell a house; so did his employer. No matter who sold the property (or, more importantly, *when* it was sold) the agent and his firm were going to get paid. Other firms (such as Didn't Do Nuthin' Realty) only make money if one of their people closes the deal, but your property is but one in a long, long list of potential sales.

No, the only person who means a darn thing to you is the one who actually brings a buyer to the table. This is the person you need to motivate, and you do this by remembering the Prime Axiom of Life. How do you turn your needs into the self-interest of an unknown salesperson?

Try this. Instead of agreeing to a straight 6 percent commission, negotiate; insist on a 5 percent commission on the deal. To make this acceptable, as part of the contract stipulate that you will pay a $5,000 bonus at closing—*but only to the agent who actually sells your house.*

Now you are now paying $25,000: $20,000 in commissions, plus a $5,000 bonus. Good heavens—that's $1,000 *more* than the standard 6 percent deal. Are you crazy?!

Yes—crazy like a fox. You almost *doubled* the amount of commission that the person who finds the actual buyer will receive.

Trust me—this will definitely get the attention of every real-estate agent on the street. It is now in their self-interest to show your house to as many truly interested, qualified, and motivated buyers as they can find . . . and to do it quickly, before some other agent snatches this windfall first.

I first tried this many years ago. I owned a property that had been on the market for over a year: not many lookers, and not a single offer. I relisted it using the above commission structure. Overnight, I had so much traffic that I had to have the carpets cleaned daily. I also had a signed offer in my hands within two weeks.

Of course, some real-estate agents will tell you flatly that they will not agree to such a bonus arrangement. Fine. Remember, there are 1.1 *million* real-estate agents out there; move on down the road until you find one who speaks your language.

Applying the above principles will help ensure that your interests will be mirrored by real-estate salespersons who otherwise might see you as part of the faceless crowd.

Of course, there are factors to keep in mind that apply to all dealings with real-estate professionals. Here are a few of the most important:

- **Be aware of the motives of all involved.**

  I once had a property that was being marketed by a real-estate agent and I had two potential buyers. One was an investor and another a family that was looking to buy it to call it *home*. But for some reason the real-estate agent kept pushing the investor as the best buyer.

  Why? Of course, because it was in his self-interest to do so.

  I found out later that the real-estate agent saw the investor as a better deal to him. Not only did he get the sale now, but there was a reasonable chance that he would get the rental agreement to rent the place and would probably get a call back much quicker to resell the property from the investor than from the home buyer.

- **Have any contract you sign reviewed by a real-estate lawyer . . .** *before* **you sign it.**

    Every line of a contract, front, back, or penciled in the margin, is a potential mantrap; real-estate professionals love the phrase "Oh, it's just a standard contract" almost as much as they enjoy trying to hide land mines in every other sentence.

    Language that says, for instance, that "in case of the buyer's default, all earnest money shall be used to pay commissions first with the balance going to the seller" means that somebody's trying to pull a fast one. It *seems* to mean that in case of a default, all earnest money goes to the seller. If you're the seller, that's good, right?

    Wrong. I was stung here myself, years ago.

    Let's use the earlier example of you selling your $400,000 home. The buyer has put down $15,000 in earnest money to hold the house until closing. But before then, the buyer changes his mind. Maybe he lost his job and can't get the loan anymore; maybe he and his wife clashed violently over dinner and a divorce is now pending.

    In any event, they are now willing to walk away from your deal and forfeit the $15,000 in earnest money.

    Okay—but if that line remains ("in case of the buyer's default, all earnest money shall be used to pay commissions first"), the $15,000 will go to the real-estate agent—*all* of it, even though the house never sold, because the $15,000 would be applied against the $24,000 commission the original deal required.

    You are left holding the bag: no sale, having lost sixty days while your house was off the market, and now having to start the sale all over again from scratch. But if you cross out that line, *you* keep the whole $15,000. That's the way it should be.

- **Pick the most realistic real-estate agent, not the one who quotes the highest asking price.**

    Human nature being what it is, we all think our property is the best, and worth far more than the market may dictate. Real-estate agents know that, and many of them play on it to get your listing. Most people will interview two or three real-estate agents before picking one—and they usually pick the agent who quotes the highest asking price.

    The typical result: six weeks later, the real-estate agent laments that the market has "softened up a bit" since you listed your parcel. He suggests that you reduce your price somewhat—usually to where it should have been in the first place.

    This could have been avoided if you, the seller, had been more realistic—and better prepared. It's not difficult to research the prevailing prices in any given market; most property sales are listed in local newspapers or at government offices where transactions are recorded. Often, this information is available via the Internet and should have been supplied by the agent to you when you signed to list the property. A few minutes spent doing your homework will help you know when a real-estate agent is giving you an honest price analysis, or simply playing to your ego and ignorance just to get the listing.

Now, for the flip side. If you are the prospective buyer rather than the seller, it's likely you will be dealing with a real-estate agent. Since the real-estate agent almost always is the legal representative of the seller, beware of everything you do or say; it could affect the price you pay. Here are a few tips for any prospective buyer:

- **Keep your emotions out of the equation; if you can't, at least keep them out of sight.**

    Translated, even if you just toured your dream home, it's unwise to dance a jig on the living-room carpet. Similarly, don't use your cell phone to rave about the house you've just visited, particularly if you're a passenger in the agent's car; the call may severely limit any subsequent negotiations.

- **Don't limit yourself to a single home; find several homes that will work for you.**

    Early in this chapter, I warned of the dangers inherent in letting your emotions influence real-estate investments. One way to limit that danger is to avoid fixing your hopes on any one parcel.

    Trust me—it's like dating in high school: if there's only one girl you want to ask to the prom, I can guarantee you that she has already accepted an invitation from someone else.

- **Always "lowball" your first offer.**

    I believe that real-estate agents tell the truth—at least, when they say in their most sincere-sounding voices that they strive mightily to get the highest possible price for the sellers they represent. They'll get no argument from me—because I understand, of course, that's how they get the highest possible commission for themselves.

    By the same measure, I cannot count the number of times a real-estate agent has shaken her head and told me, "Oh, that offer is much too low; the seller will *never* accept that."

    No argument from me here, either: in most cases, they won't.

    But I make the offer anyway, because if I make twenty lowball offers, I only need *one* seller to say yes.

    Often the broker is reluctant to do all the paperwork on a deal that will probably not fly. Too bad. By law they must present every offer to the seller, no matter how impractical it may seem to them.

    I'm not advising ridiculously below-asking-price offers; you gain nothing by insulting or otherwise offending the owner. But if the owner is asking $400,000, don't hesitate to start at $300,000. You never know the owner's true motivation for selling. If he comes back at $399,000, move on; he's sending you a strong message he is not motivated to sell. And that's okay—by making an offer, you were looking for his response in a counteroffer.

A good rule of thumb is that the higher the asking price, the more room there is for negotiation.

For example, on one recent Sunday I was in South Florida visiting open houses while on other business. One was a new 4,200-square-foot, canal-fronted home on a third-acre lot. The asking price: *$3,999,000!*

After bystanders helped revive me, I asked the real-estate agent my standard open-house question: *How much if I pay cash?*

After bystanders revived *him,* he looked me up and down for a moment, and I could see the calculator working behind his eyes.

"An offer of—oh, let's say three-point-five million would probably get the job done," he said, and watched my face closely.

Interesting. I had just witnessed a half-million-dollar price drop, on the basis of a hypothetical question.

And hypothetical it was, even if I had that amount of cash immediately available. After all, if I ultimately did buy the house, I would be paying cash. So would anybody; they'd just have to mortgage their first newborn to get it.

But my point is made, I think.

Pity the poor fool who offers just a little lower than the original asking price of $3,999,000 because he's afraid to make a low offer or the agent talks them out of it. Fear not, prospective buyers: there is no real-estate agent vigilante group that roams open houses to attack lowball bidders.

Most sellers also hate paying real-estate commissions, of course; instinctively, they know that the services provided and time spent isn't worth the money spent on commissions.

So use this to your favor.

For example, let's say that you are looking for a two-bedroom condominium in a certain high-rise building in downtown Chicago.

In a typical fifty-story building, there may be 200 units that meet your description. Prepare a concise, one-page letter stating your intentions—and note that you would like to make the purchase without the involvement of a real-estate agent. Explain how this will allow the seller to avoid any commission. Let them know that they will clear at least as much (and probably more) as they would with an agent—but that they'll make the sale immediately, not in sixty or ninety days.

Then mail it to every person in that building.

Why everybody? Why not? You cast your net, and you never

know who you are going to snare. Maybe someone has a three-bedroom unit and is willing to accept an offer only slightly higher than a two-bedroom unit would run. Perhaps someone will pass your note to a friend at a nearby building who wants to sell exactly what you want to buy. This technique has value in any type of real-estate search. Be creative; get the addresses and send the same type of letter. You never know who just filed for divorce or what widow has decided it's time to downsize. If there's a doorman, talk with him. Don't be afraid even to go door-to-door if need be in a neighborhood you particularly like. You may be very pleased with the results; I have been.

The larger profits in any deal tend to go to the bold. Be bold: for instance, when you are close to finalizing a bid with a seller but can't seem to get over that last few-thousand-dollar difference, don't hesitate to ask the real-estate agent to reduce his commissions to make up the difference.

For example, the seller wants $400,000 and you are not willing to pay a penny more than $395,000. Ask the sales agent to reduce his commissions to $19,000 from the usual $24,000 for such a deal and the sale will get done. This way the seller will net out the same amount he needs because he is paying $5,000 less in real-estate commissions and can now sell the house to you for your $395,000 offer. Real-estate agents hate it when this is pulled, but to close the deal today the agent may well swallow hard and agree, especially if his listing is ending soon.

And of course, always be on the lookout for properties that are coming off their listing with a real-estate agent. When a listed property does not sell, the disappointed owners are often the most motivated of sellers. They may have gotten a couple of offers, but now know they don't have a jewel to sell. The thought of starting over with a new real-estate agent is not a pleasant prospect for most people; they may be very willing to wheel and deal with you. Timing is indeed everything.

But most important, do your homework. Research the market, compare recent sales, wear out some shoe leather, talk to as many people as possible.

And then go for it. Good hunting, my friends.

TWELVE

ON THE AUCTION BLOCK

I'm a little reluctant to talk about auctions here—not because they aren't a carefully structured process designed to manipulate the uninitiated into a course of action that benefits those in the know at the expense of everybody else.

They are. And they're very effective at it, too.

The reason I'm not wild about providing the details of how they work is . . . is . . . well, it's because I've used them to my own benefit on a number of occasions.

There. I've said it. Isn't confession good for the soul?

I'm about to let you in on the secret world of auctions. The problem is that while I'm lifting the veil on how auctions work, I'm going to have to work hard to keep the admiration from my voice.

You've seen it since you were a kid, thumbing through the back pages of the current *Spider-Man* comic as you looked for the "magic X-ray glasses" ad. There, tucked amid the other mail-order novelties, was the picture of a Jeep, or maybe something that looked like a World War II landing craft.

In this case, the ad was touting so-called government-surplus items, but the important part was the screaming headline that urged us to BUY IT AT AUCTION FOR PENNIES ON THE DOLLAR. What a deal! How could we pass it by?

Welcome to a world where the level of excitement meets the instinct of the herd, and together—in real time, no less—they determine what any given item is worth. Where, in fact, prices are driven purely by the demand of the moment—and where it is common practice to use every facet of human nature to supercharge that demand.

Do you believe that somewhere every day people are buying "government surplus" Jeeps for less than a hundred dollars? Does the purchase of $400,000 houses for just $2,600 seem realistic? What happened—did all the other bidders fall out because the price got just a little too high?

Alas—if only any of this was true!

Of course, little of it is—at least, not in most real-estate auctions. But these and other urban legends make great stories over dinner on Saturday night with interested friends. In fact, in the majority of such auctions I have attended, the auction sale bring prices *higher* than what was being asked through more traditional methods of sale.

Contrary to conventional wisdom, in many instances property is placed at auction to sell quickly at (or above) its approximate *true* worth. Relatively few auctions involve a distress sale; while it happens occasionally, by no means is it as frequent as it is pictured in the movies.

If this comes as news to you, welcome to my old world. I myself learned how auctions worked only a short time ago. And while it shattered my illusions, it also opened up a new (and, I expect, a more profitable) real-estate awareness for me.

A few years back I had decided to purchase and renovate a twelve-year-old building that was designed as a health-care facility to house the various businesses I own. Please take note, as I suggested with a home, I bought *the deal* and didn't build new. In the process, I renovated the building for my specific uses, creating an instant 25 percent profit to my bottom line instead of the builder's.

As with all deals, it was exciting, but it would have been more fun had I not been so aware that every day, I was losing money on the other building I owned—the one that I had vacated.

I listed the property for sale the traditional way with a real-estate friend of mine. As usual, little was done in marketing the first three months and people stayed away in droves; I was informed that in ninety days, we had only one showing.

After having it sit, empty and bleeding money, for three months (each day costing me property taxes, utilities, insurance, and so on), I yanked the listing and decided to put the property up at auction. My agent's response: "Well, if you were going to *give* the place away, why didn't you just tell me in the first place?"

Now, if you check your local newspapers, selling properties through the auction system has become increasingly popular. An auction turns real-estate selling into an event, a sort of festival where the long tradition of cash-and-carry lives on.

Let me explain exactly how it works. When I contracted to auction my former office building, I paid the auction company $2,000 up front, earmarked largely to offset its costs of advertising. In return, the auction company placed boxed ads on my property and others in the *Chicago Tribune* and other local newspapers and mailed brochures widely throughout a ten-mile radius from the building, targeting zip codes of the wealthy and other business owners.

My first surprise in the process came when the auction firm recommended advertising a suggested opening-bid price that, indeed, represented just pennies on the dollar. "I won't sell at this price," I stammered. "I'd be better off renting the place out."

"Don't worry," I was told. "That's just to create interest. We did a four-hundred-thousand-dollar building last week, and our ad listed sixty thousand as a suggested opening bid. Trust me, we know what we are doing . . . just relax."

I half-heartedly agreed, still wondering what I had done.

In retrospect, it all makes perfect sense. At an auction, people are looking for a bargain. Otherwise, who would bother to attend? For an auction to succeed, the auctioneer has to rely on a person's need to find a great "once in a lifetime" deal. Having a chance to buy a $400,000 property for $60,000 appeals to the inner deal maker in all of us.

In the weeks prior to an auction, the auctioneer will hold several open houses on each of the properties in that month's auction. This attracts both the casual looker and the hard-core buyer/investor. The common denominator for the auctioneer is to find the person who has a need for the property, but, more important, who has the money to buy it, in cash. You will find no "no money down" buyers at an auction.

All auctions require buyers to have their financing in order by the time of the auction—essential, since closing on the property is usually within thirty days of the auction date.

The potential buyer can purchase a packet that explains everything about the property (surveys, deeds, lot sizes, and the specific ground rules under which the auction will be conducted) for a minimal amount, usually around twenty-five dollars. This allows the auctioneer to recoup his costs of producing the sometimes fifty-page-plus document—but even more important, it provides names and numbers for the auctioneer's staff to call and encourage interested parties to attend and bid at the auction. The twenty-five dollar fee also does an amazing job of separating the curious from the serious for his staff.

The auction itself is a masterpiece of forethought and planning. Typically, auctions are held in hotel meeting rooms that are intentionally undersized for the number of expected bidders. The appearance of standing room only is essential to creating the impression that someone is going to get a *great* bargain.

What follows is sheer genius by the auction firm. In the advertisement of all the properties to be auctioned, each individual listing requires a cashier's check to be deposited with the auctioneer the night of the auction—usually not a lot, because they don't want to scare anyone away. What is important is that *each property carries a different deposit amount!*

The reason: now the auctioneer knows exactly how many bidders there are for each property—*before* the auction starts.

This allows the auctioneer to judge exactly how much interest there is in each property, as well as schedule the sequence of the bidding. A parcel everybody wants will go later in the lineup; why risk having the auction room empty out early? It would only signal to the remaining bidders that there may not be that much interest in the remaining properties . . . lowering their potential bids.

The checks are sorted and the lineup finalized behind the scenes, while bidders are treated to a calculatedly detailed slide presentation on how the auction will be operated. If more time is needed, an assistant may even throw in a mock "demonstration auction" until the final tweaking of the program is completed.

One of the quirks of most auctions is a definite plus for the seller: each successful bidder is charged a "buyer's fee," usually ranging from 5 to 10 percent of the selling price of the property. In practice, this means that the final price of a $200,000 purchase will be between $210,000 and $220,000. Not infrequently, in a heated auction the buyer may concentrate so intently on his bid that he neglects to include this fee into his mental calculations. It's too late to squabble when the hammer goes down; the deal—and the extra fee—are legally binding.

Less commonly, some auction houses will try to split their costs evenly by charging both the buyer and seller, too—anywhere from 1 to 5 percent of the sale price. These fees are how successful auction houses offset all the up-front costs and usually make a handsome profit.

In fairness, the auction house does incur a level of risk. Typically, they advance about half the cost of all the advertising, and there is always the matter of the time involved on their part in setting up the auction. Nobody works for free.

For this reason, the auction house will do its own due-diligence research on your property before signing you to a contract. If the appraisal indicates that your property should bring between, say, $240,000 and $270,000, the auction firm requires your assurance—in advance—that you will sell the property for any bid in that range, or higher.

Most properties are contracted for auction with an *undisclosed* minimum price agreed to by you and the auction house that protects you in case all the bids fall significantly short of your true minimum-price sale. If this should happen, the salesmen of the auction house will call all interested parties over the next couple of days to try to bring the buyer and seller closer together in the old-fashioned way.

Happily for the assertiveness-trained among us, always remember when you haggle with the auction house to sell your property, its fees are usually highly negotiable. Much depends on your expectations, the property's marketability, and the auction firm's level of motivation to add your new property to its next auction list.

As you might expect, the best deals are reserved for sellers who list their properties with "no reserve"; that is, they will be sold that night regardless of the price bid. It's a risky situation for the seller— but a definite attention grabber for his property, and a gimmick that helps promote the auction as a whole. Your only way out is to buy your own property back the night of the auction, thus paying the auction company the 5 to 10 percent buyer's fee.

As with any dealings of a financial nature, there are certain cautionary items to be observed. Thoroughly check out the reputation and record of any auction company *before* signing with it. An attorney who is familiar with both real-estate issues and the auction process is a valuable resource and sounding board. And ideally, it is to your advantage to attend one of their auctions before committing to the way an auction house does business.

In my own ventures into the auction process, so far I must say that I've been favorably impressed. But remember, I was the seller.

So how did I make out in the auction of my former business headquarters? To my old real-estate agent's dismay, I *cleared $8,000 more* than he was even asking for the property when it was listed with his firm. Like most auctions, I also sold it "as is"—no one could later come back and complain about a leaky roof or a hundred different things (real or imaginary) three months down the road—*and I paid no commissions.*

Best of all for the impatient soul I am, I had a check in my hands for the whole amount thirty days after the auction.

And in the dog-eat-dog world of real estate, *that* made me a believer.

THIRTEEN

REAL-ESTATE SEMINARS AND OTHER SCAMS

They make it look *so* easy.

Full-page ads in the local newspapers proclaim that the lifestyle of the rich and famous requires only an hour or so at a seminar. Lunch is optional, but expect little more than finger food; no sense eating into the profits, eh?

Oh yes—that sixty-foot yacht, complete with supermodel, suitable for peeling the occasional grape? The late-night infomercials swear that you don't even have to leave your house: living your dream is a telephone call (and a credit card) away.

"All this," they promise, "for *twelve easy payments* of *only* $41.25! Operators are standing by, and overnight delivery is *free!*"

On and on it goes: cassette or CD, VHS or DVD, study at home or attend a weeklong seminar/cruise aboard a fabulous Caribbean luxury liner. For a few bucks (or a few thousand), you can learn the secrets of real-estate riches! Sign up a friend, and get a 25 percent discount!

Welcome to the world of real-estate scams.

It's a sad truth: wherever there is even a flicker of hope for get-rich-quick financial success, someone will devise a scam for it.

A staggering number of these schemes involve real estate, which probably says something important about our culture. I wish I could say what that is, but I can't: I'm too depressed by the sheer magnitude of the fraud being perpetrated daily on the foolish, greedy, or naive.

Make no mistake here. I have made more money in real estate than in any other venture. This includes my various businesses, media activities, investments in the stock market, and other equities—even my occasional instant-win lottery ticket.

But I also understand that my success in real estate came because I had my businesses, my radio show, my books—in fact, a range of other income sources to provide a dependable revenue stream while the property sat idle, sometimes for years. I could wait out the bad times of real estate and capitalize on the good. That's a luxury most people who dabble in real estate simply don't have.

The fact is that making money almost always requires flexibility and staying power. No investment goes up (or, thank heavens, down) forever; most depend on timing to get the best payoff. Patience is key, because it is the overly hungry who fall prey most easily to the predators out there.

I've long been fascinated with the abundance of real-estate confidence games, but the one that never fails to perplex me is the no-money-down scam. No matter how many exposés are printed in the *Wall Street Journal* or broadcast on *60 Minutes*, there's a never-slowing torrent of no-money-down seminars constantly being advertised in newspapers, on radio and TV, even through the mail.

It defies logic: by its very definition, no-money-down indicates the promise of obtaining something while paying nothing. The last time a promise like this delivered was . . . well, *never.*

The smoke and mirrors, the hype and the hyperbole, the practiced showmanship masquerading as confident expertise—they're all part of a greed-driven ritual that was ancient even before Cain coveted what belonged to Abel.

Not long ago, my curiosity chain-whipped my sense of skepticism into submission. After years of resisting the urge, I found myself escorting my long-suffering spouse to what a week's worth of almost nonstop ads on Chicago-area radio stations promised would be the Mother of All Real-Estate Seminars.

Two blocks away from the meeting site—a fashionably overpriced hotel just outside of Chicago—I found myself part of a major traffic jam, inching my way forward.

"What lousy luck," I growled to my better half, who sat patiently beside me. "The one night I decide to go to one of these things, and it's the same night the President flies in for a fund-raiser."

"Look again, sweetie," she said, nodding at the still-distant hotel entrance.

REAL ESTATE RICHES—NO MONEY DOWN SUCCESS! the banner read. SEMINAR TONIGHT!

Oh boy.

I finally found a parking space, five blocks from the hotel. It took another half hour to work our way into the hotel's grand ballroom, reconfigured tonight as a massive sea of chairs—row upon row of them, all radiating outward from a small, spotlight stage on which a single microphone had been placed. The room was filled, every seat; I later learned that a fire marshal forced the seminar organizers to turn away an overflow of prospective real-estate tycoons.

It was, I admit, quite a show. I've never been to a tent revival or a national political convention—but this real-estate "seminar" came close to how I imagine them to be. In the midst of a spellbound crowd, we listened to (*name deleted, on advice of my legal counsel*), a well-dressed bundle of energy and enthusiasm, hold forth on the untold wealth that beckoned us all.

Mr. Name Deleted spoke of foreclosures, distressed properties, property management after the purchase, quitting your day job in the near future, and scores of other topics—each subject impressive sounding (at least, to the audience of real-estate novices seated around me), but sorely lacking in information that could actually be acted upon. What few details he provided seemed intentionally designed to fly right over the head of most attendees.

But clearly, Name Deleted was an excellent salesman. He knew he had to overcome his audience's biggest obstacle: *they had no money.* If they did, they would be attending the "Screw 'Em Out of It with an All-Cash Offer" real-estate seminar, no doubt being held on the *other* side of town.

For that reason, the term *no money down* crept into his presentation in every other sentence.

All the while, on a massive video screen suspended over the stage, a sophisticated PowerPoint presentation projected page after page of charts and graphs, interspersed with such down-home wisdom homilies as "Believe in Yourself . . . and Embrace Your Own Potential!" Uplifting music—I remember hearing the *Rocky* theme, as well as Queen's "We Are the Champions," among others—provided a stimulating counterpoint to the syncopated laser-light show.

It was a whirlwind, rock-star performance—but a scant ninety minutes and a handful of Q&As later, it was over. With a regal, farewell wave of his hand to acknowledge the standing ovation, Mr. Name Deleted vanished into the night—en route, according to the sincere young staffer who took his place on the stage, to bring prosperity to another deserving audience in yet another city.

Elvis had left the building—and behind him, a new army of True Believers lined up to buy his patented no-money-down training course. Charge cards were sizzling that night. The secret of success, and at a discount price of $395 a pop—our speaker had assured us it was a one-night special for those of us present. Wait until tomorrow, and it's back up to $550.

Uh-huh.

As I was walking to my car, the one thought echoing in my mind was that I was definitely in the wrong business: if tonight's seminar was any indication, snake oil remains a growth industry.

Here's the straight dope on the no-money-down scam:

- Generally no bank is going to loan you *all* the money for any property, especially an investment property that is not going to be owner occupied. It's just another of their silly rules (albeit one designed to keep the bank solvent and its officers out of jail).

  Sure, these types of loans do exist—a number of very prosperous individuals or organizations could, on the basis of their reputation, established line of credit, track record, and/or mob affiliations, summon them virtually at will. It's just that they do not exist for *you.*

  In an interesting (but inevitable) catch-22, the only way you qualify is if the bank knows you don't need the money in the first place.

- Banks also tend to require borrowers to have a good credit rating and good steady income. Sadly, these are precisely the attributes that people most attracted to no-money-down deals (of any kind) seldom have.

In effect, such schemes require the seller to lend the "no money down" buyer the down payment for his own property. A nice deal, but only if you're the potential buyer—in this situation, you have nothing to lose: if the financial picture turns sour, you can just walk away.

- "No money down" means there is no down payment coming out of the buyer's pocket; it doesn't mean that the title is simply turned over to the new "owner" without money passing to the seller. Unless the seller agrees to act as the buyer's bank (see "selling by contract" below), if the deal is to be consummated, at some point the seller will insist that the buyer come up with the balance due. If it is indeed a NMD (no-money-down) deal, the buyer needs to use OPM (other people's money); usually, that means a bank loan.

   And by the way, good luck with *that*. In addition to those little details about credit rating and income sources I mentioned earlier, bank loan officers want to know where you got the money for the down payment. When they discover that you borrowed it (no matter from whom) they tend to get a little irritated.

- If the original owner is carrying all or part of the buyer's loan—a category called "selling by contract"—almost invariably the title remains in his name. There are substantial problems to these kinds of no-money-down arrangements, not the least of which is liability exposure. In many states, should an injury or other accident occur, by law both the new and old owner may be named in the lawsuit.

The truth of the matter is that most no-money-down programs are based only on taking money *out* . . . not putting the buyer's (often-nonexistent) cash *in*. In theory, this sounds great; in practice, it's almost always a fairy tale.

Most of these no-money-down schemes count on the rent from the tenants to pay all overhead costs, including the interest and principal on the property loan. The so-called gurus confidently tell their disciples that "cash flow from the renter is the key to success." Heaven help anyone who counts on that kind of key.

I've been a landlord, and I know many other property owners who are, too. Even with the reduced carrying costs that come with a smaller loan (for instance, one where the buyer has paid between 10 and 20 percent down), it's still rare for rental income to cover the costs involved.

Worse still, no-money-down programs tend to focus on the kind of property that requires significant repair or constant maintenance. Positive cash flow is difficult to achieve when the monthly loan payment is due at the bank—particularly if, at the same time, you have plumbers working on leaks in two units, the electrician is fishing new wire through the walls to fix the code violations an inspector found, and an exterminator is in the lobby donning what looks to be a chemical-warfare suit. If the property was in good condition, a good location, occupied by renters who paid in full and on time, or unencumbered by some other dark shadow—well, then, why didn't the seller just sell for cash or other conventional method?

More recently, those who inquire into no-money-down programs are being deluged with follow-up calls from so-called real-estate coaches who—for, typically, $2,500 and up—promise to walk you through your first closing.

Do yourself a favor. If you have that kind of dough sitting around, use it toward the down payment on a *legitimate* real-estate deal—or better, pay off your credit-card debt for this and any other scams you stumbled into over the years. If you hope to make your fortune in real estate, perhaps the best advice is to get your real-estate license (in your spare time; don't quit your day job just yet) and educate yourself on how the system *really* works.

That's the kind of logic that comes from hard experience. But the no-money-down scammers don't want to deal with the experienced (much less, the logical). Instead, they hunt out the dreamers, the innocent, and the unfortunate to purchase their CDs and DVDs, to flock to their road shows, and to buy into their fraudulent systems.

And people do, far too many of them—at the expense of their money, their trust, and their dreams.

YOU ALWAYS HURT
THE ONE YOU LOVE
(TO REPEAT:
EVERYBODY WANTS YOUR MONEY)

I am a Certified Divorce Financial Analyst, Chartered Retirement Planning Counselor, Certified Senior Advisor, and Registered Investment Advisor with a quarter-century of experience; with that kind of pedigree, there is little that I haven't seen, been told, or heard about the coldly impartial world of finance.

But my practice involves people, and I confess to a serious weakness: I *like* most people, and as a result I find it difficult to treat them like mere entries in a ledger. Some of my closest friends are people who have come to me for help in untangling their financial lives—and who have allowed me a glimpse into the personal stories that make up the rest of their lives.

You're about to meet one of these people: Ashley, the soon-to-be ex-wife of Jack. Ashley was referred to me by a long-standing client whom I had helped in a similar matter many years before. Ashley was in the final stages of the divorce negotiations, an eyeblink away from the final decree. My job: based on the proposal she was about to accept, to advise Ashley as to how to invest her divorce proceeds and help her begin her new postdivorce financial life in the most healthy condition possible.

If that sounds rather straightforward—well, in many aspects, it is. Usually, by the time a woman like Ashley comes to see me, most of the arrangements are already set in concrete. The settlement is finalized. There is X amount of assets involved and a fairly predictable level of income coming in and expenses going out. Given the financial settlement that she has to work with, many of the financial decisions we need to make are relatively clear.

And that's a large part of the problem. To protect yourself, you must know how any proposed financial settlement will impact you in the foreseeable future *before* you accept it. And remember: you also need to determine how your spouse's finances will look five, ten, or twenty years down the road, if only to determine as accurately as possible what kind of settlement is, in fact, fair to both sides.

FOURTEEN

DIVORCE—THE *REAL* EQUAL RIGHTS AMENDMENT?

For Ashley, the end of the world came not in the firestorm, but in the terrible coldness that followed.

"We had fought before," she confided to me in one of her visits to my office, after we had become friends as well as client and advisor. "Oh, how we had fought! But there had always been—I don't know. Lines, I guess. Lines that we wouldn't cross."

I nodded. Ashley and her husband, Jack, had been married for almost nine years, since shortly after Jack graduated from the college where they had met. When two people share a life for any appreciable period, each becomes privy to the fears and insecurities of the other. We know the secret vulnerabilities, the places where the most damage can be done with the minimum of effort. It is part of the price we pay for the shared intimacies that bind any couple together. In the social contract, it's the clause that says, "I allow you into *me*, into the secret parts of my very self. I trust you *that* much."

And when it is violated, as it was in Ashley and Jack's last fight, it almost always is the deal breaker.

"When I finally told him I wanted a divorce, all Jack said was 'okay,' " she said. "It hurt; I'm surprised at how much it *still* hurts. I thought I meant more to him than just an *okay.*"

What followed was a month in which they were oddly polite to each other, as icily correct as if they were strangers forced to share a too-small space. Finally, one day, Jack simply moved out. Their next communication with each other came through the lawyers they both retained to handle the divorce.

Financial Snapshot:

- Jack is thirty-eight years old; Ashley is thirty-five. They have one child, Jack Jr., age seven. Ashley and Jack had dated in college and married shortly after Jack's graduation; Ashley never did graduate. While she always planned on going back to get her degree, it hadn't happened after nine years of marriage to Jack.

- They own a home that they had purchased the first year of marriage. At that time they paid $137,000. Monthly payment: $936.34. Today the house is valued at $188,000 and has a $92,000 mortgage that will run for twelve more years.

- Jack earns $71,000 from his job as a consultant; Ashley is paid an hourly $9.50 working twenty hours per week at a part-time job. They own two cars outright, Jack's one-year-old sedan (value: $18,500) and a five-year-old SUV that Ashley drives (value: $7,000). They have $28,300 in stocks in their joint brokerage account, about $6,200 in various checking accounts, $7,800 in mutual funds, $2,300 in bonds, and $4,700 in CDs. Jack's IRA is worth $12,800 and a 401(k) pension plan has a value of $47,800. They also listed $12,000 in furniture as an asset.

- The only life insurance they carried was a $25,000 term policy on Jack, paid by his employer.

One marriage, American style; in dollars, it came to a net total of $243,400. Against this, Ashley submitted an affidavit to the divorce court that estimated her annual financial need at $34,280. Jack's affidavit stated that he would need $28,660 per year. With all the facts and figures duly recorded, the question arose: Where to start dividing everything up in an "equitable" manner?

Most lawyers start exactly where Jack's and Ashley's did, with a single-minded goal identical to that of Solomon. Straight down the middle, give or take a few dollars. Half of $243,400 is $121,700, payable to each member of the erstwhile couple.

But is "equal" the same as "equitable?"

I submit that it definitely is *not*. To show you why, let's review the final settlement that Ashley was about to accept—on, I emphasize, her lawyer's recommendation.

From the start, Ashley had made it quite clear that she wanted the house and custody of Jack Jr. Most women do. In addition to proposing a liberal child-visitation schedule, Jack's counterposition was that if Ashley got full value in the house, most other assets should go to *him*—including his 401(k) and IRA.

"Jack's lawyer told me that Jack was willing to surrender a bit more than half our assets," Ashley said, the bitterness evident in her voice, "just to bring about a 'quick and friendly' divorce." He offered an annual $3,600 per year in child support for eleven years—that is, until Jack Jr. finished high school. (In my opinion, the offer was still thousands of dollars too low.) As a final sweetener, Jack also offered annual alimony of $7,200 for three years.

Ashley wanted the divorce, and her lawyer advised her to take the deal. And so she agreed, though the settlement had not yet been legally finalized.

Let's call the following chart "Ashley and Jack's Asset Split Sheet—Plan One." On the surface, the plan appears to favor Ashley—at least, in the initial division of assets. But looks can easily deceive.

Asset Split Sheet – Plan One

Real Estate	Asset Value	Ashley	Jack
Fair Market Value	$188,000	$188,000	0
Mortgage	$92,000	$92,000	0
Equity	$96,000	$96,000	0
Working Capital			
Cash	$6,200	$3,100	$3,100
Savings	0	0	0
Stocks	$28,300	0	$28,300
Mutual Funds	$7,800	0	$7,800
Bonds	$2,300	0	$2,300
CDs	$4,700	$4,700	0
SUBTOTAL	$49,300	$7,800	$41,500
Retirement Assets			
IRA(1)	$12,800	0	$12,800
401(k)	$47,800	0	$47,800
SUBTOTAL	$60,600	0	$60,600
Non-Spreadsheet			
Furniture	$12,000	$12,000	0
Cars	$25,500	$7,000	$18,500
SUBTOTAL	$37,500	$19,000	$18,500
GRAND TOTAL	$243,400	$122,800	$120,600
PERCENTAGES		50.45%	49.55%

Plan One:
(aka, the Plan Ashley Was About to Accept . . .)

I pushed a sheet of paper across my desk to where Ashley sat, and pointed to the net-worth comparison. "See this?" I asked. "It tells you the total of yours and Jack's financial assets each year for the next twenty years based on today's available information."

She studied it, a small frown on her face.

"I don't understand," she said finally. "I mean . . . it looks as if . . . that can't be true . . ."

"It's true," I said. "Under the plan you're about to sign—with the blessing of your lawyer—you will be *dead broke* in eleven years; at the same time, your ex-husband will tally a net worth of four hundred and seventy-seven thousand dollars."

Ashley stared at me; I could guess what she was thinking, because I was thinking it, too.

Cry foul, cry *shame* on any judge who would allow such a settlement! In truth, neither judges nor lawyers are financial gurus. They are legal experts, skilled in their own area of expertise—the law. But

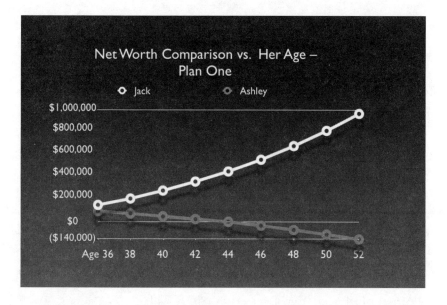

it doesn't take a financial genius to see the unfairness of a plan that impoverishes one partner while ensuring the prosperity of the other. Yet it happens every day.

But net worth alone does not tell the whole story. The next chart was entitled "Ashley's 20-Year Projection Chart—Plan One." Toward the right is a column titled "Net Cash Flow"; study the numbers, as I advised Ashley to do, noting carefully those bracketed with parentheses.

Ashley's 20-Year Projection – Plan One

Year	Pay	Child Support	Spousal Maint.	Total INCOME	Living Expenses	Mortgage	Total EXPENSES	Net Cash Flow	Net Worth
1	$7,508	$3,600	$7,200	$18,308	($23,044)	($11,236)	($35,360)	($17,052)	$97,760
2	$7,733	$3,600	$7,200	$18,533	($23,735)	($11,236)	($36,051)	($17,518)	$91,550
3	$7,965	$3,600	$7,200	$18,765	($24,447)	($11,236)	($36,763)	($17,998)	$85,420
4	$8,204	$3,600		$11,804	($25,181)	($11,236)	($36,417)	($24,613)	$73,267
5	$8,450	$3,600		$12,050	($25,936)	($11,236)	($37,172)	($25,122)	$61,233
6	$8,704	$3,600		$12,304	($26,714)	($11,236)	($37,950)	($25,646)	$49,336
7	$8,965	$3,600		$12,565	($27,516)	($11,236)	($38,752)	($26,187)	$37,602
8	$9,234	$3,600		$12,834	($28,341)	($11,236)	($39,577)	($26,743)	$26,054
9	$9,511	$3,600		$13,111	($29,191)	($11,236)	($40,427)	($27,317)	$14,721
10	$9,796	$3,600		$13,396	($30,067)	($11,236)	($41,303)	($27,907)	$3,632
11	$10,090	$3,600		$13,690	($34,569)	($11,236)	($45,805)	($32,115)	($10,780)
12	$10,393			$10,393	($35,606)	($11,236)	($46,842)	($36,449)	($28,590)
13	$10,705			$10,705	($36,674)		($36,674)	($25,970)	($46,518)
14	$11,026			$11,026	($37,775)		($37,775)	($26,749)	($64,985)
15	$11,357			$11,357	($38,908)		($38,908)	($27,551)	($84,005)
16	$11,697			$11,697	($40,075)		($40,075)	($28,378)	($103,596)
17	$12,046			$12,046	($41,277)		($41,277)	($29,229)	($123,775)
18	$12,410			$12,410	($42,516)		($42,516)	($30,106)	($144,559)
19	$12,782			$12,782	($43,791)		($43,791)	($31,009)	($165,967)
20	$13,165			$13,165	($45,105)		($45,105)	($31,940)	($188,017)

Those parentheses indicate a *negative* number.

Simply stated, Ashley is spending $17,052 *more* in the first year than she is taking in. Six months into her newfound freedom, Ashley will be forced to sell her home and find a full-time job. Otherwise, as the chart shows, she has to borrow against the house just to survive.

When I explained this chart to Ashley, she blanched. For a moment, I thought she was going to be violently ill, and I came around the desk to help her. It took several minutes before her color returned to normal.

"Do you want to continue?" I asked. "It gets worse."

Ashley swallowed hard, and I could see the effort it took her to steel her resolve.

"I want to know," she said, nodding. "I *have* to know."

I returned to my side of the desk and handed her the next sheet, entitled "Jack's 20-Year Projection Chart—Plan One."

Jack's 20-Year Projection – Plan One

Year	Pay	Total INCOME	Living Expenses	Child Support	Spousal Maint.	Total EXPENSES	Net Cash Flow	Net Worth
1	$52,540	$52,540	($28,660)	$3,600	$7,200	($37,660)	$14,880	$122,770
2	$54,116	$54,116	($29,520)	$3,600	$7,200	($38,520)	$15,596	$144,981
3	$55,740	$55,740	($30,405)	$3,600	$7,200	($39,405)	$16,334	$168,816
4	$57,412	$57,412	($31,318)	$3,600		($34,918)	$22,494	$199,763
5	$59,134	$59,134	($32,257)	$3,600		($35,857)	$23,277	$232,675
6	$60,908	$60,908	($33,225)	$3,600		($36,825)	$24,083	$267,653
7	$62,736	$62,736	($34,222)	$3,600		($37,822)	$24,914	$304,805
8	$64,618	$64,618	($35,248)	$3,600		($38,848)	$25,769	$344,243
9	$66,556	$66,556	($36,306)	$3,600		($39,906)	$26,650	$386,084
10	$68,553	$68,553	($37,395)	$3,600		($40,995)	$27,558	$430,453
11	$70,609	$70,609	($38,517)	$3,600		($42,117)	$28,493	$477,480
12	$72,728	$72,728	($39,672)			($39,672)	$33,058	$530,902
13	$74,909	$74,909	($40,862)			($40,862)	$34,047	$587,371
14	$77,157	$77,157	($42,088)			($42,088)	$35,069	$647,043
15	$79,471	$79,471	($43,351)			($43,351)	$36,121	$710,081
16	$81,856	$81,856	($44,651)			($44,651)	$37,204	$776,657
17	$84,311	$84,311	($45,991)			($45,991)	$38,320	$846,951
18	$86,841	$86,841	($47,371)			($47,371)	$39,470	$921,154
19	$89,446	$89,446	($48,792)			($48,792)	$40,654	$999,466
20	$92,129	$92,129	($50,255)			($50,255)	$41,874	$1,082,100

Jack's net-cash-flow column shows that even after paying $7,200 in alimony and $3,600 in child support to Ashley in the first year of the divorce, he is still able to put $14,880 into savings. This does not include the growth accruing in his IRA account. The bottom line: Jack's assets *increase* by $20,670 in the first year of divorce, while Ashley's total net worth *loses* $6,040.

This pattern repeats each year. Ashley gets a bit poorer, while Jack gets a lot richer. Would Ashley have agreed to such a settlement had she seen these figures beforehand?

"My God," she answered, her voice hoarse. "Of course not."

We moved on to Plan Two.

Plan Two:
Sweetening the Pot . . .

Like far too many women, when she married, Ashley had dropped out of college. In Plan Two, we increase Jack's support so that Ashley can go back to school for two years, earning her degree while still keeping her part-time job.

Ashley's 20-Year Projection – Plan Two

Year	Pay	Child Support	Spousal Maint.	Total INCOME	Living Expenses	Mortgage	Total EXPENSES	Net Cash Flow	Net Worth
1	$7,508	$3,600	$12,000	$23,108	($23,044)	($11,236)	($36,080)	($12,972)	$101,840
2	$7,733	$3,600	$12,000	$23,333	($23,735)	($11,236)	($36,771)	($13,438)	$99,710
3	$24,420	$3,600	$12,000	$40,020	($24,447)	($11,236)	($37,483)	$2,537	$114,115
4	$25,152	$3,600	$12,000	$40,752	($25,181)	($11,236)	($38,217)	$2,535	$129,110
5	$25,907	$3,600	$12,000	$41,507	($25,936)	($11,236)	($38,972)	$2,535	$144,732
6	$26,684	$3,600		$30,284	($26,714)	($11,236)	($37,950)	($7,666)	$150,875
7	$27,484	$3,600		$31,084	($27,516)	($11,236)	($38,752)	($7,668)	$157,660
8	$28,309	$3,600		$31,909	($28,341)	($11,236)	($39,577)	($7,668)	$165,188
9	$29,158	$3,600		$32,758	($29,191)	($11,236)	($40,427)	($7,669)	$173,502
10	$30,033	$3,600		$33,633	($30,067)	($11,236)	($41,303)	($7,670)	$182,649
11	$30,934	$3,600		$34,534	($34,569)	($11,236)	($45,805)	($11,271)	$189,080
12	$31,862			$31,862	($35,606)		($46,842)	($14,980)	$192,740
13	$32,818			$32,818	($36,674)		($36,674)	($3,856)	$196,925
14	$33,803			$33,803	($37,775)		($37,775)	($3,972)	$201,236
15	$34,817			$34,817	($38,908)		($38,908)	($4,091)	$205,676
16	$35,861			$35,861	($40,075)		($40,075)	($4,214)	$210,249
17	$36,937			$36,937	($41,277)		($41,277)	($4,340)	$214,959
18	$38,045			$38,045	($42,516)		($42,516)	($4,471)	$219,810
19	$39,187			$39,187	($43,791)		($43,791)	($4,604)	$224,807
20	$40,362			$40,362	($45,105)		($45,105)	($4,743)	$229,954

Plan Two changes two other important variables. First, look under the spousal-maintenance column four columns from the left. Jack is now paying Ashley $12,000 per year for *five* years instead of $7,200 for *three* years. Second, under the pay column, this plan also shows Ashley earning $24,420 in year three. The figure reflects an increase of more than $16,687, at full-time employment—the premium earned as a result of her college degree. This is just the initial impact: a sheepskin always hikes a person's earnings potential, which Ashley will see increase in upcoming years.

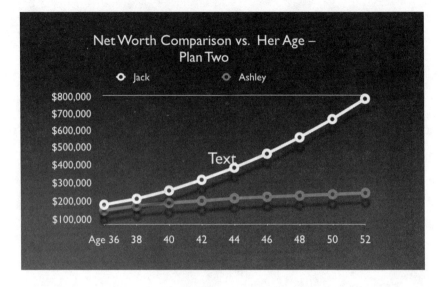

As I explained these elements, I saw a small smile cross Ashley's face; clearly, she liked the idea of finally obtaining her college degree. The new plan did help Ashley—but not enough.

"There's good news and bad news," I said. "Under this scenario, at least you won't completely run out of money in ten years."

She looked at me warily. "And the bad news?"

"For starters, take a look at the net-worth comparison for Plan Two," I said.

"Jack will still have a positive cash flow from day one. In sixteen years, he'll have a net worth of almost eight hundred thousand dollars while you will have only two hundred and thirty thousand or so. But we still haven't solved your cash-flow problem. Until you get a better-paying full-time job—you'll have to do that by year three— you'll have a negative cash flow. And under this plan, you'd better get used to it, because when Jack stops paying alimony after year five, you'll continue to have a negative cash flow *for the rest of your life.*"

"I can't imagine Jack agreeing to pay more in alimony," Ashley said.

"It would be a long shot," I agreed. "Most courts usually allow alimony payments for half the years that the couple was married. You two were married for nine years; given that, few judges would extend alimony past five years."

Ashley's shoulders slumped; clearly, she saw no hope in the situation she faced.

"But what if we don't make the property division a fifty/fifty split?" I asked, and handed her the next set of charts.

Plan Three:
Rejecting the 50/50 Split . . .

Plan Three does precisely that. It keeps all the gains for Ashley that Plan Two had brought and sweetens the alimony pot by increasing it to an annual $18,000. In addition, it calls for Ashley to receive half of the stocks, mutual funds, and bonds. Jack now receives half the value of the CDs. The net result is that Ashley has $16,850 more on her side of the ledger. Obviously, Jack will feel the effects here—he gets $16,850 *less.* This gives Ashley approximately 57 percent of the marital assets, while Jack gets 43 percent.

As the net-worth comparison in Plan Three shows, Ashley will actually have a greater net worth than Jack for the first six years they are apart.

Asset Split Sheet – Plan Three

Real Estate	Asset Value	Ashley	Jack
Fair Market Value	$188,000	$188,000	0
Mortgage	$92,000	$92,000	0
Equity	$96,000	$96,000	0
Working Capital			
Cash	$6,200	$3,100	$3,100
Savings	0	0	0
Stocks	$28,300	$14,150	$14,150
Mutual Funds	$7,800	$3,900	$3,900
Bonds	$2,300	$1,150	$1,150
CDs	$4,700	$2,350	$2,350
SUBTOTAL	$49,300	$24,650	$24,650
Retirement Assets			
IRA(1)	$12,800	0	$12,800
401(k)	$47,800	0	$47,800
SUBTOTAL	$60,600	0	$60,600
Non-Spreadsheet			
Furniture	$12,000	$12,000	0
Cars	$25,500	$7,000	$18,500
SUBTOTAL	$37,500	$19,000	$18,500
GRAND TOTAL	$243,400	$139,650	$103,750
PERCENTAGES		57.37%	42.63%

"Does that put me back on my feet, financially?" she asked me.

"It helps," I answered. "That is, if you don't mind that after year six, Jack's net worth still takes off like a rocket. In sixteen years, he's worth nine hundred and sixty-seven thousand five hundred and ninety dollars; your net worth will be two hundred and seventy-seven thousand nine hundred and forty-eight."

Ashley shrugged. "I could live with that."

"Not so fast," I cautioned her. "We still haven't solved your cash-flow problem. Even in Plan Three, you must still rely on borrowing against the house to pay your monthly bills. No banker—at least, not one who values his job—would allow this; you still face big trouble. So let's push the envelope a little bit further."

Plan Four:
Pushing the Joint-Asset Envelope . . .

I passed her a sheet of paper marked "Plan Four."

"I have kept everything the same as Plan Three—except now you

Asset Split Sheet – Plan Four

Real Estate	Asset Value	Ashley	Jack
Fair Market Value	$188,000	$188,000	0
Mortgage	$92,000	$92,000	0
Equity	$96,000	$96,000	0
Working Capital			
Cash	$6,200	$6,200	0
Savings	0	0	0
Stocks	$28,300	$28,300	0
Mutual Funds	$7,800	$7,800	0
Bonds	$2,300	$2,300	0
CDs	$4,700	$4,700	0
SUBTOTAL	$49,300	$49,300	0
Retirement Assets			
IRA(1)	$12,800	0	$12,800
401(k)	$47,800	0	$47,800
SUBTOTAL	$60,600	0	$60,600
Non-Spreadsheet			
Furniture	$12,000	$12,000	0
Cars	$25,500	$7,000	$18,500
SUBTOTAL	$37,500	$19,000	$18,500
GRAND TOTAL	$243,400	$164,300	$79,100
PERCENTAGES		67.50%	32.50%

get *all* forty-nine thousand three hundred dollars of the joint assets. Jack gets *nada*. Congratulations. You now control sixty-seven-point-five percent of all assets compared to Jack's thirty-two-point-five."

Ashley looked doubtful. "Can you even *do* that? Legally, I mean."

"The question is whether we can get Jack to agree," I said. "Or more to the point, to convince a divorce judge to approve it whether Jack likes it or not. I think it could work on the basis of simple fairness—there are clear long-term advantages to you, and you don't take a complete bath in the short run."

Reaching over, I tapped the next net-worth-comparison chart.

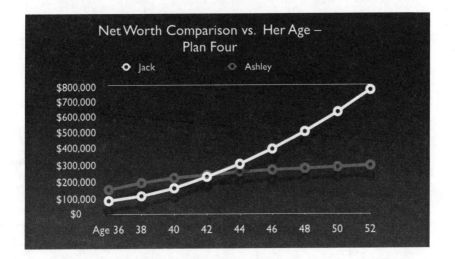

"If everything goes as scheduled, in sixteen years Jack will still have a total net worth of almost eight hundred thousand dollars. You will peak at three hundred and thirteen thousand twenty-seven. For Jack, that's almost three hundred percent more than you'll ever see—even though you receive more than two-thirds of all assets."

"Do I give up much? I mean, I can't make it without the alimony or child support . . ."

"You'd still have the eighteen thousand per year for five years in alimony, and thirty-six hundred per year for eleven years in child support."

By now, Ashley had learned to read my eyes. She looked at me for a second, then burst out laughing. It was the first truly happy expression I had seen from her, and I grinned back.

"You don't advise me to take this one either, do you?" She laughed.

"Most lawyers would jump at the chance of getting this for you," I said. "But it's still the wrong plan for you."

Ashley's 20-Year Projection – Plan Five

Year	Pay	Child Support	Spousal Maint.	Total INCOME	Living Expenses	Mortgage	Total EXPENSES	Net Cash Flow	Net Worth
1	$7,508	$3,600	$24,000	$35,108	($23,044)	($11,236)	($36,080)	($2,772)	$154,785
2	$7,733	$3,600	$24,000	$35,333	($23,735)	($11,236)	($36,771)	($3,238)	$164,295
3	$24,420	$3,600	$24,000	$52,020	($24,447)	($11,236)	($37,483)	$12,737	$190,286
4	$25,152	$3,600	$24,000	$52,752	($25,181)	($11,236)	($38,217)	$12,735	$217,291
5	$25,907	$3,600	$24,000	$53,507	($25,936)	($11,236)	($38,972)	$12,735	$245,360
6	$26,684	$3,600		$30,284	($26,714)	($11,236)	($37,950)	($7,666)	$254,139
7	$27,484	$3,600		$31,084	($27,516)	($11,236)	($38,752)	($7,668)	$263,470
8	$28,309	$3,600		$31,909	($28,341)	($11,236)	($39,577)	($7,668)	$273,391
9	$29,158	$3,600		$32,758	($29,191)	($11,236)	($40,427)	($7,669)	$283,940
10	$30,033	$3,600		$33,633	($30,067)	($11,236)	($41,303)	($7,670)	$295,159
11	$30,934	$3,600		$34,534	($34,569)	($11,236)	($45,805)	($11,271)	$303,494
12	$31,862			$31,862	($35,606)	($11,236)	($46,842)	($14,980)	$308,777
13	$32,818			$32,818	($36,674)		($36,674)	($3,856)	$314,183
14	$33,803			$33,803	($37,775)		($37,775)	($3,972)	$319,637
15	$34,817			$34,817	($38,908)		($38,908)	($4,091)	$325,135
16	$35,861			$35,861	($40,075)		($40,075)	($4,214)	$330,675
17	$36,937			$36,937	($41,277)		($41,277)	($4,340)	$336,255
18	$38,045			$38,045	($42,516)		($42,516)	($4,471)	$341,872
19	$39,187			$39,187	($43,791)		($43,791)	($4,604)	$347,524
20	$40,362			$40,362	($45,105)		($45,105)	($4,743)	$353,207

I explained that the real key is in the critically important area of net cash flow. Jack still has a positive cash flow from day one. Not so for Ashley; over the next twenty years, she will be fully solvent for only three. In the other seventeen years, she will have to borrow money each year just to pay her bills.

"And that," I told her, "is certain to turn into financial disaster somewhere down the road."

"So," Ashley said, "what do we do?"

"What do you say we inflict a tad more financial strain on Jack?" I asked.

Plan Five:
Tweaking the Settlement...

Ashley studied the next plan with what had become an experienced eye.

"Okay," she said. "In Plan Five, I get everything I would have received in Plan Four. The only change is an increase in spousal maintenance, to twenty-four thousand per year for five years from the previous eighteen thousand."

"Exactly. So you tell me—what's the problem with it?"

She frowned, looking at each column in turn. "It still doesn't solve my net-cash-flow positions."

"Very good. What else?"

"You didn't show me the net-worth-comparison chart. Where is it?" she insisted.

I handed her the next sheet.

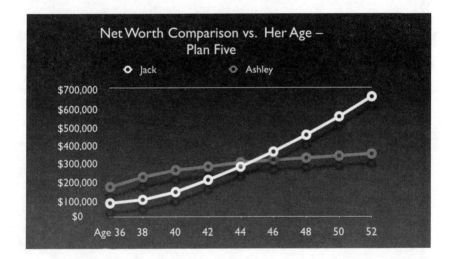

She pounced on it and said, "It will take Jack over ten years to pass me in total net worth. But when he does, his totals will skyrocket while mine level off." Ashley looked up, and I was delighted to see outrage in her eyes instead of resigned defeat. "That's not fair."

"It's partly your fault," I said.

"What?!" Ashley almost sputtered in her anger. "What do you mean by *that*?"

She hadn't seen it yet, but I can already hear all of you asking the obvious question: Why doesn't Ashley just *sell* the damn house? So I asked it myself.

"Ashley, why don't you just *sell* the damn house?"

Plan Six:
Nearly There . . .

"In Plan Six, all payments you get stay the same as in Plan Five," I said. "But this time, you sell the house in year one. You'll pay a seven percent commission, but we will invest the money from the sale of the house. Based on history, I feel there should be no problem earning a fairly conservative six percent per year return on your money over the next twenty years."

"And where do you suggest that I live with my son?"

"Ah," I said, and we both laughed this time. "There's the rub, no?"

Ashley's 20-Year Projection – Plan Six

Year	Pay	Child Support	Spousal Maint.	Total INCOME	Living Expenses	Mortgage	Total EXPENSES	Net Cash Flow	Net Worth
1	$7,508	$3,600	$24,000	$35,108	($34,280)		($40,280)	($5,172)	$227,171
2	$7,733	$3,600	$24,000	$35,333	($35,308)		($41,308)	($5,975)	$234,826
3	$24,420	$3,600	$24,000	$52,020	($36,368)		($42,368)	$9,652	$258,568
4	$25,152	$3,600	$24,000	$52,752	($37,459)		($43,459)	$9,293	$283,376
5	$25,907	$3,600	$24,000	$53,507	($38,582)		($44,582)	$8,925	$309,303
6	$26,684	$3,600		$30,284	($39,740)		($39,740)	($9,456)	$318,405
7	$27,484	$3,600		$31,084	($40,932)		($40,932)	($9,848)	$327,661
8	$28,309	$3,600		$31,909	($42,160)		($42,160)	($10,251)	$337,070
9	$29,158	$3,600		$32,758	($43,425)		($43,425)	($10,667)	$346,627
10	$30,033	$3,600		$33,633	($44,728)		($44,728)	($11,095)	$356,330
11	$30,934	$3,600		$34,534	($49,669)		($49,669)	($15,135)	$362,574
12	$31,862			$31,862	($51,160)		($51,160)	($19,298)	$365,031
13	$32,818			$32,818	($52,694)		($52,694)	($19,876)	$367,057
14	$33,803			$33,803	($54,275)		($54,275)	($20,472)	$368,608
15	$34,817			$34,817	($55,903)		($55,903)	($21,086)	$369,638
16	$35,861			$35,861	($57,581)		($57,581)	($21,720)	$370,097
17	$36,937			$36,937	($59,308)		($59,308)	($22,371)	$369,932
18	$38,045			$38,045	($61,087)		($61,087)	($23,042)	$369,086
19	$39,187			$39,187	($62,920)		($62,920)	($23,733)	$367,498
20	$40,362			$40,362	($64,807)		($64,807)	($24,445)	$365,103

Selling the house has very little impact on Ashley's situation. After sixteen years, the net-worth charts say that Jack will *still* have twice as much in net worth as Ashley: more than seven hundred thousand dollars, versus Ashley's three hundred sixty-five thousand one hundred three dollars.

She gains virtually nothing by selling her residence.

Why? *Because she's paying a house payment of $11,236 per year or $936 per month.* And, after all, she has to live *somewhere* with her son. All that really happens is that Ashley trades her mortgage payment for a rent payment of equal value. She loses here because she

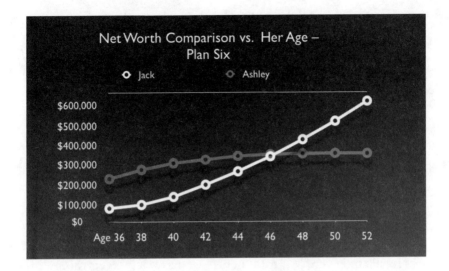

no longer gets any tax advantages for the interest payments and builds no equity or appreciation in her house.

For this reason, you will see that Ashley only builds up approximately $12,000 more in total equity over the next *twenty* years by selling the house and living in an apartment. Remember, we incorporated a 3-percent-inflation scenario on everything for Jack and Ashley. This means Ashley is no longer gaining a 3 percent increase on her home's value each year while she is paying 3 percent more for rent each year.

Ashley looked relieved. "So I keep the house, right?"

"Unfortunately," I said, "no."

I pointed to the numbers. "As you can see from the chart under net cash flow, you're still trapped into running a deficit seventeen of the next twenty years. That's better than the federal government, but still an unworkable situation for a real person."

"Then what's the advantage in selling?" she pressed.

"You'll at least have the resources to pay your monthly bills directly from your working capital," I responded. "In the first year, see how under your working-capital column your funds increase from forty-nine thousand three hundred to two hundred and twenty-seven one hundred and seventy-one after the sale of the house? But don't get used to this money. You'll need to continually tap these funds to survive, and even with an increase to a six percent annual return, this barely keeps your lips dry."

Her face tightened in exasperation. "So *is* there an acceptable answer?"

"Would we have come all this way otherwise?" I said. "Let's look at how total return on investments can change a financial picture—specifically, *yours.*"

Plan Seven:
The Final Answer . . .

With no small sense of ceremony, I handed Ashley the final packet of charts from her folder.

"In Plan Seven," I told her, "we have left everything un-changed—except instead of crediting you with six-percent-a-year return on working capital, I bumped that figure up to seven-point-five percent per year. In essence, we have more working capital for a cushion to deal with; as a result, we can use asset allocation to give you a more effective mix of investments—which means we can take a bit more risk with part of it, in exchange for a better return."

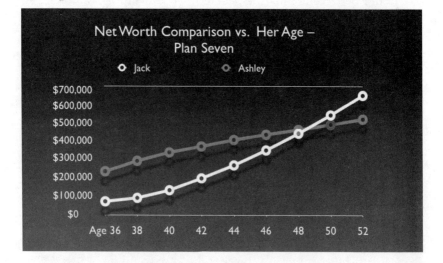

Ashley examined the chart marked "Ashley's Net Worth"; a smile lit her face. "And that increases my total net worth from three hundred and sixty-five thousand one hundred and three dollars to five hundred and fifty-three thousand seven hundred and seventy-six over the sixteen-year period." She looked very impressed. "That's a gain of over a hundred and eighty-eight thousand dollars."

"I don't know what to say," Ashley said, her voice almost a whisper. "You kept me from making a terrible mistake. It was almost too late for me."

"The point is, it's *not* too late," I said. "For you or for any other woman like you."

———

Essentially, Plan Seven is where I envision most divorce battles being fought in the future. There's a growing concern in the legal profession about malpractice suits; maybe this is fair considering the hell and havoc lawyers have been wreaking on society for decades. Having an independent financial counselor review the projected long-term consequences of divorce settlements before the court approves them is logical self-protection.

But as you might suspect, men have (and will continue to have) a hard time accepting all of this. I have never talked to a divorced man who didn't think he got the short end of the divorce stick, even when the numbers prove the opposite. Imagine the response when he is told he must give up more than 50 percent of the marital assets—and remember, I had Jack give up 100 percent of their joint assets—and *still* pay marital support for years longer and at substantially higher amounts than he ever dreamed possible.

But things tend to even out, it appears. These days, I'm seeing more and more men coming in for divorce advice—because their wives are earning more than they do.

Is twenty years to far to look into the future? Maybe, maybe not. Each set of circumstances will ultimately determine this. Will judges want to review the plans after every five years? That would not be unusual. Should the husband be compensated or relieved of his financial obligations in the future because he took more risk than deemed appropriate and lost his share to faulty investments? Can anybody raise a child on three hundred dollars per month?

Also in the above case, Jack agrees to pay half of their son's college education bills *when Jack Jr. enters college*. Promises are nice, but I'd rather see that money coming out of his paycheck monthly (or even in one lump sum) into a side account to cover that future expense . . . starting today. If so, that would shed a new light on all the numbers in the case.

Remember, Jack's financial obligation should not and does not end with his wife. Today's cost to Jack? Hundreds of dollars a month for a college fund, and we're not talking about his kid going to Harvard here. But if Jack doesn't have the money today, I seriously doubt he will have it (or give it) in ten years either. A court-ordered mandate requiring monthly payments to a preestablished fund would solve this problem quickly.

The bottom line? Again the above goes to show how everything most people think about money and divorce is wrong. Sure, Plan Seven, as presented in the above example, may never materialize. But no longer should Plan One become the goal. With a good legal and financial team, and a little financial education for the judge, never again should one party live on Park Avenue while the other is forced to take up residence in the park.

And it must start now, in fairness to spouses like Ashley—and very likely, with U.S. divorce rates still above the 50 percent mark, in fairness to people like *you*.

FIFTEEN

MEN ARE DOGS

Men are dogs.

I say this as a man, and as a fairly representative example of my gender. This is neither a boast nor a confession; it is simple fact. So let me reiterate: men are dogs.

Some of us admit it, albeit sheepishly; others—thankfully, relatively few—proclaim it as a badge of their self-professed masculinity. I've heard human-male dogness rationalized as a sociological after-effect of our common patriarchal/tribal heritage, or as the logical interpretation of the biblical exhortation to "be fruitful and multiply." I've even heard pseudoscientific research cited to prove men are genetically hardwired into our dog instincts; blame it on that dastardly Y chromosome . . .

Be that as it may: the problem is not that men are dogs—after all, at its best, a dog can be a lovable, loyal beast. The problem is that some men *act* like dogs and, in so doing, betray both their own higher nature and the loving trust of their wives and children.

Case in point: Diane, who came to my office after her dog of a husband slipped the leash and mauled everyone who had been close to him.

Poor Diane.

"I never expected this," she told me, from the comfortable chair across from my desk in my office. Her expression and body language were unmistakable; I've seen this many times. She was bewildered, humiliated, and doubtful of her own self-worth.

Diane was an attractive woman of twenty-eight years, lively and smart—in total, she seemed to be the kind of woman that men naturally seek out.

For all too many men, the bottom line is this: you can give him everything he wants, needs, and desires—and in far too many cases, in his mind that's simply not enough. He is Genghis Khan, Napoléon, Alexander the Great; he will never feel fulfilled until he has conquered all that he surveys.

Given that, the real problem for the unfortunate wives of such men is how they ultimately will handle and react to their mates' cheating. My personal opinions aside (kind of a hybrid combination of "vows are vows" and "in this day of HIV and other sexually transmitted diseases, sexual responsibility goes hand in glove with marital fidelity"), that's a choice only you can make for yourself.

But there are practical ramifications here, too. In working with clients who encountered this issue, I've found that what happened and who it happened with will determine not only if the wife files for divorce, but also the manner in which the divorce proceedings will be handled. A woman whose ego has been shattered by an act of outrageous adultery is far more likely to declare unrestricted war, opting for a scorched-earth policy in the subsequent divorce proceedings.

Such a response is understandable. After all, the world as she had known it has collapsed; "someone will have to pay" is an appealing battle cry to adopt.

If anything can be good news for the wife at this point, it is the possibility that the husband has retained even one ounce of moral fiber; that, or a healthy dose of shame. Overwhelming guilt for breaking up the happy home can make him much more agreeable to signing away the farm to his wife and children. Sadly, neither guilt nor shame nor morality seems to carry much weight these days, at least when balanced against the "practical" advice the husband will get from his own lawyer.

Still, an episode of infidelity doesn't necessarily mean the end of a marriage. Professional counseling remains the option of choice for many. It allows for a controlled setting, creating the potential not just to work through the immediate cause of the marital rift but also to work on the underlying issues of the relationship as a whole.

I don't recommend a knee-jerk reaction of rushing yourself and your spouse into therapy (see below for the reason). But clearly, couples therapy/counseling is an option if both parties agree.

And of course, some couples find the strength to once again find each other, with or without outside help.

Unfortunately, this was not the case for Diane, the heroine of our story.

Diane and John had met in college; the attention that John paid to her was like a chapter out of a romance novel. He was funny, romantic, and ambitious. They married upon graduation. Their only child, Jessica, was born a year later, and the family seemed destined for a storybook life together.

But as Diane continued to talk, I noticed something odd. Amid the stories of Jessica's first steps, first day of preschool, and so on, there was very little mention of her husband. Somewhere, John had slipped out of the picture. When I asked, Diana's response was studiously noncommittal. John was, she said, very busy building his business.

The outcome was predictable; but the specifics of how it occurred were nothing short of tragic.

Jessica missed her daddy, who had adopted the practice of working later and later. So one day, Diane and Jessica spent the afternoon baking chocolate chip cookies to take to him that evening—as a surprise.

Some surprise, indeed.

They arrived at John's offices shortly after six, past the rest of the staff's quitting time. Diane unlocked the main doors to John's offices, and Jessica quickly took off down the finely carpeted hallways, cookies in hand, directly to her destination—her daddy's office door. It was closed, but for Jessica that meant nothing.

"Surprise, Daddy!" Jessica shouted as she threw open her father's door.

Then, silence.

As Diane stepped in the doorway, she could feel and hear the sound of cookies crunching under her shoes. Jessica had turned into a statue of stone, the plateful of cookies scattered at her feet.

I need not describe the triple-X-rated scene that was being played out on John's executive-style desk. It was all Diane could do to scoop up Jessica in her arms and rush her from the building.

Needless to say, the next several weeks at Diane's house were not filled with joy.

———————

Let's stop here for some tips and pointers. Obviously, I urge you to share these with your attorney; in a legal process like divorce, you should always follow the advice of competent legal counsel. But for any wife in this position, there are some very important steps *not* to take at this juncture:

- **Don't give in to temptation.** Picking up the first heavy item you see to use as a weapon might make you feel better, but the relief would be temporary and the act a mistake. I have found no jurisdiction in this country where the police or the courts deem such violence acceptable behavior.

  Even nonphysical conflict is dangerous; it can escalate easily into what law enforcement terms a "domestic call." Not only will it make things worse, it just might land you in jail and, during the divorce, could have a significant impact on financial settlement and child-custody issues.

  For the same reason, don't play out the "eye for an eye, tooth for a tooth" scenario; you'll only feel cheapened yourself, and your own sexual history may become part of the divorce proceedings. Besides, a quick tryst without thought may just end up getting you nothing more than one of the many social diseases being passed around so freely these days, including AIDS.

- **Do not confront the woman with whom your husband had the affair.** Again, it may give you some internal satisfaction—but in today's litigious society, you risk turning yourself from the injured party into the defendant in a civil (or even criminal) trial. You should also resist the impulse to inform the husband, boyfriend, or domestic partner of "the other woman" of the affair. Targeting an angry, potentially violent, and possibly unstable person on those who have hurt you may *sound* appealing, but it is never a good idea on any level. You (and your children, if you have any) could come into physical danger from one or another of the parties involved. Also, in most cases, such action will make any future reconciliation with your husband (should you so desire) far more difficult.

- **Don't tell the world your business, particularly at your place of work.** This is hard advice to follow. You'll probably want to tell someone—maybe even everyone—the sordid facts of your devastated life. People being people, this is a virtual guarantee that all manner of rumors will be flying—at your workplace, your child's school, at your favorite coffee shop. At best, you will only end up with a lot of bad advice; you'll be getting enough of that from family and personal friends anyway. Besides, do you want to risk having a well-meaning friend or relative subpoenaed to testify in court against you in the future?

- **Do not automatically sign you and your husband up for six months of marital counseling.** Men do not react well to *anybody* telling them they need help. My theory is that it is related to the male disinclination to stop and ask directions . . . about anything. If you have any inclination to try saving the marriage, seek marital counseling for *yourself* first. See where that leads before you try to bring your erstwhile soul mate along.

- **Do not run to the yellow pages to find a divorce attorney.** This is far too important a matter to trust to chance; you don't want to play eenie meenie minie moe with the rest of your life. (And don't be influenced by the size of the ad in the phone book, either; a law firm may be able to afford that costly ad because it overcharges its clients.)

Your lawyer will be the quarterback of your all-star team of advisors; in many ways, the buck is going to stop with them.

Your financial future as well as those of your children hinges on your decision here. Don't take it lightly . . . and don't make it quickly.

- **Do not assume you have all the financial information, or that what you do have is accurate.** After all, you thought you knew your spouse; well, you don't need any more surprises in your suddenly uncertain life.

    Locate and copy every financial and legal document you can before they have a chance to start to disappear. Examples include the last five years of income tax returns and as many bank statements, stocks or bonds quarterly statements, pension-account reports, and other documentation of assets or income.

    It might be very valuable for you to even consider commissioning a detailed investigation of your spouse.

    But in any event, *do not destroy any documents you obtain,* even if you and your husband decide to reconcile. Unfortunately, habits are hard to break—and if there is a next time, he may cover his tracks better.

- **Do not trust anyone to keep your secrets.** Sad to say, this includes friends, family, or even your own mother. With the exception of your legal representation (with whom you're protected by attorney-client privilege), do not provide anyone with information you would rather not hear repeated in court.

- **Do not write down your plan of action, anywhere.** Remember, you are reading this book, looking for informed advice, and finding out how to obtain an advantage in your divorce proceedings; almost inevitably, your husband is doing the same. It's best not to make it too easy for him.

- **Do not go on an indiscriminate spending spree.** Getting back at a cheating husband is tempting; it may seem to you that running up "his" charge accounts is both fitting and justified. But don't do it. In divorce proceedings, both your judgment and your indiscretions will be brought into court; what you do now might adversely affect your settlement in a major way. And of course, if you reconcile with your husband, someone has to eventually pay those Visa and MasterCard bills . . . and you know who that someone will be.

Let's return to Diane's story for a brief postscript.

Diane had called an attorney and met with him before she met with me. Not surprisingly, none of the points listed above was brought up in their initial conversations. In all too many such consultations, the attorney is focused on asking Diane what *she* wants *him* to do for her.

Does it seem to you that the flow of information should go in the other direction? You're absolutely right; if your lawyer is so bereft of either experience or ideas that you're asked to chart your own legal strategy, it may well be time to find another attorney. Diane pondered exactly that question; in short order, the first attorney was replaced.

She eventually filed for divorce from her husband, despite the joint marital counseling they received. Even with professional help, Diane could neither forgive nor forget.

Nor could daughter Jessica, whose innocence was shattered one evening when she opened her father's office door. I'm sorry to say that Jessica remains a victim of that episode. She continues to receive counseling, on and off, to deal with the issues of trust raised on that traumatic day.

SIXTEEN

KIDS: TO HEIR IS HUMAN

Like virtually every parent, I love my kids. There's very little I wouldn't do to help them or to protect them from the many pitfalls of life. I live for those moments in life when I see that something I was able to do brought happiness to them. I take pride in their achievements, encourage them to pursue new and higher goals, consider them as talented and intelligent individuals in their own right.

But I have no illusions, either.

The fact is that kids are a work in progress for most of their lives . . . and that includes much of their *adult* life. They learn precisely the same way the rest of us do: through formal education, where we study theory; through observation and analysis, where we play connect the dots between the theoretical and the actual; and through experience, where we take what we have learned and lived over a long enough period so as to bring us to competence.

To put all this into practical terms: if you hand a submachine gun to any four-year-old, the little darling will—in all innocence—proceed to spray his immediate surroundings with a hail of bullets. If you allow a slightly older child behind the wheel of your car, the odds are she will find a way to impact your insurance rates, dramatically.

Or if you turn your financial decisions over to a child of *any* age—even if he or she has long passed the age of legal majority—the odds are good that you will witness nothing less than a catastrophe.

Trust me on this; I've seen it happen, all too often.

How can their decisions always seem to be so wide of the mark?

In fact, the leading reason that I decline to accept certain new clients—and, occasionally, am forced to ask veteran clients to move their accounts elsewhere—is that they decide to involve their adult offspring in the relationship. I've learned to recognize the catchphrases that signal this problem is on the horizon.

"My son works for a bank, and he knows all about money." "My daughter made a profit trading stocks in her IRA account." More recently, I heard this most memorable line: "My son *must* know what he is doing. He and his wife have such a big house and they always drive an expensive new car."

In my practice, I advise a number of bankers—the smartest of whom readily admit that banking experience does not equate to money-management expertise. Playing the market with a $2,000 IRA fund—particularly when one is young enough to survive the inevitable missteps—differs greatly from supervising an older person's life savings. Carrying a huge mortgage and driving a car leased from Mercedes-Benz is evidence of many character traits—but fiscal prudence may not be one of them.

In short, be proud of your childrens' achievements in their life—but think about it. Are you really proud because they are truly among the financial elite and trendsetters in their areas of expertise, or simply proud because they have finally pulled their life together and have stopped asking you for help in paying their daily bills?

But unless you wish to court disaster, don't turn your life over to them. Is your son-in-law Warren Buffett? If not, it is likely that any knowledge he has about managing often-complex financial issues is purely theoretical—that is, obtained by reading the latest *Money* magazine (a few bucks, available at any newsstand) or by talking to the guy sitting next to him on the bus on his way to work.

Now don't misunderstand me: children should be a comfort to their parents and provide whatever support is needed. In fact, kids have the right (indeed, the duty) to ensure that their parents' welfare is being served in all financial and emotional concerns they face. This is what is called love—the very love that may give the illness-stricken parent the will to live, or the new widow the strength to continue on with life after losing her life's partner of decades.

But love and money don't mix well. When it involves their parents, very few children can be completely objective in money matters—and even the most loving of them have a difficult time silencing an inner voice that whispers, "This is my inheritance."

This chapter was by far the hardest for me to write. Lack of ideas? Hardly. The biggest problem was narrowing the choices of stories down to just two or three.

To illustrate what can happen when children take control, let me start by relating my experience with the Jamisons, who walked wide-eyed into one of the biggest blunders I have ever encountered in twenty-five years.

Mr. Jamison—at seventy, a short, energetic man with graying hair and startlingly intense eyes—had experienced a satisfactory degree of success in life. He had attended one of my seminars, expressed interest in becoming a client, and had taken me up on my standing offer of a free analysis of his portfolio.

According to my review of their tax returns, Mrs. Jamison, age sixty-four, was "at home." She was also a woman who took obvious pride in her appearance. I wish I could tell you more about her— but after our introduction, despite my prodding, she sat primly, hands folded, while her husband did the talking for both of them. (NOTE: In my experience, this is invariably a yellow flag; we'll discuss why in a moment.)

Financially, the Jamisons were in surprisingly good condition. He had retired from a relatively prosperous business career that had provided a good life for his family, a reasonable pension, and investable assets in excess of a million dollars. On paper, it was evident that with a little planning he and his wife could live a comfortable retirement and still leave a sizable estate.

The couple had visited my office several times since the seminar. At Mr. Jamison's request, I had made several suggestions on investments that had *no* up-front fees, *no* surrender charges, and were completely liquid.

"Sounds good," Jamison had said, smiling as we shook hands. "Sounds *very* good. But I want to run your ideas past my son before I make any final decisions."

"Fair enough," I said, but in the back of my mind a small red light had started to flash.

Fast-forward almost a month, during which I had not heard from the Jamisons. Finally, I called to follow up on their decision.

Jamison answered, and we exchanged the usual pleasantries.

Then I said, "So—on those investments we discussed. Are we good to go?"

"Well, not exactly," Jamison said. "In fact, we've decided to go a different route."

I was taken somewhat aback. "Of course, that's your decision. But may I ask why?"

There was a moment of awkward silence. Then: "Actually, my son had a few ideas of his own . . ."

I listened to the details in growing disbelief. Acting on the advice of their son—supported, the elder Jamison assured me, by a broker the son had brought in for the purpose—here's what happened:

1. They had paid $3,500 for a "comprehensive" financial plan— ignoring a similar plan that I had provided at no charge. Thirty-five hundred dollars that could have paid for a set of braces for one of the Jamisons' teenage grandchildren. Now the broker's child would be receiving the equivalent of free dental care.

2. They had decided, in Jamison's words, "to follow the *general* outline of what you recommended." He listed the investments they had made, some with the very same companies I had suggested. The difference: the funds they had been guided toward by their son's friend carried up-front commissions to the broker—*of more than $75,000!* We would have received none. Seventy-five thousand dollars that could have been used to fund one of their grandchildren's college education. Instead, the broker's child just received the equivalent of a four-year all-expenses-paid scholarship.

3. Tied to these staggering up-front commissions, most of their investments carried an eight-year surrender charge; if they wanted their money out early, they'd pay an 8 percent penalty (that comes to a little over $80,000) on all their funds in the first year alone. Remember, I had recommended investments with no surrender charges; all their money would have been

fully liquid to respond to any need, emergency, or change in the tax code.

4. Finally, adding insult to injury, the son's broker would charge them an ongoing, annual management fee of 1 percent of the account value. For the Jamisons, that totaled about $10,000 annually; this, on money they surely wouldn't move because of the early-surrender penalties. It was the equivalent of an all-expenses-paid vacation for the two of them for ten days each year for the rest of their lives. I hope the broker at least sends them a postcard.

I pointed out the multitude of problems I saw with his decision—detailing the costs Jamison had incurred on the advice of his son and his broker.

And where was Mrs. Jamison during all of this? Sitting in the backseat with blinders on, letting her husband and son decide what would most likely be her last personal financial road map, without any input from her. Sad, because statistics say she will outlive her husband by seven to ten years, and that does not include the fact that he was already six years her senior. Poor Mrs. Jamison . . . and all the future widows just like her.

Jamison heard me out, then spoke the last words we would ever exchange.

"Well," he said, "when I die, everything will be handled by my son anyway. He may as well get started with someone he knows."

You can't argue with logic like that.

———————

As I write this, *Forbes* magazine has announced that Warren Buffett is still the second richest man in the world; his net worth exceeds $40 billion. Buffett is brilliant in his own right—but he's also savvy enough to surround himself with the best financial minds that money can buy.

The Jamisons were not the only people who have mistaken family loyalty for sound guidance; they're not even the saddest example I've seen.

That dubious distinction goes to poor Betty—at seventy-six years of age, among the most lively ladies I've been privileged to know. She had been a client of mine for almost two decades, ever since she and her husband came to me seeking counseling on their upcoming retirement.

"I never had much interest in finance," Betty confided to me, shortly after Bill died several years ago, "because Bill told me I didn't."

It could have been a new beginning for her—a fact that I could see intrigued her as much as it frightened her. Fear won out; as far too many new widows do, she turned are all financial decisions directly to her son.

By today's standards, her account with me was relatively modest: $300,000 or so. The majority of the money was placed in fixed-income vehicles—at Betty's age, about the only investments suitable for a woman whose return to the job market was unlikely at best. Only a very small percentage was in growth-related funds, and those in the most conservative funds I could find.

Part of our strategy for Betty was to remain constantly on the lookout for investments that would provide a locked-in return; it sometimes required a bit of agility, but the extra percentage point or two could provide the difference between annual financial comfort and hardship for Betty. She was a friend, and I never considered the extra effort an imposition.

Until, that is, she turned decision making over to her son, Carl.

One fine spring morning, one of my staff found a strong fixed investment that was paying a straight 6 percent return—a premium over a money-market fund that at the time paid 2 percent from which we could move some of Betty's idle money. The best part: the return was locked in for a year, but Betty could access the money free of charge should the need arise.

As is my practice, I called Betty for authorization.

"I promised Carl that he would make those decisions now," she told me, and she gave me his home and work telephone numbers.

I called both; no answer. I left a message at each; no return call. For several days, I played phone tag with Carl; in between, I had repeated conversations with Betty, who would only direct me to contact her son.

By now, the investment was no longer at 6 percent. One can only do so much; I left a final message for Betty and Carl and moved on to more productive tasks.

Several months later, after more calls, I finally heard from the missing Carl. This time, I urged him to authorize a reallocation that would bring his mother 5 percent . . . a great rate for *that* point in time.

"What happened to six percent?" he demanded. "Call me when you can get what you promised the first time." The phone went dead in my hand. I again informed Betty of Carl's response; she was adamant about her position regarding Carl's role.

Again, the money sat idle in a money-market fund that now paid less than 1 percent.

Another couple of months passed, and an opportunity for what had originally been a 6 percent return had now fallen to 4 percent. Another call to Betty led to another call to Carl.

"Your mother's money is paying half of one percent in the money market," I said. "Just let me *do* this. It is absolutely in her best interest."

"Send me the information," Carl said. "I'll get back to you."

I did; he didn't.

And, for me, that was the end.

Betty's response to all this? She was the eternal mom. She told me she would stand by her son no matter what the cost; in her eyes, he could do no wrong.

The loss to Betty during all this? By my calculations, it came to about $20,000 in lost income.

I still consider Betty a friend, but I no longer handle her financial affairs. I can't, because I can't compete with a mother's loyalty for her son—a stubborn determination that, through foolish procrastination, cost her dearly.

Gee, I wonder what Warren Buffett would have to say to that?

————————

Gina was as typical as a client who comes to our office gets. She was a widow, age sixty-six, who had lost her husband several years back to an untimely accident at work. He left her with an estate that included a wrongful-death settlement and a $100,000 life-insurance policy. Gina's net worth was about $600,000, not including a house that was free and clear, currently valued at $225,000.

Gina was always open to ideas, relying on me for advice for everything from buying a car to maybe selling the family home. Gina would listen carefully, ask questions that invariably cut to the heart of the matter, and decide.

She had two children, son Greg and daughter Laura, whom Gina had kept at arm's length from her financial affairs, despite her obvious pride in their accomplishments. Laura taught school, and Greg owned a well-known area restaurant.

But one day, during a scheduled midsummer review of her portfolio, Gina abruptly indicated an interest in taking more risk than she had previously.

"It's up to you," I said, "but for a woman in your situation, I'd deem it less than advisable to take on *any* additional risk."

She nodded, obviously troubled by my words.

"I'll think about your advice," Gina said, and by her tone I knew we would discuss the topic again, soon.

A few days later, very uncharacteristically, Gina was back in my office.

"I want to push the envelope," she said firmly.

"Gina, what's going on?" I asked, counting on our long friendship. "This isn't like you."

The answer surprised me, though it probably should not have.

"Greg has a few ideas about investments I should make," she said, and reached into her purse for a slip of paper. "To bring in a better return."

I examined it, and my eyebrows arched involuntarily.

"Gina, these aren't just higher-risk investments," I said. "They're akin to walking a tightrope over a poolful of sharks. The risk level is *very* high—so high that I would consider them inappropriate for a thirty-year-old, let alone a sixty-six-year-old widow."

"Greg says—" she began, and I broke in.

"Greg runs a restaurant," I said, grinning to take the sting from my words. "Let me see his credentials to suggest how you invest your life savings. C'mon, Gina—we've known each other a long time. What's this *really* about?"

She was silent for a long moment before she spoke.

"Greg needs money," she said, in a soft voice.

He did, indeed. And, as it turned out, not a small amount: $50,000. Restaurants are often dicey business ventures; many, even established ones, fail each year. And so it was with Greg's restaurant. Business had fallen off, revenue was down; nonetheless, his employees, suppliers, and the tax man all wanted their money, on time and in full.

It's a catch-22 situation. When you're doing well, financial institutions fall over themselves to offer loans you don't need. But when you *do* need it, the loan offers disappear. Money is almost impossible to obtain.

Frantic, Greg turned to the only source of cash he knew. In the arithmetic of the desperate, Greg calculated that if Gina earned more money from her investments, she could loan it to him to save his failing restaurant.

Gina was not the first of my clients to face this situation. I always advise them against such requests—but I know that most of them are going to do it anyway. In such cases, I advise them to set *some* basic ground rules before letting their children borrow from the First National Bank of Mom. For your edification, here are three:

1. Set a limit depending on what you can afford to never see again in your lifetime, because you very likely won't.

2. Never loan a single dollar past that limit unless the first loan has been repaid.

3. Get it in writing, legalized, collateralized, and recorded by your child and his or her spouse. You'll see in a moment why this is extremely important.

For Gina, rule number one started with a definite amount. She would provide Greg with no more than $50,000. In my opinion, even that total was far too high, based on her age and total financial picture.

But Gina had made up her mind. "He's my son," she said, "and he's in trouble." She tried to laugh, but it came out like a sob.

I handed her my ever-ready box of facial tissues. When she could speak once more, she tried to turn it into a joke.

"After all, David—he's going to get the money sooner or later," she said.

"Later would be a lot better," I said. "At least, for you."

With floundering businesses, it's not uncommon to find yourself throwing good money after bad; this scenario fit Greg all too well. That's what rule two is intended to shortstop—when it is faithfully applied.

Gina found herself unable to refuse her son. Over a few short months $50,000 turned into $70,000; $70,000 into $100,000— and it didn't stop there.

After it reached $225,000 worth of withdrawals, I asked Gina to visit; it was time for tough love, and not just for Greg. I reviewed her situation, carefully noting the steady decline in her assets.

"Based on everything I've seen, you're determined to bankrupt yourself," I said. "I can't stand by and be a part of this, Gina. You don't need a financial advisor anymore; you merely need a with-drawal window."

"What are you saying, David?"

"I can't work with you anymore," I said, as firmly as I could. "I have to ask you to move your account elsewhere. If you like, I can recommend several other financial advisors who—"

My words may have made the difference; more likely, knowing Gina as I did, she had already made her decision, possibly without realizing that she had done so.

"No," she said, with more spirit than I had heard from her in months. "I don't want another advisor. The 'bank' is closed to Greg, as of today. Will you reconsider?"

I nodded, knowing how much all this had cost Gina—and not just in monetary terms.

She was as good as her word; the cash tap shut down, and after a few weeks, Greg's restaurant closed with little fanfare.

It might have ended there—except that Gina never followed rule three. She neglected to get the terms of her loans to Greg in writing and recorded. It was a dire oversight, because shortly after Greg's business failed, so did his marriage.

The only equity to share was his house. Greg's wife had never allowed him to use it as collateral; in the divorce settlement, the house garnered about $60,000 in equity when it was sold, divided evenly between Greg and his wife.

It didn't help Gina. With nothing in writing to indicate that Gina's infusions of cash were loans to Greg, the divorce-court judge ruled that the money had been a gift to her son—and as such, the half that went to Greg's ex-wife was unrecoverable.

Three simple stories, all different yet so close in the common denominator. Could I go on?

Probably indefinitely.

I could have included the story about the kid who *demanded* his share of the family inheritance—while his parents were both still living. Or the one where the child wanted to live in the family home with *his* wife and kids—and moved his poor mother to an apartment because "she really didn't need the space."

Also of note were the three kids who together sued their mother for their "fair" share after the father died and left no will. Most recently was the son who threatened to never again talk to his newly divorced mother if she didn't invest her postdivorce settlement with his best friend—who had graduated from college just six months earlier.

Kids: ya gotta love 'em. Otherwise you'd be tempted to *shoot* them.

SEVENTEEN

BONANZA!
(OR, LEAVING YOUR CHILDREN
ALL YOUR MONEY . . . AT ONE TIME)

Let me tell you a story about a client of mine we'll call Kathy—or, more to the point, let me tell you about what happened a few days after her death.

Kathy was a widow, having lost her husband, Jim, to a massive heart attack at age fifty-six. The next nine years dragged by for Kathy, as they often do for people whose soul mates have been the focus of their lives. When the doctors diagnosed Kathy with a particularly aggressive form of lymphoma, it may well have come as a relief to her.

Kathy and I worked together many hours in those last weeks, making sure her affairs were in order. Jim and Kathy had not been rich; still, the flower shop they had owned had provided for them and their three sons during Jim's life. The proceeds from the shop's sale, plus a life-insurance policy Jim had carried, allowed Kathy to build an estate of almost $750,000 dollars by the time she fell ill. The three sons were to be the sole heirs of this sum.

I try not to speak ill of the dead—but of those they leave behind, I have seldom seen as selfish a trio as Kathy's three sons. These were young men who were afire with a sense of their own destinies—so much so that, after Jim's death, operating a flower shop was out of the question. They had pressured Kathy to sell it; when she finally did, they had pressured her for loans that all concerned knew would never be repaid.

I told Kathy stories about other disasters that had happened to families in similar circumstances. Sadly, my advice fell on deaf ears, as it has so many times with parents in similar situations. Everybody thinks *their kids are different*—more wise, or more mature, or simply not as greedy. Kathy trusted her sons, and trusted their wives, too.

And so it was no surprise that on the day of Kathy's wake, all three sons buttonholed me in a corner at the funeral home—not to reminisce, but to demand information on the value of Kathy's estate. Their behavior was less unique—sadly, it happens more often than not—than it was inappropriate.

In fact, statistics we keep at my firm's office indicate an interesting, if sad, truth: in slightly more than 52 percent of cases when the surviving parent dies, the children have contacted us to inquire about the size of the final payment due to them before that parent is even buried.

Prior to her death, I had put Kathy in touch with a good trust attorney. Three-quarters of a million dollars is no mean sum; but a trio of determined spendthrifts could easily burn through it to no good end. I know the thought of such waste had pained her.

I had suggested that she set up her estate to spread out the payments over five, ten, or even twenty years.

"Protect the kids from themselves," I urged her—and deep down, I knew she agreed.

But there were always other issues to deal with. The last months of her life I almost pleaded with her to keep her appointments with the attorney. "Do whatever you want," I urged her, ". . . but *listen*, then decide."

Finally, as happens so many times in this situation, she simply ran out of time.

Several days after the burial, I faced Kathy's sons across the desk from me. They were barely restraining themselves; each looked as if he had hit the jackpot at Caesars Palace.

As is my practice, I had sent them preprinted forms—questionnaires to help guide them in planning how to handle their inheritance. Invested wisely, the quarter of a million dollars each received could form an assured basis for financial security.

But it seldom does, as it did not this time.

One by one, each brother delivered variations of the same speech. I've heard it often, and it usually goes like this: "David, I've given it a lot of thought—but I need to pay off some bills. The wife and I each really need a new car, and if we're ever going to buy a new house, it should probably be now. So why don't you just give me a check for whatever I have coming?"

The only question I am ever left with is whether they want us to withhold any taxes that might be due. (And the typical answer to that, as you might expect, is no.)

The resolution of all this didn't take long; it seldom does.

In short order, each had a new car to drive (as an asset, cars are short-lived indeed); credit cards were paid off in full (if only temporarily); several once-in-a-lifetime trips (including those first-class-cabin snapshots of Kathy's kids sipping champagne); and they had moved into new, larger homes (which carry with them higher property taxes, maintenance costs, and utility bills) packed with a dizzying array of newly purchased electronic gadgets. Best Buy should hang a banner on every store that says BIG-SCREEN TVs—SPEND YOUR INHERITANCE HERE!

Oh, did I mention that two of the three children are now divorced? Half of the money put into that new house as well as 50 percent of any money that they might have neglected to spend now sits in Kathy's ex-daughter-in-laws' bank accounts.

It didn't have to work out this way. But without wise estate planning, it almost always does.

My advice? Your sons and daughters will despise it (but only half as much as their spouses). In fact, if you decide to follow this advice, I strongly suggest you not tell them what you did. There will be plenty of time for them to learn when you are long departed. Why? Because in twenty-five years, I have never known of a son, daughter, or in-law who jumped up and down for joy when getting the news that they were going to receive their inheritance in dribs and drabs.

Look at the size of your estate and consider how you want it divided. Go ahead and give the kids the money immediately from the sale of the house when you die. That will at least provide them with some money to blow right away and keep them coming to put flowers on your grave around the holidays.

The rest of the funds can be set up so as to pay them out over time . . . five years, ten years, or even their lifetime. In effect, you will be guiding their financial lives from beyond the grave. And isn't that a parent's job?

Now you can truly rest in peace and with a smile on your face.

SIMPLY, WHEELS

EIGHTEEN

IT'S THE WHEEL THING: AUTOMOBILES AND YOU

New or used, buy or lease, pay in cash or take a loan—even leather versus cloth. When it comes to people and their cars, the list of available options isn't limited to what a dealership offers; there are some real choices involved, and the potential for bewilderment is sky-high.

That's the reason why, aside from questions about retirement investments, concerns about how to buy and pay for a car arise among my clients more than any other.

Not even buying a house elicits the same level of interest, though the investment at stake there is many times higher. I suspect it's because no matter how passionate one may get about buying a house, purchasing a car taps into other emotions entirely. With a house—even if you make a mistake in size, color, or furnishings—in today's marketplace there's the expectation that, willy-nilly, inflation is your salvation.

But with a car—which loses a substantial part of its value as soon as it leaves the dealer's lot—the financial gamble being taken has a real, and immediate, impact.

Prospective buyers know they are at a disadvantage, that they are swimming among the smiling, white-shirt-sleeved sharks. The foreknowledge that they are about to be taken for a ride—an apt expression, no?—makes the entire experience somewhat less than joyful.

In all humility, I do consider myself somewhat of an expert in the field of car buying. Oh, I may not be a world-beater when it comes to which manufacturer offers the best designs, features, or safety record—some of that involves personal taste and aesthetics, and I'm a meat-and-potatoes sort of hard-nosed pragmatist. Still, I have helped hundreds of people understand the intricacies of the retail automobile business, and I possess more than a layman's knowledge of the financial maneuvering involved.

But more to the point, I have gone through this ritual more than three hundred times in my life to date—sometimes six or eight times *in a single year.* I buy a *lot* of cars, if only because I enjoy driving a finely engineered vehicle. The fact that I've usually sold them for what I paid for them (occasionally, even more) is an added benefit—but one not to be disregarded.

I'm able to do this because I focus on limited-edition vehicles, in which the demand tends to be higher than the supply. I also have the luxury of being patient, until I see an opportunity to acquire one of these autos at a good price, even if the price is not conducive to profitable, relatively short-term resale.

My education in auto economics started at the age of thirteen as I watched my father guide my older brother through the process of buying his first car. We trudged through showrooms and used-car lots for days (though it seemed shorter: few American males would find this activity burdensome).

I very quickly learned two critical facts that serve me to this day:

- Cars that were, to all appearances, *identical* could vary dramatically in price from dealer to dealer.

- Not all cars depreciate at the same rate. Thus they must be viewed as an investment—albeit lousy ones: with most investments, you try to pick the ones that will make you the most money; here the object is to lose the least amount every year.

But even those insights, as valuable as they are, pale in comparison to what I've come to call the Prime Axiom of Auto Buying:

Unless You Are Willing to Walk Away—from Any *Prospective Car Deal—You Cannot (and Will Not) Prevail.*

Two facts and an axiom—not much to remember, is it?

But understanding how each of them influences your auto purchase will allow you to do as I have done. You will get the best possible deal on every car you buy. More important, you'll also have a chance to *make* money—the goal with any investment—when you trade up to a different (note that I don't use the word *new*) car.

In the process of following my own advice, I have owned and driven what most deem to be among the most exotic cars in the world—limited-production Mercedes, BMWs, Porsche Turbos, and even Ferraris.

There are literally thousands of Web sites that provide tips on buying automobiles; any bookstore has shelves full of how-to books, many of them penned by former car salespersons.

Most focus on the painfully obvious: "never tell the salesman you are trading in a car in advance," "only buy the options you *truly* want," "shop around for the best interest rate when financing your car"—clichés that are generally worthless to any reasonably intelligent human.

Worse, car salesmen read the same "how-to" information that you do; if they're still working on the sales lot, they've already prepared their defenses to counter these ploys.

To get the best deal for the least outlay of money, flexibility is the key; leave your emotions at home (at least, until you pull into your driveway after the deal is struck). Understand that fixating on any specific vehicle is shortsighted: after all, they manufacture these things in *factories,* where (with the few exceptions I've noted) they pump out thousands of any particular model or style.

In purchasing a car, you must practice the kind of Zen-like detachment that guides most successful negotiators. You may have envisioned your dream car in fire-hydrant red, but if sunrise silver is the better deal, don't be afraid to revise your fantasies. When you were growing up, your father might have been a Chevy man—but don't walk past a Ford, if the numbers come out right.

Buying a car need not be an experience either perilous or disheartening. You can emerge the winner (or at least call it a tie) in most any automobile deal—if you remember the Prime Axiom of Auto Buying and hold firmly to the following seven tips, which I follow in every automobile transaction.

Tip 1: New vs. Used

With only a few exceptions, there are few transactions more ill considered than buying a straight-from-the-factory new car—yet millions of people do it every year. If losing money (usually, *lots* of it) is your idea of a good time, ask your friends for an invitation to their monthly poker game; but if you appreciate prudent stewardship of your own personal finances, stay away from the new-car showroom at all costs.

Okay, okay—I know that I won't have your full attention until I disclose the exceptions to this rule. At the risk of deflating egos out there, let me state that the first exception involves the kind of cars that most of us will never *see*, let alone own.

For instance, if you can find a new Ferrari 430 Spider for anywhere near its "official" list price (around $220,000, with a couple of key options)—mortgage the house and *buy it immediately*!

Why is this particular Ferrari an exception to the rule? Well, only a few hundred of these cars roll out of the Ferrari factory each year earmarked for export to the United States. Given the propensity of many professional athletes, hot-at-the-moment entertainers, and profligate children of the vulgar rich to obtain "bling" of any sort, Ferrari could probably sell twice that many in L.A. and New York alone.

At the time I write the words, there is a waiting list of approximately three years to get a Ferrari 430 Spider. Thus this supply-and-demand equation has the current model selling for $25,000 *over* sticker price the moment you drive it off the lot. (Which raises the intriguing question of why the dealer wouldn't simply hike the price tag by that amount and take the profit himself—except that our old nemesis, supply and demand, would immediately compensate for *that,* creating an endless logic loop that would ultimately cause the universe to implode. But I digress . . .)

Occasionally you will also find some limited-edition Bentleys,

Mercedes, BMWs and other rare production models that will not give you a huge profit, but can be bought at sticker and sold six months down the road for approximately what you paid. I know each and every one—but only because I make it my job to beat the system. My goal is to drive the finest vehicles the world has to offer, at as small a depreciation cost to me as possible.

A word of caution. This only works while interest rates on money are very low. If you can get a car loan for 3 or 4 percent or so, buying that high-line exotic won't cost you much in interest payments. The same holds true if you pay cash and the rate of return on that money is very low. But a 10 percent loan on a $200,000 car makes no financial sense, no matter how great the residual value of the vehicle.

The second exception is infinitely more plausible. Let's say that the car you *really* want happens to have a significant rebate offer in effect. If you can purchase a vehicle that has a MSRP (manufacturer's suggested retail price, in dealer-speak) of $35,000 for, say, $24,000 after all discounts and zero percent interest for five years to boot—well, as onetime Chrysler CEO and pitchman Lee Iacocca urged in his heyday, "Buy it!" (But be on the lookout for the countless other markups the salesman may try to factor into the final price; add-on charges are a time-honored dealer tactic.)

A word of caution here: if you are trading in a one- or two-year-old car of the same model, all bets are off. Your old beast just depreciated substantially because of the rebate on the new model. If you can afford it, buy without a trade-in (unless it is a model from a different manufacturer that doesn't currently have a rebate) and then sell your used one after the rebates have ended.

A third exception to the "never buy new cars" rule involves certain high-residual models from Honda, Toyota, Nissan, and a few others.

For example, Sandy has been a client for about as long as I have had a broker's license. A seventy-eight-year-old widow, one of her life's joys is to drive to see friends. Despite a substantial account with my firm that allows her to live quite comfortably, she has long known the benefits of keeping life simple as well as fiscally frugal. One result is that she tends toward owning small, relatively inexpensive imported autos that give her great reliability as well as sensational resale values.

Sandy had given her previous car—a six-year-old Toyota—as a college-graduation present to a granddaughter. To replace it, she was considering buying a three-year-old Toyota with 41,000 miles, but—as with many used cars—no warranty or guarantees.

"I've done my homework, David," she told me proudly. "I know that a new car loses so much value in the first year. So I only buy used cars now."

"That's usually a wise decision," I agreed. "But let's run the numbers, just to make certain."

I fired up my desk calculator. "Okay—the used Toyota you're looking at will cost about eighteen thousand," I said, punching in the numbers. "Given that it's in good condition, that's a fair price, according to the auto guides."

"I know." She smiled. "I checked that, too."

"Still, you tend to keep your cars for longer than most people," I reminded her. "That makes repairs and maintenance more important to you."

"Now, for about ten thousand more than you plan to pay for that used car with *no* warranty, you could buy a new one—but with a three-year bumper-to-bumper manufacturer's warranty, which eliminates the repairs you'd otherwise have to pay for out of pocket yourself."

I showed Sandy the calculator.

"Essentially, buying a new car will cost you about ten thousand more than the used model, but it will be a three-year-newer car for resale purposes three years down the road," I pointed out. "Three years from now, you'll have a three-year-old car that has not lost much more in value than a three-year-old car if you bought it now—but in the interim, you've eliminated the costs—and just as important, the headaches—of most upkeep and repairs."

Sandy saw the merit in my suggestion: in effect, she was spending a little more—not to "buy a new car," but in large part to simplify her life by minimizing the potential hassles and out-of-pocket costs.

If, like Sandy, you can swing it financially (Sandy could) and you're at an age where you're willing to spend a little more to avoid a few of life's speed bumps, and are willing to buy certain foreign models with exceptional resale values instead of Detroit iron—well, these are acceptable reasons to opt for new over used.

So there they are, a short list indeed: ultrahigh-end cars, verifiable once-in-a-lifetime rebate deals, and a few economically priced/high-resale hassle avoiders.

If the new car you're considering doesn't fit any of these criteria, you'd be well advised to head for what dealers today have renamed the "previously driven" lot.

Yet every year millions of people still buy factory-new anyway—and after all, doesn't that keep the auto industry out of the bankruptcy courts?

I'd love for federal law to require every new-car sticker to include the resale value of the car projected two, three, or even five years down the road. It could easily be done: banks and finance companies do it all the time. They have to. The business of loaning money and setting long-term-lease payments depends on it.

Why not provide this same information to consumers before they purchase *any* new car?

Until then, let me make this absolutely clear: unlike oxygen, nourishment, or the ability to rationalize our own dubious deeds, nobody really *needs* a new car.

Some people see certain cars as a testament to virility or as public scoreboards proclaiming their financial achievements. These individuals seek validation through the simple fact of conspicuous consumption, and for them no satisfaction is greater than the sight of envy on a neighbor's face.

Is this how *you* see yourself, or want to?

For that reason, the first step is to figure out what type of person you *want* to be; it will help define the type of car buyer you *are*.

Aside from these aspects of self-analysis, you must also consider the simple economics involved. Each year millions of people talk themselves into buying new cars—and a surprising number of them simply shouldn't. The reason is what the accounting trade calls "depreciation." For the person concerned with the financial and not the egotistical, this is where all car buying must start.

So, what is your best deal? Well, unless you are the type who buys a ten-year-old car and then runs the wheels off it, often one of the best vehicles to buy is a two or three years old. It should be low mileage, and still be under the original manufacturer's warranty. If it comes loaded with optional equipment or performance packages, such a car can be a real steal for you.

Also, *never* buy an extended warranty from *anyone* except the original manufacturer of the car you are buying. Over-the-counter no-name warranties may be accepted by the dealer who sold you the warranty—but heaven forbid you're on vacation when you need help. Sadly, some dealers simply pocket the premium, never even purchasing the warranty, playing the odds that they'll never hear from you again.

But let's assume that you found your dream car—used, under manufacturer's warranty, and priced a little over wholesale. Your job is still not done.

• *Do your due diligence.* Always have the dealer certify on your contract—*in writing*—that the car has never been in an accident or sustained other serious damage (for example, that it was not one of the autos caught in the flooding caused by hurricanes in 2005. Don't laugh—hundreds of them were shipped inland, "reconditioned," and sold after being under water for periods as long as a week). If you end up in court, a signed declaration is far more valuable than the "he said/she said" routine.

And don't allow use of the phrase *to the best of my knowledge.* This is a loophole you may regret—and besides, the dealer knows darn well if any work has been done on any particular car. In fact, the VIN of many cars can be input into a computer at the dealership; within seconds, up pops the history of any service done at any of the manufacturer's dealerships. Always get a copy of this before signing on the dotted line.

• You can also get most of the vehicle's history (previous owners, locales, and problems); tracking companies such as Carfax provide this service for a nominal fee of around twenty dollars. If a more personal inspection is desired, use your own (not the dealership's) mechanic. If you don't have a regular independent mechanic, a number of companies will do an inspection for around a hundred dollars.

Several national chains provide this service; check the yellow pages or the Internet for "automobile inspections" and pick one. Among the national firms is one called Carchex, which promises a fifty-five-point inspection sent to you via e-mail within forty-eight hours of your call. All you do is provide the seller's name and contact information; they handle the rest.

This inspection is an important step at any time, but it's essential when you're buying a vehicle from an out-of-state seller. In addition, with cars being sold sight unseen today via such online services as eBay—well, if there were a word stronger than *essential,* I'd use it here.

Of course, dealers hate anything that smacks of "independent" inspections; usually, individual sellers like it even less—they have nothing to gain from such inspections and everything to lose.

But then, you aren't looking to make a new friend, are you?

Tip 2: Add-on Options and Resale Values

Tricking out your new SUV in those über-popular twenty-two-inch chrome wheels may have a certain appeal, despite a price tag that can run as high as $5,000 to $8,000—but if you opt to buy them, the Law of Unintended Consequences will quickly come into play.

Looks aside, the low-profile styling of these wheels will make the vehicle ride even more like a truck and could actually be a true safety hazard; sadly, their popularity among certain elements of society makes it more likely they will be stolen some dark night. If you live in a northern climate, you'll need to protect the wheels in the winter (to say nothing about merely *moving* on ice and snow); that means you must buy another set of winter tires and wheels (estimated cost: $1,000). Add to this the cost of the changing, rebalancing, and storage each spring and fall.

But even worse, at least to the financially astute, those $8,000 worth of tires and wheels will usually be worthless come trade-in time. The same can be said for $3,000 stereos, $2,500 chrome grilles, $5,000 video systems, and $4,000 exotic exhaust systems. In some extreme cases, these luxuries can actually make the car worth less at trade-in time. Not everyone enjoys twelve-inch subwoofers in the trunk or listening to a "custom-tuned" exhaust system that sounds like an ice pick punched holes in the muffler.

If you must have these kinds of "pimp my ride" trick items, search the used-car lots and Internet sites for a used model. That's where you will get a lot of bling for your buck.

Another point here, if you like the fancy *factory*-installed stuff that all manufacturers offer (as I do), but don't want to pay rock-star prices (as I won't), there's a simple rule: always buy the top-of-the-line, fully loaded model—*but buy it used!* The cost is already deeply discounted because the car is "previously driven."

But know this: When it comes to trade-in time, none of these options will really matter.

What?!

Indeed. We've all played out the scene, as the used-car manager inspects the car we're offering in trade, on his face a skeptical frown. One by one, we tick off for him all those extra features that make *this* trade-in worth so much more.

It never works. While we prattle on, the dealer is focusing in on the Big Three of the used-car business: color, condition, and mileage. These elements, when applied to the current used-car market at the wholesale auctions, will determine the value of the vehicle.

It's simple economics: he knows what sells . . . and for how much.

He also understands the unique psychology involved in the used-car business. For instance, if you want the best value, try to time your trade-in before nearing the 20,000-, 30,000-, or 50,000-mile marks. It's psychological, sure—but that doesn't make it less important to the bottom line: your 38,600-mile car will be far easier for the dealer to resell than one with 40,300 miles, and he knows it.

But even if you have the right color, mileage, and it looks like it just drove off the showroom floor, be prepared for the dealer's final assault on your vehicle's value. Whatever car you're looking at buying is hot, hot, hot, and he will tell you the ugly story about how he just had one just like yours on the lot and no one opened the door on it for sixty days.

This helps him pull off a major coup that I have seen more and more dealers trying to pull on unsuspecting sellers over the last couple of years. It used to be that dealers were happy giving you a good wholesale price for your trade-in knowing that if it did not sell on their lot in a reasonable amount of time, they could always whole-sale it to another dealer or sell it at auction for about what they gave you for it at trade-in time.

Now they want to give you much less (sometimes several thou-sand dollars less, depending on the car's value) so that they can sell it at auction *to another dealer for a fat profit.*

When this happens, you have really been taken. But not by the dealer: you did it to yourself, because you didn't do your home-work.

Tip 3: Always Buy Your Used Cadillac from the Mercedes Dealer

This tip is simple, and I try to make it a practice to use it *every* time I buy a "previously driven" car.

Here's how it works. Let's say, for whatever twisted reasons of your own, that your dream car is a Cadillac STS. Since you now see the logic of never buying a new car (unless it fits one of my three categories for buying new—and this model definitely does not), you have focused on finding a fully loaded two-year-old model.

So how did Jason, a relatively new client of mine, proceed?

Like most everyone else, he started by visiting his local Cadillac dealership to peruse his lot. Twenty minutes later, he made a phone call that saved him from a several-thousand-dollar mistake.

My phone rang, and I heard a familiar voice. "Mr. Latko, you know how you told me to call you if I ever need advice? Well, I'm over at the Cadillac dealer, about to buy a used car—and this is my call."

"Jason," I said, "here's my professional advice. First, call me 'David.' Second, if you're about to buy a used Cadillac at the Cadil-lac dealership, you're probably shopping in the wrong place."

And almost everybody does; it's a misstep that, like so many other rookie mistakes, appears initially to be rooted firmly in logic. You want a Caddy, so you go to where the Cadillacs are. This means locating the closest Cadillac dealer to let the shopping commence, right?

Wrong.

My advice to Jason is the same as what I follow myself. As a smart consumer, if you want to buy a Cadillac, the most savvy move is to head for the local Lincoln, Mercedes, or BMW dealer—because this is where your best deals will usually be found.

The Cadillac you covet is a high-end model; for that reason, it's likely that the previous owner traded it in on another high-priced car. He may have been a die-hard Caddy owner—but if not, he's created an opportunity for you to save a lot of money.

Let's say he drove off in a new BMW. Before the deal was consummated, the used-car manager at BWM was already on the telephone obtaining wholesale bids on his old Cadillac from Cadillac dealers to put the final deal together.

In the used-car business, it's axiomatic that a vehicle sitting unsold on the lot represents a ticking financial time bomb.

Our BMW staffer now has a choice to make. He can gamble on selling the car himself for, say, $28,000 (a $4,000 profit over the wholesale price he received from the Cadillac dealer), or sell it immediately at a wholesale price to another dealer and receive less money, but get his money right away. Depending on his own inventory and time of year, he may decide to keep the car, taking a shot at making more money at least temporarily.

If the dealer decides to keep the car and you see such an "alien" car on his lot, it can present you with a potential negotiating advantage because of two basic factors: marketing and timing.

- **Marketing:** The BMW dealer will usually price a Cadillac on his lot *lower* than what a Cadillac dealer would ask for a similar model. He's forced to, for the same reason he called those Caddy dealerships first: he knows most people who want a Cadillac look for them at Cadillac dealerships. He must attract them to his BMW store but has to give them a reason to come in—preferably, by offering them a chance to save money.

- **Timing:** Just as important is how long the car has been on his lot. After a certain duration—thirty days is a typical cycle, though many high-volume dealerships get fidgety after as little as a week—the used-car manager is ready to make a deal, *any* deal—as long as (a) he gets his investment back, and (b) he can earn even a small amount over the $24,000 he would have received by selling it wholesale to the Cadillac dealer or by sending it to an auto auction.

In a logical world, both these factors can help you, the consumer, get a great deal on the car you want. Of course, logic doesn't always rule—and when it doesn't, there're often nefarious dealings afoot.

There's a lucrative under-the-table trade in used cars, perpetrated by insiders who see an opportunity to skim from their employers. In the example I cite above, the used-car manager might sell the car to an independent car dealer for, say, $23,500. His friend then pays him back $500 under the table (tax-free) for the favor.

Of course, the dealership loses $500 on the deal—but the average used-car manager can hide that in his monthly profit-and-loss statement without breaking a sweat, and most people will not even know what happened. If he does this just ten times a month, it creates a pretty lucrative side business (at least, until he gets caught).

Finally, on a rare occasion, you may encounter a manager who resembles the south end of a northbound horse; I have. Despite your best bargaining efforts and in the face of all logic, he *still* sells the vehicle you want to another dealer for less money than you offer him.

Some people just can't stand being beaten at their own game.

Tip 4: I'll Always Get a Better Deal from an Individual . . . Right?

After all the cautions I've listed involving dealerships, it's not surprising that you may be ready to consider almost any alternative. And of course, alternatives exist—many of them delivered to your doorstep each morning in your newspaper or listed on Internet sites like eBay and Cars.com. You may like the idea of dealing with an individual either in person or on-line; and most people believe that they get a better deal (and even a better car) than they would find in a dealer's showroom.

I have found the exact opposite to be true. In fact, I rarely even consider a used car sold by a private individual. I find some degree of financial comfort in knowing that when I step on a dealer's lot, he has already done the hard work of convincing the individual his car is worth nothing and thus already screwed the previous buyer out of his car financially.

Even in the best of circumstances, though, the fact is that while an individual has one car to sell—in effect, he's trying to move his entire inventory at once—a dealer is subject to many concerns, pressures, and influences—and has many cars on the lot. As a result, a dealer can afford to be more flexible.

Can I convince the dealer to sell me a car for just a few dollars over what he paid the previous owner? If he just took the car in on trade, if it is the only model like it on his showroom floor—well then, I am probably out of luck.

But if he has three similar models in stock and none has sold in the past thirty days, there is an excellent chance I will be driving home in one of those three cars—and at a price very close to what he paid or sometimes even less. In any event, it's probably less than I would pay an individual, less time shopping, and incalculably less dangerous than visiting a stranger's house.

Also, with all the stolen cars out there, you never know what you are buying or if the seller really does own the car and have a good title to the car. I find it much easier dealing with an established franchised dealer in case something goes wrong.

I also find that the bigger-franchised car dealers tend to keep only the best cars to resell. They don't need the aggravation of selling cars that have been piecemealed back together and having you show up on their doorstep with your attorney some Monday morning.

Two extra tips for dealing with a dealer should you go this route:

- Some make each new customer sign an arbitration agreement stating that if something goes wrong with your deal you cannot sue them. Ask the dealer if he does this even before you ask about the mileage on the car in which you are interested. If he says it is a prerequisite . . . *this is always a deal breaker; walk out immediately.*

- If you are trading in a car on which you still have an outstanding loan, have the dealer sign a letter stating that he will pay off your old vehicle within five days.

Many dealers just "forget" (whenever possible) to pay off your old loan until they sell the car. That allows them to use your credit to finance their inventory—a bonus for the dealer, especially if you are paying less interest than they would pay through their financing sources.

Check with your bank to make sure he has retired your loan within the five-day period. Otherwise, the next time you try to purchase something on credit, you could find the credit report lists you as sixty or more days late on your last car-loan payment.

Tip 5: How States' Sales Tax May Be the Most Important Tip of All

Oddly enough for a guy who likes cars as much as I do, before I ever think about the next car I am going to buy, there is one question that *must* always be answered: *How will my state's sales taxes impact the final price?* Given the economics involved, this is a critical factor when it comes to the party from whom I will buy (or lease) my next car, as well as what kind of vehicle it will be.

The tax impact will be different from state to state; more confusing, the amount will differ each year, as states come up with new ideas on how to soak us for additional tax dollars.

It troubles me how little attention most people pay to the impact of taxes on their car purchases. People will spend days looking for the right vehicle, and take hours to negotiate the price down to the last hundred dollars—only to give their state, county, or local government *thousands* of dollars in sales taxes when there is often a much better alternative.

I'll use my home state of Illinois as an example; it's pretty typical, so it will give you the general picture. But don't forget to check out the tax code for your own state.

In Illinois, as buyer, you are responsible for the tax levied by the state, the individual county, and the municipality. This can be a considerable sum, because any new or used car purchased from an *Illinois* dealer is taxed on the *entire* amount of the transaction.

For example, let's say that the purchase price is $42,000 and the tax is 8 percent. Well, 8 percent of $42,000 is $3,360 in sales tax. If you're buying that new Bentley convertible for $330,000, in Illinois you'll fork over $26,400 in sales taxes; that's the price of a new Honda.

In contrast, a few states don't even have sales taxes, making these same purchases tax-free—that is, if you're a resident of these tax-haven states, or if your own state doesn't levy its own sales tax on cars you buy and "import" into your home state.

In Illinois and several other states, trading in a car as part of purchasing another car gives you a tax credit on the amount of the trade-in. A $42,000 deal that includes a $20,000 trade-in leaves a $22,000 balance; you would pay the 8 percent tax on the $22,000, for a total of $1,760. That's a tax savings of $1,600, as a result of trading in your old car.

Interestingly, if you sold that same car to a friend for $20,000 and then purchased your new car for $42,000 from a dealer, you would have to pay the sales tax on the entire $42,000. Car dealers play on this fact; they know they have a built-in $1,600 sales-tax advantage. They don't hesitate to tell you that you'll need to get $21,600 from your friend to match the $20,000 they're offering as a trade-in value.

But in other states, there is no sales-tax credit given on dealer trade-ins, making it all that much more advantageous to sell your trade-in outright by yourself.

There is a benefit, at least in Illinois: when you buy a car from an individual, the maximum sales tax you pay is $1,500—it caps out, no matter how high the price of the vehicle. So buying that $330,000 Bentley from an individual will cost "only" $1,500 in sales taxes, rather than $26,400. In Illinois, the more expensive the car you buy, the more advantageous it is to buy from an individual rather than a dealer.

Tax impact is also important when leasing a vehicle. In many states, the tax is based only on the monthly payment. That is, if your lease payment is $500 per month and your sales tax is 6 percent, expect to pay $30 per month in taxes (6 percent times the $500). That's a total of $530 per month in lease and tax costs.

Not in Illinois, where you'll pay a tax based on the total valuation of the car. It matters not that you are only *leasing* the car; even though the title never transfers to you, you're on the tax hook as if you bought the vehicle. Other states have similarly illogical tax laws that apply to lease agreements; there's little consistency, aside from the sheer unfairness of the statutes.

In Illinois, it gets worse. Let's assume you signed a three-year lease; you like the car, and when the lease expires you decide to buy it instead of turning it in. Prepare to pay the sales tax *again* on the end-of-lease purchase amount—in effect, you are forced to pay tax on the same car *twice*.

Everyone wants your money, and governments are no exception.

Tip 6: "The Holdback" and "The Money in the Trunk"

Once upon a time, most car buyers dreamed of buying a new car on the basis of what experts called "dealer invoice"—that is, the price the manufacturer charged the dealership for the car.

That was then; this is now—and now most people know that dealer invoice is a myth—a ploy designed to trip up the unwary consumer.

Yet even today, some dealers continue to use it as a sales tactic. They swear that they will show you the actual manufacturer's invoice for any car on their lot—and sell it to you at that price.

Yeah, right: he buys a car for X dollars and sells it for the same amount. How would he pay the electric bill, mortgage payments, property taxes, and the salaries of his staff?

Well, I'm here to tell you that the manufacturer's invoice does indeed exist—and that it's not uncommon for a dealer to sell you a car for the price it lists. Moreover, it is an *actual* invoice, not a phony he jobbed up on the office computer.

And yet the dealer still makes a profit on the sale. Will miracles never cease?

The secret is a little-understood entity called the "dealer holdback." It's a 2 percent to 3 percent cash bonanza for the dealership, paid by the manufacturer. The holdback is a level of profitability that provides the dealer with a cushion that ranges from a few hundred to a thousand dollars (or more) on each car the dealership sells in any given year.

For example, that new car you are considering may have a $30,000 MSRP list price and a $27,000 invoice price—a 10 percent difference, which the dealer will cite as his profit (minus such incidental charges as regional advertising charge-backs). But when that car sells, the dealer will receive somewhere between $600 and $900 back from the manufacturer—not immediately, but at a later date.

So in reality, "invoice price" doesn't equal "dealer cost," and it has virtually nothing to do with "dealer profit." This shell game is one reason dealerships generally remain a profitable enterprise, but there's no law that says the dealer holdback can't be a factor in your negotiations.

But getting dealers to share this money with you is another story entirely. To them, that money is sacred—and they'd prefer to deny it even exists. Moreover, don't even *think* about this money on popular or hard-to-find models. You may not even get a dime off sticker price, let alone touch his holdback. Your best chance of tapping this fiscal mother lode happens when the new model year is several months old and the dealership has an oversupply of last year's cars still on his lot. You may also have a chance if sales are very, very slow during the current model year and the dealer needs to move his inventory before his floor-financing costs drown him in red ink.

Another game dealers often play is called "money in the trunk." This is money the manufacturer pays directly to the dealer (not the customer) to help sell slow-moving models. Many of the luxury-car companies use money in the trunk to avoid diluting the image of their cars by having to place full-page ads that scream "THESE CARS ARE NOT MOVING." Placing a $5,000 rebate on their top-of-the-line models is a signal they'd prefer to avoid sending. Offering a money in the truck sales bounty to dealers doesn't have quite the same sting.

It's good for the dealer, too. He can use that $5,000 any way he pleases. He can reduce the price as much as needed to sell the car, and if there's any left over, he can pocket the difference. Alternately, he can inflate the price of your trade-in by $2,000 and keep the extra $3,000 you didn't get. Unlike a customer rebate, the dealer is usually under no obligation to give you *any* of the money. But I guarantee you that some dealer out there will be willing to share some of the wealth with you.

Here's a fun way to watch a dealer turn purple. Demand that he put in writing that he has told you about any and *all* dealer incentives and holdbacks. He probably won't.

Funny how dealers hate to put things in writing that might come back to bite them where the sun doesn't shine.

Tip 7: Car Salesmen—"But He *Said* He Was My Friend" . . .

He lied.

Make no mistake: your salesperson is not your friend.

Oh, sure—salespeople are generally cheerful, enthusiastic types who ask about the spouse and kids, who glad-hand you when you enter the showroom, who may even send you Christmas card or a little note on your birthday.

But as friendly as they may act, *they are not your friends!*

They have sales quotas, labor long hours, and have experienced a level of personal rejection that would have the average person braiding a rope to toss over the nearest rafter. They eke out a living (some of them, a very good living) by selling you a product. They may swear that "if it was up to *me,* I'd give you the car for nothing"; it's a lie. They are there to sell you a car, at the highest price possible.

It is a job, and the paycheck each salesperson takes home reflects how well he does it.

Precisely how is your salesperson paid? On what basis is he (or, increasingly, she) compensated and motivated to "put you in that sweet little buggy . . . *right now?*"

Believe me—there are more commission scales than there are grains of sand at any given beach; many plans change each month, or even more often. All are devised by the owner of the dealership to focus on the particular type of sales activity that will bring maximum profitability to his business.

Are used cars moving well, or have they turned into "lot hogs," where the dealer's investment is sitting idle? Conversely, is the manufacturer pushing new-car sales by boosting rebates or money in the trunk? Different compensation schemes will be used to motivate the sales force to focus on the strategic needs of the moment.

What you must understand is that perilously few auto-sales staffers are paid a regular, dependable salary. Their livelihood is measured one sale at a time. So is career progress: becoming a sales manager (and general manager, if the salesperson is not related to the owner) simply indicates that over the years, said salesperson has done a consistently successful job of extracting the maximum volume of money from buyers.

An owner needs to push the buying public to buy, and buy from his dealership. There is little that motivates salesmen more than knowing that if a prospect doesn't sign on the dotted line, the salesman's house payment may not get paid this month. And of course, every sales person knows that if the dealership owner could operate with robots or stickmen, every salesman would be replaced tomorrow.

Depending on the dealership, most salespeople are paid a stipend (not much larger than minimum wage) that is guaranteed every month, but which must be paid back against future sales commissions. Sometimes the best salesmen, who hit monthly or annual sales goals, receive the perk of driving a new car (known sometimes as a demonstrator) for free.

But they essentially write their own check based on their performance. Most are paid a percentage of the profits from the sale of the car. For example, if the dealer makes $2,000 on the sale of the car, the salesman may get 20 percent, or $400. For the particularly productive salesperson, who can sell ten or more used cars, that percentage may go higher; occasionally, the dealership may make that higher rate retroactive to the first car sold that month. So much for "giving" you the car at cost.

By necessity, there will always be a special commission paid on the purple station wagon that has squatted on the lot unsold for ninety days. A dealer may be forced to surrender *any* profit, just to motivate his sales staff to make "loser" cars go away.

Of course, these numbers are relative, depending on the type of cars he is selling. Selling fifteen new high-line Mercedes in a month might be quite an accomplishment in some areas. Selling fifteen Fords might get you unemployed.

Salespeople will usually do whatever is required to make their sales quota. Recently, I was enjoying a cup of coffee at a dealership as I waited for my salesman as he labored to get his manager's approval on an offer I had made on a car. Behind me, I could hear another salesman in the next booth making callback after callback to prospects. Every single call sounded something like this:

"John, we still have that car you were asking about. But I have to warn you: we need to get you in here *today* if you want it. I don't want you to lose out. See, one of the other salesmen has someone else driving in from out of state."

I made a mental note to stay off the roads; apparently, a lot of people were "coming in from out of state" that day.

Also disregard all the phony sales ads with their "now reduced to" prices; ignore the urgent warnings screaming "sale ends today!" Unless it is a manufacturer's "factory incentive" (which does last for only a limited period), the sale price will almost certainly be available tomorrow; as the car sits unsold, with a little luck an even lower price might become acceptable until that car *is* sold.

The best time to buy a car is when few other buyers are available. Holidays are good, especially around Christmas. Dealerships are virtually deserted between Thanksgiving and the New Year's holiday. This sparks a definite need to "move some iron" and remove it from the ledger. As a result, you're likely to find a much better deal than when buyer demand is high and showrooms are packed.

But no matter when you venture forth, shop around; there's always a deal waiting for you to seize it.

Shop wisely, using these tips—and that deal will be among the best you've ever made.

SCAMS, CONFIDENCE GAMES, AND IDENTITY THEFT— WELCOME TO THE NEW WILD WEST

NINETEEN

WHO ARE YOU? TALES FROM THE WORLD OF IDENTITY THEFT

Not long ago, I invited a special guest to appear on my nationally broadcast radio program, *David Latko's Money & More*. He was an FBI agent who was an expert in what the Justice Department has termed "the fastest-growing crime in the United States."

I speak, of course, of identity theft—a crime that directly evokes the adage "Who robs me of gold steals rubbish; who steals my good name steals what is beyond price." When it comes to ID theft, you lose both money *and* reputation.

During the program, my guest recounted tales of innocent citizens whose credit was ruined—and, as a result, lost jobs, child-custody cases, homes . . . and sometimes hope itself. Among victims of ID theft, bankruptcy is not uncommon, and suicide not unknown.

But it was a conversation we had between segments, during our commercial break, that I remember most vividly.

"What can we tell the audience to do?" I asked. "How can people protect themselves against identity theft?"

"I can give you some tips," the FBI man said with a shrug. "But as a practical matter, nobody has figured out how to stop these people. And between us, it's going to get a lot worse."

I was stunned. Here was a representative of the FBI—arguably, the premier crime-fighting law enforcement agency in the world—

telling me that they couldn't stop the country's fastest-growing criminal enterprise.

It should have prepared me for the headlines in the first half of 2005, but they still came as a shock—in fact, as a series of shocks:

- The financial records of almost 4 million customers of Citi-group's CitiFinancial disappeared mysteriously while being transported between "secure" facilities; as of this writing, they have neither been recovered nor has the manner of their disappearance been determined. What is known is that CitiFinancial was forced to inform millions of its customers that detailed information regarding their most private financial matters was gone and presumed stolen.

- In an apparent inside job, credit and identity information on more than 650,000 customers and depositors of Bank of America was stolen and sold into the shadowy underworld of international identity-theft rings.

- DSW, the shoe retailer, also found its computers looted by hackers, who downloaded credit-card numbers and other critical information of almost a million and a half DSW customers.

- After crooks set up phony companies, ChoicePoint—an information clearinghouse that keeps records on virtually every American—"inadvertently" sold these fake companies the Social Security numbers and computerized files on credit cards, loans, and other highly confidential information of at least 130,000 U.S. citizens, and probably more.

- Around the same time, persons unknown hacked into the computerized data banks of CardSystems, a credit-services clearinghouse that serves virtually every major credit-card company in the United States. The hackers obtained highly confidential credit information, gathered for research purposes but improperly retained in the data bank by CardSystems, which put at risk the identities of more than 40 million persons. As of this writing, it remains the largest such crime of its type in the United States.

I could continue, but my point is clear: my FBI-agent guest was indubitably right, and his prediction that things will get worse is becoming truer every day.

The fact is that you or I could, at this very moment, be victims of this particularly heinous crime. Not even our elected officials are immune: in the spring of 2005, federal officials admitted that information on the finances and pensions of members of Congress had been stolen; the investigation continues today.

Not that they should have been surprised. In June of 2004, a special subcommittee of the House Ways and Means Committee heard days of testimony on the subject. Under the chairmanship of Florida congressman E. Clay Shaw, the House Subcommittee on Social Security turned what had been planned as an examination of the misuse of Social Security numbers into a stunning examination of identity and credit theft in today's America.

Said Congressman Shaw, "[Use of Social Security numbers] is woven into the fabric of many of our dealings with governments and businesses. They are widely used as personal identifiers even though the original purpose was simply to track earnings for determining eligibility and benefit amounts under Social Security.

"Some of the uses of the Social Security numbers help us achieve important goals like reducing waste, fraud, and abuse in government programs; enforcing child support; and aiding law enforcement," Shaw noted. "Unfortunately there is also wide use of Social Security numbers for everyday business transactions. Concerns about identity theft are rapidly growing. According to the Federal Trade Commission (FTC), identity theft is the *number one* [italics mine] consumer complaint, amounting to 42 percent of complaints received in 2003."

Another senior member of the subcommittee, Representative Ben Cardin of Maryland, put the extent of identity theft in clear terms. "The FTC has received more than a half-million calls on the identity fraud line, and they have projected that about 5 percent of our adult population in the United States were victims of some kind of identity theft in just the last 12 months."

Five percent. That equals about 12.5 million people—and that's a lot of victims in a one-year period.

Of that number, according to J. H. Beales, director of the FTC's Bureau of Consumer Protection, about 3.2 million persons discovered that an identity thief had opened new accounts—credit cards, bank loans, and others—in their names. An additional 6.6 million people learned of the misuse of an *existing* account—again, all in the same twelve-month span.

"Federal laws do not do enough," Shaw said. "As a result, Social Security numbers are sought-after tools for identity theft; worse yet, terrorists use of SSN fraud and identity theft to assimilate themselves into our society."

"Identity theft," he concluded, "continues to threaten our individual and national security."

Frightening words, indeed.

As a financial advisor, I'm privy to a great deal of highly confidential information on the financial lives of my clients. Security concerns keep me awake at night, despite the extensive system of document shredding, database-access limitations, electronic firewalls, and other precautions that we have in place.

We've done everything that the best minds in data security recommend—and I'm still wide-awake in the middle of the night, certain that there is some twisted genius working at that very moment to circumvent our efforts.

And to be fair, the government has made *some* effort to give us private citizens a few tools to fight identity theft.

The Fair and Accurate Credit Transactions Act of 2003 provides several new measures to prevent identity theft and make recovery less hellish for the victims involved. FACT is why we can now get one free copy of our credit reports each year. And when it is finally put into place, the National Fraud Alert System—which includes a "red flag" requirement requiring financial institutions and creditors to analyze spending patterns and act to *prevent* a crime from taking place—will let many consumers know when someone is trying to hijack their identity.

But the illness is growing faster than the proposed cures; Shaw first proposed legislation restricting use of Social Security numbers in 2003—and that's a long time to wait while the Huns are looting and pillaging.

Still, knowledge is power—and knowing what these bottom-feeders are looking for is an important step in denying them access to *your* identity.

Below, I've provided a checklist of what identity thieves want, and some tips on how to protect yourself. None of them is fool-proof, but there's a story that illustrates the value of making the effort:

Two friends are camping, and have just crawled out of their sleeping bags when a hungry-looking bear happens upon their campsite. The bear rears high, preparing to charge.

One camper turns and stumbles for the woods, wincing as he feels the rocks and twigs under his bare feet; then he looks back and sees his companion hurriedly pulling on jogging shoes.

"You fool," he shouts over his shoulder, "you can't outrun a *bear.*"

"I don't have to," says the now-shod companion as he breaks into a sprint. "I just have to outrun *you.*"

You can't protect yourself from an identity thief who targets you; but if you make it harder for him, he might just decide to move on to the next target.

Your name and home address: This is, of course, the basic information needed by anyone looking to abscond with your identity. The good news is that, alone, knowing a name and address won't do much for the ID thief, at least as far as actually establishing a phony identity. The bad news is that it certainly helps him winnow down the list of potential victims—and may even be the reason he selects *you* instead of someone else.

The fact is that a simple database search of almost any individual's name can produce a wealth of information. If you haven't done it (or haven't done it for a while; it's an eye-opening experience to see how often information is updated on the World Wide Web), get on your computer and go to any one of the Internet search engines. I like Google, but Yahoo! has a good search function, as does Lycos, Alta Vista, and a distressing number of other online companies.

Then input your own name. Ever fired off a letter to the editor, written a learned paper, or made a speech? Perhaps you once won an award. Or have you ever done anything that merited mention in a newspaper article, organizational newsletter, or other publication?

If so, the odds are alarmingly high that you'll show up during even the most cursory search; when you do, up pops everything about you that was included in the article, sidebar biography, or introduction—for instance, where you work, whether you're married, and maybe even the names of your children.

Your address is a similar gateway to information about you. For years, direct-marketing firms have used lists of mailing addresses to target specific demographic groups. Much of this selection is done on the basis of the zip code in which you live.

For an identity thief, the premise is that stealing the ID of someone who is well-off (or at least resides in a more affluent neighborhood) is preferable to pretending to be someone who lives in a working-class area; the odds are better that the thief will qualify for heftier loans or higher-charge-card limits without setting off alarm bells.

Unless you want to live like Unabomber Ted Kaczynski, it's virtually impossible in today's world for your name and address to remain unknown (or even hard to find). To see how easy it is, check out the "people finder" function on Yahoo! or Google; in most cases, along with address and phone number, they'll even provide a detailed map with a dotted line leading to your home.

Even so-called unlisted telephone numbers are accessible; not long ago, I used a city directory at my local library to obtain such numbers, knowing that even people who pay extra for them frequently give them out to solicitors, handwrite them on their checks, or otherwise provide them as verification when asked.

Remember, Kaczynski's one-room, "off the grid" shack was *still* located by persistent people who were determined to find him; by comparison, you're easy meat.

Personal information: It's terrible how often I've forgotten my wife's birthday. It's also inexcusable, given the fact that I could get the information with a few keystrokes.

You see, not too long ago some very dear friends of our family thought it would be amusing to post one of those ads in the personals section of our town's newspaper—you know, those one-column ads with the boldfaced type that says "Guess who's turning 40?" and photo, name, and birthday prominently displayed.

It would have been more amusing had I not known that many banks, credit-card companies, department-store billing departments, and other financial operations use a person's birthday as one (sometimes, as the *only*) way to verify that a telephone inquiry or order is coming from an authorized caller.

This certainly illustrates the large number of people who, usually with the best of intentions, have obtained one of the most intimate details of our lives. It also underscores the dangers of blithely sharing such knowledge with strangers who might know how to misuse it.

Somehow, the wisdom of broadcasting such potentially useful information escapes me. I can only hope it also escaped those who seek such data for their own dark designs—but in my most dismal moments, I know how unlikely *that* is.

Credit-card identification numbers: "Okay," I hear you saying, "what are we supposed to do about this one? If you buy something, how do you not give out your card number?!"

Granted, one has to provide the card numbers to merchants (whether at a store counter, online, or via telephone) if one wants to use the card to actually *make* a purchase.

And the answer is as simple as it is depressing: as far as the card number goes, there's not much you *can* do. It's part of the price we pay for a financial system that is user-friendly enough to work for most people.

It's also one reason why the major credit-card companies foot the bill for so much credit fraud, and why laws have been passed that limit the liability of an individual cardholder. After all, credit-card fraud is a major part of what Deborah Majoras—chairman of the Federal Trade Commission, and herself an ID-theft victim (she bought shoes at DSW)—estimates to be $53 *billion* lost in 2004 to identity-theft crime.

But we're not completely helpless; there are certain safeguards we can employ when we use our credit cards—and while none of them guarantees ironclad protection, each can at minimum make it more difficult for the bad guys.

For instance, if a thief does not have actual physical possession of one of our cards, it is less likely that he has an important piece of information: the secondary security number that authenticates credit-card purchases.

This number—in the credit industry, it's known as the "CW-2 code"—is printed on every legitimate credit card. Implemented several years ago, it is an attempt by financial/credit companies to shortstop the use of stolen or fraudulent numbers. Without it, a transaction is voided before it can be completed.

The sad news is that here, the crooks have already begun to modify their actions.

Last spring, news reports trumpeted a story about how Interpol had broken up an international credit-card theft ring based in the Ukraine. The gang was engaged in a thriving wholesale operation: they sold stolen card numbers in bulk to other thieves, with the going rate for 1,000 "raw" card numbers—that is, cards without the CW-2 numbers included—going for the equivalent of $500 U.S.

But the Ukrainians also offered a package deal: for cards with a valid CW-2 included, the asking price was about three dollars per card.

So the bad guys are closing in on the CW-2. But until the card industry counters with a new (and, one hopes, a more secure) system, guard your CW-2 zealously.

I have one client—who is himself in the banking industry—who has blacked out the CW-2s on his card with indelible marker. When he uses the card in a traditional setting—i.e., not online or over the phone—he counts on his memory to provide the number . . . if the establishment asks. Surprisingly, many don't.

Social Security and driver's-license numbers: For anyone seeking to steal your identity, these numbers are the Holy Grail of data, the mother lode from which all things can flow (at least, from your pocket to theirs).

With even *one* of these two identifying serial numbers, an ID thief can wreak havoc on your credit; with both of them, he can literally become you, often elbowing you out of your own life and taking your place. *You* become the interloper, the suspect, the one who has to prove your bona fides.

Despite the oft-stated intentions of those who implemented the Social Security program back in the 1930s, our Social Security cards have become our de facto national ID numbers. Today, the fear is less focused on the potential of Big Brother watching us than it is on the criminal element's use of these digits to loot every aspect of our lives.

The danger is real, because we've made it so easy.

In the case of Social Security numbers, they are routinely used at colleges, posted on the bulletin board alongside your daughter's midterm-test score; they're input into your computerized cable-TV billing account; they've become part of every standardized form—from a department-store credit-card request to a passport application—in America today. In many locales, they're used to track your overdue video rentals.

This cavalier treatment extends into the most mundane of commercial transactions, usually without a second thought. Consider: how often have you been asked for "the last four digits of your Social Security number" over the telephone? It's touted as a security measure, but what it really means is that the computer of the asker has your *full* number—and in a few paragraphs, we'll see how dangerous this fact is.

Even the military has given up the fight; for more than two decades, "name, rank, and serial number" has meant "name, rank, and Social Security number." They're stamped on dog tags and stenciled on duffel bags—hardly the kind of top secret treatment one might expect for a number of such critical importance.

Or maybe it's not so surprising at that. During the June 2004 Subcommittee on Social Security hearings, a representative of the Social Security Administration was asked if the agency still took a liberal approach to investigating repeated requests to reissue "lost" Social Security cards.

The question was relevant, given the thriving market for Social

Security cards among those who don't have one (notably, undocumented aliens and prospective terrorist infiltrators). It was also timely, in light of prominent news stories that noted one instance where a card was replaced *eighty times* by the Social Security Administration, without question or comment.

This was the exchange, taken verbatim from the subcommittee's transcript:

> **Question** (from Congressman JOHNSON): Just one follow-up. Are you still waiting to 80 before you check them out?
> **Answer:** The number has dropped considerably on the number of replacements. It is not up to 80. What we are looking for now is 20 in the lifetime.

Twenty replacement cards before somebody asks why; what a relief! Everybody needs at *least* that many, no?

Drivers' licenses are second in importance only to Social Security cards in our daily identity. Aside from the driving privileges they confer, you can't cash a check, rent a car, or board an airplane without showing one.

Given all this, it's appalling how little thought we give to protect these numbers. I'm guilty myself; until recently, each check I issued to pay suppliers or freelance employees of my businesses included, to facilitate accounting and tracking, *the payee's Social Security number*!

It was only when a cashed check passed over my desk—with the freelancer's driver's license number hand-printed on the front by the helpful bank teller who cashed it—did I realize what a treasure trove of information we were providing to anyone dishonest enough to use it for criminal purposes.

Consider how many people *you* provide with the same information; now consider how many of them have an opportunity to use it for evil, or to sell it to somebody with that intent.

By the way, an oft-aired television ad—you've seen it: the ad shows a cocky identity thief poking through a prospective victim's trash can before pocketing a discarded envelope—appears to be another instance of wasted effort.

Interestingly enough, according to the U.S. Postal Inspection Service (which should know) only about 4 percent of identity-theft crimes result from information obtained from stolen mail. (Not that you should return that shredder to Office Max—after all, why make anything easy for those unimaginative ID thieves who get their idea from watching public-service spots on TV?)

But, as I noted, there is no shortage of other sources for this information.

Several states, including California, traditionally a bellwether for imminent change on the national level, have enacted laws restricting display and use of Social Security numbers, and such limitations have caused a few private companies to alter their policies, in some cases on a nationwide basis. (And, by the way, hurray for the Golden State—it was only in 2004, after the California legislature passed a law requiring companies to openly disclose security breaches of confidential records that the American public came to realize how often identity thieves strike.)

Nevertheless, at present no law restricts use and display of your Social Security number in *all* industries, or in *all* locations. In fact, frequently it is the government that posts this information for the public to see. For instance, individual Social Security numbers continue to be displayed on such ubiquitous public documents as your Medicare card.

Worse, many state, county, and local agencies (and no small number of federal agencies) maintain public records that contain Social Security numbers. Since public records are routinely made available to the public—this includes, by the way, marriage licenses, property transactions, court records, uniform commercial-code filings, and professional licensing records—there's no shortage of "official" leaks of this highly sensitive data.

In short, the potential for misuse remains staggeringly high—and the bad guys are capitalizing on it.

Here again, the only defense we have is cold comfort indeed. Congressman Shaw's still-pending legislation would provide some safeguards by limiting the free and easy access all too often given to our identity numbers. But even the strictest legislation is useless—unless it is vigorously enforced.

Until then, we're stuck with the pessimistic (though accurate) assessment of my FBI radio-show guest.

At best, all we can hope for is for our financial ruin to be quick and complete—because, as a good (though cynical) friend of mine is fond of saying, "The only defense against identity theft is to have an identity so tainted that no thief wants to steal it."

TWENTY

WE ALL LIVE IN TODAY'S WILD WEST—AND THE BLACK HATS ARE WINNING . . .

If it weren't for the fact that scams cost Americans literally billions of dollars, one would have to admire the energy and sheer chutzpah of the scammers.

I've made a sort of hobby of following the various scams and confidence games that victimize millions of people every day. You could call it a matter of professional curiosity (I can't advise my clients on avoiding scams if I don't study them closely); I prefer to call it a matter of personal survival.

And so should you.

If you're fortunate, you've only heard of some of them. But more likely, you've had a far closer relationship with at least one of them: the FTC estimates that 1 in every 10 Americans has been victimized; according to the same estimate, *fewer* than 1 in every 700 cases results in an arrest and conviction.

In addition to the resources expended by the various government agencies to monitor the burgeoning online scams, there are some very dedicated private groups that specialize in the area.

One of them is the National Consumer League's National Fraud Watch, and for a number of years they've pulled together a list of the scams most frequently encountered. You can review their annual lists on the National Fraud Watch Web site: http://www.fraud

.org/internet/inttip/inttip.htm. It's readable and informative, and includes a pageful of links to other valuable telephone numbers and Web sites, including the Federal Trade Commission (1-877-FTC-HELP), and Federal Bureau of Investigation's Web page for Internet fraud (https://www.ifccfbi.gov/).

But I've also maintained my own list of scams. Below, in wildly abbreviated form, are a few of my current favorites.

The Fake ATM Scam: A few months ago, in a New Jersey neighborhood with a spectacular view of the New York City skyscape, one of the ubiquitous symbols of today's financial life—an automatic teller machine, or ATM—was wheeled into place sometime during the night.

Located a few steps from a popular pizza parlor, the ATM was an immediate success. Literally hundreds of people used it over a two-week period—usually obtaining between twenty and fifty dollars in cash, with the amounts charged against their credit or debit cards.

But then people who used the ATM began to notice strange occurences. Bank accounts were being electronically looted, and charge-card accounts began to post a flood of purchases at stores and online sites that the cardholders had never visited.

Soon authorities had pieced together the common denominator that linked the victims: all had used the pizza-parlor ATM. Days later, the assaults on their finances began.

The machine, of course, was a scammer's tool. It dispensed cash, to be sure; but in so doing, it also recorded the wealth of cardholder data employed in each transaction. The information was quickly transferred to what police believe was a gang linked to organized crime in the Garden State area.

The scam—which has come to be known as "ATM spoofing"—has been made far less difficult by the relative ease of obtaining the ATM units themselves; a quick search of the Internet indicates a long list of suppliers, which sell the machines to independent investors—much like a person would buy a candy machine, stock it, and drop by weekly to collect the quarters. No laws currently regulate such sales of ATMs or their use.

A similar scam occurred at a busy mall in Connecticut, where another fake ATM was used to obtain card information and personal identification numbers (PINs) from unwary shoppers. In that case, several thousand dollars were stolen by the scammers, who ensured high patronage of their machine by disabling two legitimate ATMs in the same mall by feeding Super Glue–coated cards into them.

Not to be outdone by their East Coast counterparts, scammers in San Francisco took the scam one step further. In March of last year, San Francisco police issued an urgent warning about ATMs throughout the city, many of which had been in place for years and were legitimately linked to nationally known banks and financial institutions.

There, thieves attached a phony facade consisting of microscopic chips and circuitry electronics to an ATM. Within hours of using the booby-trapped ATM, Elaine Flaherty, a San Francisco nurse, had lost about $4,000. The money was electronically removed from her bank account in transactions that were recorded along the California coast from San Mateo to Los Angeles. At least one other woman was victimized by the same machine, police reported.

These women were victims of a scam that has become known as "fascia overlay," where thieves install a phony ATM facade over a *real* machine. The parasitic device includes a card reader that is connected to the real machine's input slot; it scans the magnetic strip from the victim's card and in some cases—as in San Francisco—even "swallows" the card itself.

An "out of order" notice is displayed on the real machine's monitor, and the frustrated victim leaves the card, which is collected by the thieves. Sensors or miniature video cameras record the PIN being entered.

The "Ma Bell Scam": Sarah, one of the clients I advise on her investments, was the first person to call my attention to a particularly insidious sort of telephone confidence game. I learned of it one afternoon when she visited my office—oddly for her, without calling to arrange an appointment.

When I noted this unusual fact, Sarah's eyes clenched tight and she took a deep breath.

"I'm afraid to even *use* my phone, David," she said, and burst into tears.

Fearing that she had been receiving obscene calls or other threats, I pressed her for details.

"It's my phone bill," she wailed. "My bill was more than two thousand dollars this month—most of it in calls to those . . . those . . . you know! *Those* kinds of Internet sites."

I studied Sarah; at sixty-eight, she is the epitome of everybody's favorite grandmother. It didn't take Sherlock Holmes to guess what she meant.

"Ah yes." I nodded. "*Those* kinds of sites. Sarah, what happened?"

It's called "the Ma Bell Scam" by law enforcement, and it has become relatively common. In its most typical form, it's often perpetrated by prison inmates with payphone privileges and a warped sense of humor.

Here's how it works. You receive a phone call from someone who identifies himself as a telephone-company employee or emergency-services official, or even a police officer.

They ask you to dial a three-digit code; *72 is the most common, but other combinations will also work in certain areas. The codes activate a telephone feature available on almost any phone line: it allows another telephone to literally take command of your phone and to make telephone calls on *your* account.

The result can be embarrassing as well as expensive; there are a large number of telephone-sex hotlines that will charge the caller through their telephone bills. If your phone has been "captured," you can guess where *that* bill will go.

But even if the phone calls made on your account are of the more conventional kind, it's not unheard of for them to involve international long distance or lengthy calls inside the U.S. that quickly mount up to hefty bills.

As I advised Sarah, I now advise you: naturally, don't pay the bill. In most cases, the telephone company will write off any charges for calls not made by, or with the permission of, whoever holds the phone account.

The same is not always true of third-party bills. Even though the telephone company will enter into agreements wherein it bills the consumer for pay-per-call "services," Ma Bell and her regional sisters adamantly refuse to accept any responsibility for the accuracy or validity of the fees she collects for them. That is to say, it may be on the phone bill the phone company sends to you, but—in the event of a billing dispute—they claim it's none of their business.

You can try to negotiate with entities who advertise their services with such taglines as "Hot Co-Eds Calling!" or "Spanking Sisters International," but I don't recommend making the effort. Instead, I again offer you the same advice I offered Sarah.

For Sarah, the solution ultimately involved a new phone number and a significant volume of correspondence between her and a list of phone-sex companies, her own telephone-service provider—and both the Federal Trade Commission and the attorney general of her home state.

Oh yes—and never, *ever* respond to the requests of strangers— but certainly not over the telephone or the Internet. They're both part of the modern-day Wild West, lawless and filled with predators.

The Nigerian Letter Scam: This just in from Nigeria: there's some good news and some bad news.

First, the good news: the Nigerian government has announced a major crackdown on the rampant cyber-scamming from its country that has become legendary among computer users around the world. Government police have cracked down on the famed Nigerian Internet Fraud network, having raided a number of the Internet cafés in the capital city of Lagos.

The bad news: it's not making a significant difference in the tons of Nigerian-made spam filling e-mail boxes throughout the world.

And so it goes; Internet scamming has joined death and taxes in our pantheon of the inevitable. It's become a fact of life, made ever pervasive by the spread of computer usage—oh, yes: and by the surprising fact that such scams actually *work*. Despite the fact that Nigerian Web scams have become hoary clichés—literally, the subject of scornful monologues on both Leno and Letterman—they're still profitable enough to form a virtual cottage industry for an impoverished, third-world African nation.

Here's how it works. It's early evening in Nigeria, which makes it morning in North America: time to go to work.

You leave your apartment in the section of Lagos known as Festac Town for a short stroll to the corner cybercafe. Here, for a small fee you can buy a cup of sweet Nigerian café au lait and rent an Internet-connected computer terminal. Once online, you join the thousands of other Nigerians at the terminals in other Lagos cafés—all of them, it would seem at times, merrily sending off one or another version of the "Nigerian Scam Letter."

You know this letter; if you've ever logged onto the Internet, you've received one. In one variant, you've won an international lottery; millions of U.S. dollars await you—and all you need to do is to authorize a modest transfer of funds from your bank to cover "transfer fees."

Or perhaps you've been selected because of your famed humanitarianism: a violent military coup has overthrown the government of an African nation (so small that you don't even recognize its name). The minister of the treasury has, at risk of his own life, somehow obtained control of tens of millions of dollars, which you must help him keep from the hands of the newly installed despots. In return for your assistance, you will receive *several million dollars*—not a bad return for a good deed, eh?

All you have to do is to e-mail the minister all your banking-account numbers so they'll know where you want these millions sent. Of course it's safe—what harm could happen just by sending your confidential financial information to a stranger on the other side of the world?

These scams are just two of the con games known collectively as "419 scams," named after the provision of Nigerian legal code that outlaws them. To many of us, the real mystery is that *anybody* falls for this sort of scheme.

But fall they do, if only because the Nigerian Letter Scam is a simple game of numbers. Otherwise-out-of-work Nigerian software engineers peddle home-written programs that automatically collect millions of e-mail addresses in the United States and Europe; scammers pay a fee for the list, and millions of Nigerian letters fill millions of electronic mailboxes.

All it takes is one sucker, and there's a new one born every minute.

According to the Nigerian Economic and Financial Crimes Commission, cash and assets worth more than $700 million were recovered from Nigerian scam suspects between May 2003 and June 2004. And that is only a small fraction of the estimated amount gullible Americans have lost to this otherwise-laughable confidence game.

It goes without saying (or should); but since the Nigerian scam shows no signs of withering away, here goes:

Every swindle is predicated on the misbegotten belief that one can get something for nothing. You cannot—and even if you could, the odds are astronomically against such windfalls coming to you in the form of an unsolicited e-mail.

If you wish someone unknown to you to have access to your bank accounts, by all means send them the account numbers they seek. But you'd be better advised to call a lawyer—and petition a court to have *yourself* declared incompetent to manage your own life.

"Phishing" for Profits: Pronounced "fishing"—and with apologies to the iconoclastic rock group Phish—this scam involves the act of sending an e-mail to a user in which the sender claims to be a legitimate business entity. The goal is to trick the recipient into disclosing private information that will be used for identity theft.

A friend of mine who has an account with AOL reports that "phishers" have become remarkably sophisticated in their ability to mimic "real" sites. In the past year, he's received an almost weekly barrage of official-sounding e-mails that state his AOL account faces revocation "due to incorrect credit-card information." Some of these e-mails are sent in HTML, a graphic format that allows for illustrations; the AOL logo is, my friend tells me, indistinguishable from the real thing.

As with all "phish" attempts, the e-mail directs the user to click on a link that transfers him to a Web site where she will be asked to update personal information, such as passwords and credit-card, Social Security, and bank-account numbers—information already on file with the real company. *Do not do this!*

If you are unwise enough to click on the link, it will take you to an official-looking Web site; this site is counterfeit. Its purpose is to steal your information, but it can also be a trap that can download a computer virus or a so-called Trojan Horse program that can literally hijack your computer.

According to conventional wisdom, one way to tell if a link is bogus is to hold the cursor over the link. If only numbers are displayed—and not the name of the supposed company, such as AOL—you can assume this is an attempted phishing.

But I've seen too many changes during the time I've been using the Internet; if I've learned anything, it is that hackers and phishers never rest. By the time you read this, it's quite possible they will have found a way to contravene the "test" outlined in the previous paragraph.

For that reason, an ounce of prevention remains the best way to avoid the need for tons of cure.

Be wary of sites or e-mail that want more information than they should need, or that you know they already have. Be particularly careful not to divulge such information as bank-account or credit-card numbers, PINs, the CW-2 number found on your credit cards, your Social Security number, your city of birth, or your mother's maiden name.

The latter two bits of data, as innocuous as they seem, are frequently used as confirmation to authorize online purchases or even to verify one's identity. They are worth gold to the savvy information thief; keep them confidential.

Spoofing: Internet spoofing allows a hacker to create a "shadow copy" of the entire World Wide Web. Anytime the victim goes online, his Web access is funneled through the attacker's machine. This allows the attacker to monitor all of the victim's activities—including, of course, any passwords or account numbers he may transmit.

Online Auction Scams: As I've noted elsewhere in this book, I'm quite active in buying and selling automobiles. These days, the Internet has become a valuable tool to all manner of auto buffs.

And, of course, that fact has opened the door to the unscrupulous who prey on the unsuspecting. There are many different scams being pulled, but one in particular struck close to home with me.

In that instance, a client with similar car-buying interests sold one of his cars. The buyer, whom my client had met only online, sent him a check for several thousand dollars more than the total purchase price—and, when he realized his "mistake," asked my friend to simply send *him* a check for the overpayment.

You've probably guessed the outcome here: the seller's original check bounced—but not before the check my friend sent to him was cashed. The "buyer" never intended to purchase my friend's car; for him, it was only an opportunity to steal a few thousand dollars in "change."

Credit Repair Scams: This confidence game infuriates me, if only because it preys on the hopes of those who have little hope to spare. The most common version of this scam ropes in unfortunates who have, for whatever reasons, destroyed their credit rating to the point that they cannot qualify for even the worst interest rates or credit terms.

Credit-repair companies buy lists that contain the contact information of these people. They contact them and promise, for a fee, to "fix" their credit.

"We'll handle everything," they tell their victims. "We call the credit-tracking companies, and we'll make sure your credit report is changed."

The fact is, they carry through on this promise. They do contact Equfax, Trans Union, and Experion—the three major credit-reporting companies.

And they do "fix" your credit rating—at least, temporarily. What happens is that they file a formal denial of all the blemishes that keep a person from obtaining credit—in essence, they say the missed payments and defaults are incorrect and never happened.

These days, having been stung by horrendous media stories detailing actual abuses, the credit-reporting companies are extremely sensitive to contested credit reports. They'll investigate the claims your credit fixers have contested—and while they do, in the interim they delete those claims from your file.

Presto! Your credit is "fixed"—that is, until the original information is confirmed. Then you're back in the credit toilet. Worse, any loans or credit you obtained during the brief period of creditworthiness will be revoked or recalled immediately.

It's even possible that those creditors may decide to file fraud charges against you—but in any case, this fraudulent "fix" will be added to your credit record, making it even more radioactive if you ever seek credit again.

When it comes to protecting yourself from the predators who lie in wait along the information highway, vigilance is the best defense; indeed, with the apparent inability of law enforcement and government to stem the tidal wave of scams, it seems to be the *only* defense we currently have.

So diligently monitor *every aspect of your life*. Check your billing statements carefully, and don't hesitate to call the store or credit-card company if you note any questionable items.

On the larger playing field, remember that by law you are entitled to one free credit report annually from each of the three major credit-reporting companies. Take advantage of this. What you find may surprise you, but it's far better to find any damaging items yourself than it is to have credit denied (or certainly, made significantly more costly due to your "bad risk" rating).

Here's the contact information of each credit-reporting company so you can request your credit report:

- EQUIFAX (http://www.equifax.com/) or call 800-685-1111

- EXPERIAN (http://www.experian.com/consumer/index.html) or call 888-397-3747

- TRANS UNION (http://www.transunion.com/) or call 800-888-4213

As an alternative to contacting each of the individual companies, you can go to www.annualcreditreport.com or call 877-322-8228.

I've touched on only a few of the many scams out there today. Entire books could be penned on the subject (and several excellent ones have been).

The good news is that we're finally beginning to fight back, as indicated by the news headlines on the subject of modern-day fraud and the number of organizations that are gearing up to combat it.

But there's bad news, too. Despite all these efforts and the best of intentions by people who care . . . right now, we're still losing.

TWENTY-ONE

UNCLE SAM, THE FLIMFLAM MAN

After all that I've written in this section about how the scammers succeed in fleecing us on a seemingly ceaseless basis, I would be remiss if I neglected to touch briefly on what many victims consider the single largest player of confidence games in today's United States.

I mean, of course, the United States itself—or rather, the system of governance thereof, at the national, state, and local levels.

Before any government agents in the audience hit their cellphone speed dial to call the Enforcement Department, don't worry—I am not about to launch into a screed involving the U.S. tax code (all several million, special-interest-riddled line items of it), or rant about under-the-table deals with defense contractors, or bark in scorn about the annual Congressional Pork Barrel Festival, or recite the scandal-screaming headlines in just about any big-city newspaper. As social protest, that's all been covered elsewhere, ad infinitum (not to mention ad nauseam).

But it is important to understand that even many of the private-sector hands that we feel in our pockets are enabled (and sometimes, even *encouraged*) in their trespass therein by our elected representatives.

Take, for instance, the matter of . . . bicycle helmets?

Now, I'm not an insurance actuary; nor do I have specific knowledge of the extent to which bike helmets have prevented death or serious injury to two-wheelers of all ages.

But as a lad, I rode a bicycle on a daily basis—in the predawn hours as I delivered newspapers, to and from school, and so on. In point of fact, I logged countless miles on the streets and sidewalks of the city where I was raised, as did most of my friends.

None of us ever suffered a head injury as a result of this activity—this, despite the occasionally . . . well, the occasionally *unwise* uses to which we put our bikes, which included daredevil stunts that would have made Evel Knievel blanch.

Nonetheless, in the past decade or two, countless cities and even states have passed ordinances or legislation that mandate use of bicycle helmets. Even where such laws do not exist, factors such as peer pressure or the perceived fear of injury have led to a level of helmet wearing estimated by the Consumer Product Safety Commission as slightly more than *half* of all bike riders. While some groups dispute this estimate, it is a fact that an item of safety gear that was virtually unknown a generation ago has become commonplace.

Why?

As I may have suggested previously in this book, whenever there's a question that begs for an answer, it's hard to go wrong by taking a page from the Watergate years and—as Deep Throat urged—"follow the money."

A quick search of the Internet lists page upon page of references to "bike helmets," "bicycle helmet wars," "helmet legislation," and similar entries. A surprising number of these sites are referenced to, sponsored by, or otherwise linked with the country's leading manufacturers of helmets, with organizations like the Snell Association (an advocate for increased use of helmets) or with other groups that promote helmet use. Similarly, the Internet is top-heavy with studies commissioned by these helmet-advocacy groups.

In short, a cynic might suspect that there has emerged a thriving cottage industry of groups with a vested interest in seeing a helmet atop every cranium in America, presumably on a 24/7 basis and regardless of whether that head is being transported by vehicle or on foot.

I priced a bike helmet at a local store last week. A decent one runs about ten dollars, though you can find them for significantly more. I've never commissioned a statistical study on helmet safety (or anything else, for that matter), but I imagine it's a not-inconsiderable cost.

But I do know how most legislation is written. Contrary to what the movies or TV shows like *The West Wing* might portray, few senators or congressmen sit down with their staffers, roll up their sleeves, and pound out a proposed bill to take in for a vote.

Instead, most bills are authored by the very people that bill is intended to legislate over: for instance, in legislation involving health care, lobbyists hired by insurance companies, corporate hospital groups, and the American Medical Association will all show up for the bill-writing party, pencils in hand.

Commonly, the end product of these groups' efforts will then make the rounds of selected legislators—selected, that is, on the basis of how friendly that legislator is to the special interests involved.

Politics being politics, "friendship" is usually tallied in terms of quid pro quo—with the "quid" being campaign contributions, or membership endorsement of the incumbent, or something of similar value to the typical citizen statesman. The "quo," of course, is the politician's support for the proposed legislation.

Sponsors and cosponsors are found, hearings are held, favors are called in, and logrolling deals ("you vote for my bill, I'll vote for yours") are struck.

Not that this is one-sided. If *other* groups have a vested interest in opposing the proposed bill, they, too, will mobilize the shock troops and prepare their own position before seeking a legislative sponsor. But the process is virtually identical, no matter *which* side is working the system.

Which brings us back to bicycle helmets.

I have no idea whether the ongoing movement toward equipping every living American with a helmet ($10 $\times$ 250 million heads = big $) originated as a brilliant flash of inspiration in the mind of someone who owned an underutilized helmet factory.

Rather, I am quite willing to accept that it involved a spontaneous mobilization of like-minded individuals who saw a critical safety need and came together to create a solution to a problem that didn't exist when I rode a bike.

It certainly *might* have happened that way. But it doesn't happen often.

One of the more interesting exercises of combined lobbyist/legislative power came to light a little more than a year ago.

That was when the Check Clearing for the Twenty-first Century Act became the law of the land, going into effect at midnight on October 28, 2004.

Check 21, as it came to be known, was a relatively underpublicized bit of legislation that had been signed into law a year earlier, in late October of 2003.

When it was discussed in the media at all, Check 21 was touted as the means to "foster innovation in the payments system and to enhance efficiency by reducing some of the legal impediments to check truncation."

As enlightening as *that* is—translated, it means the banking industry was being helped to modernize how it handles the checks you write—it failed to convey the real impact most consumers would feel.

Up until Check 21 went into effect, banks were required to physically transport each check from the bank, where it was deposited *back* to the bank where the account existed. Only then was payment authorized and monies transferred.

But Check 21 changed all that.

To illustrate how, let me quote from the Federal Reserve Board's official Web site: "The law facilitates check truncation by creating a new negotiable instrument called a substitute check, which permits banks to truncate original checks, to process check information electronically, and to deliver substitute checks to banks that want to continue receiving paper checks. A substitute check is the legal equivalent of the original check . . . ."

Whoa! In case it slipped past you amid the bureaucratese, what Congress did was to render paper checks obsolete. Oh, you can still write one at your local grocery store, as before; they'll send it to their local bank, as before . . .

. . . but as of October 28, 2004, that bank scans it into a collection of electrons, which are sent—literally, at the speed of light—to *your* bank, which immediately transfers the money *out* of your account.

Transaction completed. Next, please . . .

And for the millions of us who had become accustomed to depending on the "float"—that is, the cushion of time between writing a check and having it credited against our account balance— well, suffice it to say that millions of us had a rude awakening in October 2004.

Certainly, one should never write checks unless the money is in the account. But most people have done it, at one time or another, and many people did it on a regular basis. Check 21 changed the landscape forever.

Well and good, you might say. After the September 11, 2001, terrorist attacks, the banking industry was slowed to a crawl as planes were stranded and checks could not be returned to their original banks for processing. And certainly, sending tons of paper around the country is an antiquated and inefficient practice that *needed* to be changed.

To be fair, all of that is true; in addition to eliminating the delay in processing, the move is saving the banking industry about $3 billion annually. Efficiency is not only good—as banks have proven with Check 21, it can be profitable, too.

But here the dark beauty of Check 21's carefully drafted provisions comes into play. Under Check 21, the checks you write are processed immediately—*but the checks you deposit are not!* Those funds are not credited to your account until several business days have elapsed—giving the *banks* the benefit of the float that Check 21 took away from you.

In a bank, money is never idle; even if it is only in the bank overnight, the bank can "park" it in short-term vehicles that earn a profit, if only a tiny one for every dollar involved. But mountains are made of tiny motes of dust; all that "float" money can add up to a staggering profit for the banking industry as a whole.

If you sense some level of collusion here between the banks and Congress, you're not alone. Consumer groups continue to howl about how the float has shifted—thus far, to no avail.

If shifting the benefits of the float were the only boondoggle that Check 21 hath wrought for the bankers, it might be defensible. But of course, it isn't.

As it turns out, in the year between passage of the law and the date it went into effect, banks around the U.S. started to quietly ratchet up the fees they charged for overdrafts.

The result: an initial windfall that has been estimated at upward of *$170 million* in each of the first six months after Check 21 became law.

Of course, humans are an adaptable species; over time, we'll forget that there was once a golden era when one could float a check on Thursday, deposit a paycheck on Friday, and not worry that an overdraft penalty would show up on our next bank statement. As people learn not to risk a bounced check, that $170 million monthly windfall for the banks will, one presumes, winnow down to an infrequent trickle of what is, literally, chump change.

But when special-interest groups score such a blatant win over the public—a victory secured with the knowledge and consent of those we have elected to serve *our* interests—it tends to leave a sour taste in the collective mouth of the people.

Everybody wants your money—but why should your government help them get it?

Bankruptcy has never been a pleasant topic of conversation—but based on conversations I've had with people who've hit that particular speed bump on the road of life, talking about it is far easier than experiencing it.

But the original intention was anything but hard. Particularly in American law, bankruptcy was designed as a parachute that could allow the desperate a chance to stop the horrifying free fall that is part and parcel of financial insolvency.

For a surprisingly long time, that's just what it did. The various forms of bankruptcy—Chapter 11, Chapter 7, and so on, named after the sections within the overall law—were intentionally crafted to provide the maximum level of flexibility in dealing with each specific bankruptcy situation.

Taken as a whole, the American approach to bankruptcy was far superior to the alternative it was intended to supplant: debtors' prison, the Dickensian nightmare of the old world that condemned the debtor (and often, the debtor's family) to a state where neither debt repayment nor personal recovery was possible.

Traditionally—that is, until October 2005—debt relief via bankruptcy was available to virtually everybody.

But that was then, this is now—or rather, this is the time after October 17, 2005. On that date, a new bankruptcy code became law in the United States—and things got a lot worse for the country's insolvent.

Written largely by lobbyists—many of them from the credit-card industry—the new law simply bars many people from filing under Chapter 7, the least onerous form of bankruptcy. If your income is above your state's median (in some states, this is a stunningly low figure) and you can pay $100 per month to creditors—well, forget about filing. Worse (if you are the debtor), the question of whether you can afford to pony up $100 or more each month is determined not by your actual income and expenses, but by IRS rules that define "reasonable" expenses.

In addition to this rather novel—if draconian—approach, the new law makes it far more difficult for those who *can* still use Chapter 7 to avoid often-aggressive collection tactics by creditors that were previously outlawed. It also defines strict prerequisites before allowing repayment proposals.

If you don't qualify for a Chapter-7 bankruptcy, your choices are limited indeed: either file for Chapter-13 bankruptcy and come up with an "acceptable" three- to five-year repayment plan . . . or simply resign yourself to being swallowed up by your existing debt load.

Women's groups vigorously fought against the new law, rightly seeing it as yet another millstone hung around the necks of their gender.

The issue is not merely that women (particularly those impoverished by divorce: see the chapter on this subject in this book) would have a harder time obtaining financial relief through bankruptcy for themselves; rather, it was the realization that the combination of Chapter-7 bankruptcy ineligibility and an inability to wipe out credit-card balances would simply make less money available to pay other debts. For instance, an ex-husband might be unable to pay child support, court order or not.

These new provisions alone would have radically altered bankruptcy in America. But the new law contains a witches' brew of other changes.

Among these are new limitations on the so-called automatic stay. This refers to rules that halted—automatically and immediately—virtually all collection actions and lawsuits against a bankruptcy filer.

No more. Today, the automatic stay no longer stops or postpones:

- evictions

- actions to withhold, suspend, or restrict a professional or occupational license

- lawsuits to establish paternity, child custody, or child support

- actions to withhold, suspend, or restrict a driver's license

- divorce proceedings

or

- lawsuits related to domestic violence

I could go on, but the fact is that much already has been written about the new bankruptcy law. My intention is not to list all the problems with it, but to point out that the law itself is the result of an intensive (and multiyear) effort by the credit industry to get it through Congress.

Credit-card companies—yes, the same ones who blithely mass-mail credit-card applications to anyone who can draw a breath (and more than a few who cannot, having died long years before)—pushed hardest for the law.

A few days before the new bankruptcy law went into effect, Nora Raum—a veteran journalist with National Public Radio and a practicing attorney—was a guest on my radio program, *Money & More*.

Nora is the author of one of the best books I've read on the subject of bankruptcy, *Surviving Personal Bankruptcy*, which provides a step-by-step guide for the financially insolvent among us. She's handled hundreds of bankruptcy cases, and she's not optimistic about the direction taken under the law.

"I think there's something very mean-spirited in the new law," she said. "It was a solution in search of a problem, and was pushed hard for eight years by the credit companies, who felt too many people were using bankruptcy simply to avoid paying their debts. I simply don't believe that is the case. I don't see people who are gaming the system by declaring bankruptcy; they're desperate people looking for a way out.

"My reading of the new law is that it was aimed at the little guy rather than at business—and the changes in the law really do hurt the average person who is forced to file."

In a detailed online discussion of the new law, Portland, Oregon–based bankruptcy attorney Jeffrey Wong noted that under the old law, more than 90 percent of people filing for bankruptcy were able to discharge all their debt without being ordered to make installment payments. "In that respect, the new bankruptcy code probably enhances a business's prospect of some recovery," Wong says.

Still, he notes, "The changes in the new code are all about *consumer* debt, not business debt," says Wong. "This is pounding *small* America, not big America. Big business with unsecured debts will still be able to file for bankruptcy protection. Small businesses who are owed money still won't be able to do much."

In fairness, Congress did not simply make a gift of the new law to the credit industry. As part of the deal, they pressured the credit-card companies to increase the monthly minimum payment required of their cardholders . . . to $100.

As it happened, this was precisely high enough to cause cash-flow problems for the lowest-income cardholders, but far too low to make much of a dent in the increasing debt load Americans owe on their AmEx, Visa, or MasterCard accounts.

What the new law *has* succeeded in doing is to tip those cardholders with the most precarious finances over the edge—and into the abyss.

The safety net previously provided by a less stringent bankruptcy law no longer exists.

It will be a long, long fall.

WE HAVE MET THE ENEMY—
AND HE IS US . . .

TWENTY-TWO

THE "FIENDISH FIVE": THE BIGGEST, BADDEST FINANCIAL MISTAKES AROUND . . .

Over a quarter of a century, a lot of people have told me their stories. Sometimes they have related tales that have left both of us roaring with laughter; at other times, what I've heard would keep me awake much of the night, staring wide-eyed into the darkness.

Sadly, as a financial advisor, I see the latter category most often.

Some mistakes are inconsequential and easily correctable. Others are anything but minor, and have cost people their home, or their retirement, or their children's inheritance.

Most frequently, the mistakes I encounter are the result of a stubborn refusal to accept change—a head-in-the-sand attitude that leaves one vulnerable to an often-indifferent world that can turn fiercely Darwinian at any given moment.

In the following stories, I've used actual, real-life examples to illustrate what I call the "Fiendish Five"—five financial pitfalls that dot life's journey, and that I've encountered time and again. To protect the privacy of the individuals involved, I've changed some of the details and all of the names.

Nonetheless, I have no doubt that you will see friends, neighbors, your kids—and if you are being brutally honest, very likely *yourself*—in one or more of the following points.

The reason is simple. With few exceptions, *most humans resist change*. A desire for stability and continuity is hardwired into us, a genetic survival mechanism that allows us to recognize patterns, to remember the location of the water hole, and to find our way back to the cave that shelters us.

As a result, we see change as dangerous—when in reality it is the inability to alter our attitudes and behavior that leaves us most at risk.

Ironically, we even seek to create these patterns of stability in the mistakes we make. Below, I explore five basic mistakes that I've seen people make, year after year.

In some instances, I've been able to help them see what they were doing, and assist them to embrace a new set of actions. I'm proud of these successes, and in helping these clients, I've also learned much that I've been able to apply to my own life.

But sadly, in the majority of cases, I've failed dismally. I've stood by, helpless—my hand figuratively outstretched in a futile attempt to save people from the financial sinkhole into which they've charged, taking spouses and family down, too.

Up until now, this book has focused on how *others* try to get their hands in your pocket.

In concluding my book, I wanted this chapter to be a little different. Here, we'll examine instances where *we* rob *ourselves,* and become our own worst enemy.

Procrastination . . . Stealing from Yourself

Jerry was a slender man, slight to the point of frailness; he sported the ill-advised comb-over so common to men in denial of their middle years. I met Jerry several years ago, when as a guest of one of my clients, he attended one of the financial seminars I hold throughout the year.

I've led such seminars for many years; inevitably, there's at least one attendee who comes less for advice or information than to be the star of the show. Most commonly, these participants play "stump the chump"—peppering the "expert" (me) with involved and convoluted "what if" financial scenarios that could perhaps exist in a distant dimension, but seldom in real life.

Such behavior typically comes from an alpha male in the company of his spouse or a group of friends.

Jerry was different. I encourage questions, but Jerry's arm was seldom lowered that night. Still, he did not appear intent on impressing the audience. He was polite and did not stray from the scope of my presentation—so much so, in fact, that I feared the other attendees might think I had placed a shill among them.

As is customary, that night Jerry signed the form requesting an appointment to discuss his future and his finances. Three weeks later, he was sitting across from me in my office.

Jerry came well prepared—tax returns, bank-account statements, and the other paperwork we require from prospective clients. It was an excellent sign—but I've been in my business for a long time, and it was also a clear signal to me that this was not Jerry's first experience with a financial advisor.

With little preamble, we got down to business.

"I need my investments to earn more money," Jerry said—not an unusual opening for a new client. "I want to retire early."

As I examined his paperwork, it was clear that Jerry had done relatively well for himself. He was forty-nine and had never married. He owned his home and car outright and had amassed a total of almost $490,000 in investable assets—that is, funds available to invest, not including his house and car.

I did note a few oddities. Jerry's funds were deposited in several different banks—all of them in money-market accounts or *very* short-term certificates of deposit.

As it turned out, Jerry had never owned a stock, bond, or mutual fund in his entire life. Even a small 401(k) plan was still in his former employer's money-market fund.

I also noticed that Jerry had marked "deceased" in the boxes that asked for parental information, and that the lion's share of Jerry's assets—$300,000, in fact—had been inherited.

"I lost my father when I was sixteen and my mother eleven years ago," he said. "Cancer. It took both of them."

"I'm very sorry," I replied.

"Life's like that," he said. "A person had better be ready for bad things to happen, because they're going to."

It was obvious from our subsequent conversations that Jerry's experiences had taught him that one must never take risks—and Jerry had learned this lesson well.

I also learned that Jerry was quite a student of the financial arena; he subscribed to most of the major financial publications. He was, in fact, one of the more financially astute people I had ever met.

Jerry could talk with a fair degree of accuracy about P/E ratios, historical returns of the markets—virtually any financial topic. He rattled off statistics like a ten-year-old who had memorized his favorite baseball stars' batting averages.

On one occasion, Jerry paid me a decent compliment. "David, you are the most straighforward advisor I have come across," he said, nodding his head. "And I should know—I've been to . . . let me see . . . thirteen seminars in the last eleven years."

Thirteen seminars? Nothing in Jerry's paperwork indicated that his finances had been managed by a professional financial expert: money-market accounts and CDs are stopgap measures at best, and no competent advisor would recommend maintaining several hundred thousand dollars in such low-yielding vehicles.

As we spoke, I had began to form a more complete picture of Jerry—and it wasn't completely favorable. Jerry was what some of my colleagues term a "financial-theory wonk." It's a term that describes the armchair amateurs who never miss the Saturday-morning financial programs on cable TV and whose idea of an investment strategy is determined by what they've most recently read in the financial section of newspapers.

This was Jerry, to a tee. He was not unlike the proverbial student, who has received good grades all his life; but the thought of graduating into the real world, where theory would have to be translated into action, was a terrifying prospect to him.

Jerry knew his stuff; we spoke for almost an hour during this first visit, and the topics ranged across the full spectrum, touching on such subjects as asset allocation and portfolio diversification.

"Jerry, let me show you something," I said, and turned to my computer. He leaned over my shoulder as my fingers flew over the keyboard.

"Based on your age, experience, and knowledge," I said, "you're a perfect candidate for an asset-allocation plan that would split your money equally between stock and bond funds. The growth and income projections are greatly improved over your current"—I couldn't bring myself to call it a plan—"uh . . . status. Take a look here."

On the screen, a chart indicated that the investments I was suggesting would have had an approximate return of 8.2 percent—compared to the 4 percent or so Jerry had actually earned during that same time period.

"In other words," I said, "your three hundred thousand would have turned into seven hundred and thirteen or so. That extra four percent return amounts to about two hundred and fifty-three thousand *more* than you earned on your CDs and money-market returns."

He studied the chart, his face impassive. "Of course, past performance doesn't mean future results would follow the same pattern," he said, his voice flat.

"Absolutely right," I agreed. "But there are different plans that can allocate your assets to allow you as much risk—or as little—as you want."

And therein lay the problem. To meet his stated objective—a secure, early retirement—Jerry knew he needed to take more risk.

But he was utterly unable to pull the trigger. He harbored one of the worst cases of procrastination I have ever seen.

I detailed a number of potential investment-plan options, but Jerry's reaction never changed. The market was too high or too low. The presidential elections were coming. If it was October, "don't the markets always do poorly in October?" He couldn't buy at the end of the year ("there might be year-end tax consequences, and besides—don't all mutual-fund companies churn their investment portfolios to make their end-of-the-year audits look better?").

Whatever the suggestion, Jerry had a reason for not investing. For Jerry, it was an old story: year after year—for the past eleven years, to be precise—he had been unable to find anyone who could truthfully promise complete safety and rising profitability for his money.

I couldn't either. Instead, I tried to soothe his fears by coaxing him into investing a smaller amount of his money in stocks and bonds.

"Let's put fifty thousand out there," I urged, "just so you can test the waters."

To my relief, Jerry smiled broadly. "I like it; I'll give it a try," he said, and we set an appointment eleven days away, when Jerry would drop off a check and sign the required forms.

We shook hands—but in the back of my mind, the warning light still blinked steadily. I wondered if I would ever see Jerry again.

Eight days later, he called to cancel his appointment. "Too much happening at work, David. Let's try for—oh, how about in two weeks?"

Two weeks later, on the morning of the appointment, he called again to cancel: a neighbor needed his help. Appointment number three was set for a week later, with the same result.

When he called to cancel that time, I had already made my decision. "I'm sorry, Jerry," I said, as politely as I could. "I'm just not interested in handling your account."

He took the news calmly—so calmly that I knew it was a relief to him.

I figured that I had seen the last of Jerry, but I was wrong. At a seminar about two years later, there he was—front row (again), the guest of a current client (again), asking and answering questions (again).

It was hard not to admire his perseverance. Afterward, I could not help myself; I had talk to Jerry, if only for a minute.

"Jerry, how have you been?" I said, shaking his hand. "Have you finally taken the plunge into the markets?"

With a big smile, he replied, "Not yet, Dave. But I'm *definitely* getting closer."

You can start out small or start out big . . . but at some point, you have to *start*.

TWENTY-THREE

PENNY-WISE, POUND-FOOLISH . . .

Magazines, newspapers, or talk-show hosts, rarely mention it, but there's a sure way to hamstring the overall performance of your investment portfolio: focus on finding the investment that charges the lowest fee rather than one that earns you the most profit.

If this sounds simplistic—well, it's not; it's only simple, as in "simpleminded."

Fee fixation is becoming rampant, in large part because so-called money experts are filling the airwaves and financial-magazine columns with a statement that is as outrageous as it is inaccurate: "all investments are the same, generally; pick the one with the lowest fees."

Investments are "all the same"?! Try telling *that* to anyone who has ever lost a bundle by being heavily into the wrong one. Select your holdings on the basis of "the lowest fees"?! You never want to pay more than necessary for *anything*—but the fee of any investment is only *one* of a multitude of factors to be considered, and only idiots and incompetents believe otherwise.

Okay—I think I've calmed myself enough to rationally explain this issue.

At present, there are more than 17,000 mutual funds from which an investor can choose. Given this, it's probably no mystery why the advice of so many magazines and so-called financial gurus has popular appeal.

It would indeed be comforting to believe that you can slash the Gordian knot, simply pick the three or four mutual funds that charge the least in internal costs and up-front fees, and sit back sipping a margarita while the profits roll in.

Well, you can't. If you could, there would be 16,997 fewer mutual funds out there, and we'd all be staggering around on a beach—stinking drunk but filthy rich.

If you still need someone to illustrate all this, let's use Larry as a prime example.

Larry was one of my mistakes; I knew better than to accept him as a client, but I caved when his wife—a close friend of my spouse—pleaded for assistance.

You see, previously Larry had commanded his own financial ship. He had closely monitored how much he paid in fees, and to whom he paid them—in the process, saving at least $20,000 he otherwise would have paid an advisor.

While he was thus occupied, he managed to turn a $3.5 million portfolio into one worth a little over $1.5 million.

Larry watched a *lot* of cable TV, particularly the financial shows; he was inordinately well read, at least insofar as he religiously followed the writing of every financial columnist who published in the English language.

This led him to question *every* suggestion I made *every* time for his family's accounts. This is not necessarily bad; in fact, I wish every client displayed his level of enthusiasm for garnering information. An informed investor makes for a good client.

But oddly, Larry never questioned the reasons behind, tax consequences of, or possible outcomes for my proposals. His single concern was the fees that he would pay.

"C'mon, David," he would say. "I know how the game works. Is it gonna be more or less than what we're already invested in?"

He adamantly refused to consider anything else. That an investment that offered more benefits, liquidity, and had a very strong track record over a couple of decades—to Larry, that was irrelevant.

Larry had listened closely to the media's financial experts (at least the ones he *wanted* to listen to) who said that "if you spend .4 percent less a year in fees on a hundred thousand dollars account over ten years, you keep almost five thousand that would otherwise line the pockets of someone else."

Seems logical, no?

But if a fund with a higher fee has consistently returned 2 percent more each year for the last ten years, should *that* not be a major consideration? If another prospective investment can guarantee that, in the event of the investor's untimely demise, his family will receive a *full return of all money invested*—plus a 5 percent annual growth bonus—why would that not merit a closer look, regardless of the fee structure?

Not for Larry—and surprisingly, not for a number of other entities whom one would expect to have a less myopic viewpoint.

In fact, this "lowest fee" malarky has even reached the hierarchy of the NASD and other regulating groups that monitor and control financial advisors' activities. Much that I see emanating from these rule makers and enforcers no longer seems to consider what may be in the client's best interests. Like Larry, the main goal seems to be to ensure that every client is investing in the *cheapest* way possible . . . not the *wisest*.

Take, for instance, the question of mutual-fund investments. Pretend that you have $1 million to invest; after careful consideration, you decide mutual funds are the best route for you. (They're diversified for safety, or perhaps you simply have no interest in overseeing your investments yourself.)

I'll make it easy: we'll assume that you have an excellent advisor who passed my 10-point questionnaire (see Chapter 5) with flying colors. The only problem: he charges up-front fees.

Program A: Here, your advisor provides a list of twelve different, asset-diversified, front-loaded mutual funds to buy. Some are large-cap-growth funds, others in mid-cap-value stock; some are overseas funds, others focus on high-yield bonds. You notice that each recommendation involves a different fund family—an Oppenheimer, a Fidelity, a Van Kampen or two, and so on. It's a veritable Chinese-restaurant menu ("one from column A, one from column B") of mutual funds.

Why?

In the mutual-fund industry, the big dogs are companies with names like Fidelity, Oppenheimer, Vanguard, and dozens of others.

Each company has hundreds of individual funds under their flag, reflecting the multitude of investment strategies (i.e., high risk and income, low risk and growth, etc.) each is meant to support.

Will any one mutual-fund company have all the best-performing funds in each investment category?

Of course not.

The mere fact that your advisor's list is so diversified is evidence that she's probably doing her job correctly. It indicates that she's likely to have painstakingly researched each individual fund and asset class. He's made certain that each fund has a minimum ten-year track record of constantly performing in the top 10 percent of its category. He's confirmed that the manager currently running the fund has been in control for at least as long.

Now, because of the size of each fund order in this example, you will pay approximately 4 percent in commissions, up front.

And, given what you now know, isn't this worth it?

Program B: If you're still not sure, let's look at the "fee fixation" option.

Here everything stays the same as in Program A, with a single exception. Your advisor has been instructed by the powers that be (i.e., NASD, or even *you*) that in order to save you money, he *must* place your entire million dollars with a *single* mutual-fund family, diversified only with the funds it offers regardless of quality.

You are again sent a proposal, this one composed of:

- one high-performing fund

- eight also-ran funds, managed by mediocre managers (i.e., ones who performed in the bottom half of all funds over the last ten years), and

- three funds in the bottom 10 percent of their fund peers

This decision will save the client money, up front; that is absolutely, positively, undeniably true. With most mutual-fund families, the commissions charged decrease as you invest more money. Your million-dollar buy-in now qualifies you to a onetime, bargain-rate up-front commission: 1 percent or so, which saves you about 3 percent compared to Program A.

So, decide: Who do you want managing your money over the next ten years?

Do you want Program A—offering the dream team, the very best financial minds that Wall Street has to offer, with a proven track record over decades? Or do you prefer Program B—a system-imposed bunch of has-beens and never-will-bes at the helm of your financial ship?

Surprise: it really doesn't matter what *you* want. You *have* to pick Program B—or the regulators and his firm's compliance arm will have your advisor's backside, simply for doing what was right for his client.

This situation can be a major problem for you—but one neither my clients nor I need to worry about it. Neither will you, if you change to an advisor who charges no up-front commissions.

If you need help, find an advisor who operates like me. I charge (a) annual fees based on a percentage of the size of the account, or (b) an hourly rate, if that is what the client deems in his best interest.

Frankly, I find that charging any commissions up front is usually not in the client's best interest. But that is a personal choice; all financial advisors (or the firm for which they work) must make it for themselves. I believe it would have made much more sense for the regulator just to eliminate up-front commissions altogether and make all funds available only through annual fees.

So what of Larry and his fee fixation?

For a while, Larry allowed me to steer him back to financial health. I held hopes that Larry had revised his views and had learned how to weigh the cost/benefit ratio of paying experts to handle complex issues.

But sadly, you can't teach an old dog new tricks.

Larry recently fell off the wagon; when financial markets stabilized, he turned to a focus on finding the cheapest, not the best. With regret, I fired Larry as a client.

But I do wish him well, and I expect I'll deal with his portfolio somewhere down the road.

After all, our spouses remain good friends—and much of my client list is composed of widows and divorcées.

Not Knowing What You Own—or *Why* You Own It

In my career, I have discussed the world of finance and investments before literally millions of people—at seminars, during my own radio show, and in guest appearances on such radio and television programs as CBS's *Morning Show.* I've been blessed with a wide forum for my viewpoints and enjoyed sharing my ideas with other people.

But often I've had the tables turned in the forum I like the best: one-on-one sessions in my offices, where I have personally interviewed thousands of people regarding their finances. This is where I've learned from *them*—and I've used the life lessons they taught me to try to assist others achieve peace and security.

But not all I hear is comforting. For instance, I've encountered one recurring common denominator, and it still shocks me.

Most people have no idea what they own in their portfolios or why it is there!

Since I started tracking my findings many years ago, I've found that of all the prospective new clients I interview, a full 91 percent had no information on two or more of the following points:

1. How much they paid in commissions to purchase what is in their accounts.

2. Whether there were surrender charges associated with their holdings.

3. How the mutual funds they owned performed against similar funds.

4. Why the broker suggested the various purchases.

5. How long they owned the position.

6. How their account had performed over time versus the overall market.

7. How their holdings fit into an asset-allocation program.

8. If—based on their age, income needs, and current portfolio value—they had any idea if or when they would run out of money in their lifetime.

Ignorance may be bliss—but when it comes to your personal finances, it is an undeniable signpost on the road to ruin.

Now, I'm not talking about what some in the trade call "financial virgins"—the innocents who have never before worked with a financial professional. The vast majority of the "Clueless Ninety-one Percenters" were already working with some type of a broker or advisor, on a regular basis.

Still, none of them had a list of prepared questions to ask their broker before signing on with him or her. None understood how brokers can tie up money for years, fattening the commission checks and ignoring the less expensive, no-surrender-charge alternatives that exist. These clients endured broker abuse without protest, despite poorly performing investments, ignored telephone entreaties, and a complete lack of ongoing educational seminars programs to keep them up-to-date on new ideas and new opportunities.

And yet more than two-thirds of them had taken this abuse without complaint—even declining to change financial advisors or brokers—even after learning of the abuse!

If the above examples reflect your own lack of knowledge (or if you're suddenly feeling an abuse-kindled outrage), there is hope for you. It's time to take one of two steps:

1. Start learning the business—today—so you can handle all your own financial decisions and investments.

2. Fire your present financial broker immediately—and start searching for a new advisor right now.

Elsewhere in this book, I've provided a list of my ten questions that will tell you how to find a good financial advisor. Use them, and take control of your financial life.

Meeting Mr. (or Ms.) Know-It-All . . .

Someday, genetic research probing the human DNA will identify the gene that forces men to drive on, aimlessly and endlessly, rather than stop and ask for directions. I know it's in there, because I suffer from it. I also know it's not a recessive gene, because far too many others of my gender (and more than a few women, too) exhibit its effects.

But it shows up in places other than behind a steering wheel. Ask any competent financial advisor: we've been known to diagnose it in our clients in a matter of minutes.

The symptoms are a dead giveaway to those trained in the financial arts. They include:

- Severe and constant verbal discharge from the oral cavity (most of it, on topics of which they obviously know little)

- Paralysis of the *obstinateus maximus,* the organ that forms and retains ironclad opinions (in severe cases, based on little or no supporting evidence), which is located in close proximity to the *gleutus maximus,* the muscle surrounding the orafice from which victims frequently emit the aforementioned opinions)

- Disorientation, seen particularly in an inability to understand why they are meeting with a financial advisor in the first place

- An oft-expressed willingness to die rather than change their preexisting views

- Paranoia, presented in loud statements that all investment advisors are nothing more than highly paid salesmen and/or thieves. *(NOTE: depending on whom they deal with, such statements may not be indicative of delusion.)*

As I said, the majority of those whom the above symptoms describe are males—but women are not immune, whether they are active carriers or simply enablers for their infected spouses. If you're not part of the solution, ladies—well, you're part of the problem.

Levity aside, I will not even set an appointment with a married couple about their joint finances unless both parties are present.

The reason is simple: a person seeks my services because he (or she) has faith that I can make money perform better than she (or he) can alone. For a married couple, we're dealing with money that is jointly owned by both spouses; both of their lives will ultimately be impacted by the choice made during any consultation with me.

Candidly speaking, in such cases it is almost always the female partner who initiates the visit to my office. (As I said, it's usually not a woman who would rather eat ground glass than ask for driving directions.) Oddly enough, though, it is seldom the woman who takes the lead role when a married couple meets with me; often, the session passes without a word from the female species.

Why one party would not take an active role in what is potentially the biggest investment decisions she will ever make—well, it baffles me, particularly because the Silent Partner is usually the one who will still be around in the long run.

In an earlier book I authored, *Financial Strategies for Today's Widow*, I mused over this question at length. After all, the average age of an American widow is fifty-five; nine out of ten husbands will precede their wives in death.

Ultimately, I fear, it is a matter of the male ego. Men tend to see the family finances as their territory; women tend to prefer household harmony to contesting the question.

But contest it they should; ego and outdated gender-role definitions cannot be allowed to endanger anyone's financial future.

Clearly, most people can learn to build their own houses or rewire their home's electrical system (all traditionally male activities, but ones in which women have made significant inroads in the past few decades). There are plenty of how-to books on just about every subject under the sun—including finances. But few take advantage, and those who do, often read just enough to be dangerous to themselves and those they love.

Investing is not a four-minute-mile run; it is a lifetime marathon.

Would you turn over your health care to a person whose knowledge was obtained by watching *ER* on television? Your financial health is at least as important, and far too critical to be based on information learned thirty years ago in a high-school economics class, supplemented by a casual reading of *Money* magazine.

Some of the biggest financial catastrophes I've witnessed came from such "talented amateurs" who based their portfolio decisions on the latest financial-rag headline that touted EIGHT MUTUAL FUNDS TO BUY—RIGHT NOW!

And therein rests the most significant problem of know-it-all investors—simply stated, they *don't*.

Patience Is a Virtue . . .

It's very difficult—for some people, impossible—not to constantly monitor their investments.

It's not uncommon for a client to tell me that he or she has become pathologically compulsive on the issue: they check the market value of their holdings at the opening bell, at the midday reports, and at the closing bell. It is as if they believe that constant vigilance is key to shaping the daily outcome of their accounts.

Vigilance is good; but in plain, nonjudgmental English, this degree of obsession is *nuts*.

Sure—always check any account statements or confirmations you receive carefully to confirm that the broker is playing it straight and not taking advantage of you by, for instance, excessively trading your holdings. Certainly, you want to ensure that your account is being managed, not looted.

But end it there. Don't become overly fixated on the inevitable fluctuations that are the normal up and down of the financial universe. Choose your broker carefully (preferably, based on his ranking in my finding-a-broker test, printed elsewhere in this book). But unless there's a reason not to—and if there is, we're talking about a situation that is far more serious than your fixation with daily ticker prices—you need to trust the professional you hired.

In addition to *being* nuts, excessive focus on daily results will make *other* people nuts, too. For instance, don't fall into the trap of comparing your portfolio's returns to the earnings statement for your most recent certificate of deposit. The professional lifetime of virtually every financial advisor has been themed to the chorus of "I should have put all my money in a bank CD. It's doing so much better than the market."

Well . . . *today,* maybe. Still, it's remarkable how those same people forget how to compare statements after the stock market posts
a 12 percent gain for the year.

Different people can tolerate different levels of risk. As with any
investment, the more risk you take, the higher the potential
return—but the larger the loss if things go south on you.

As a result, in some cases the investment approach that best fits a
specific client's risk tolerance is one that has a measurable, historical
average return—proven, typically, over decades. For the sake of example, let's say a specific investment has averaged a 7 percent annual return.

Work with me here; this may sound far too obvious. That means
that over a long-term, specified period, the investment can be expected to *average* 7 percent. It may be 4 percent in one year, 9 percent in another, and even lose 6 percent some year in the future; the
average is 7 percent.

I take every measure possible to explain this to my clients: in five
of the next ten years, they may actually *lose* money. Be patient. Sadly,
that advice is hard to accept if those five losing years occur consecu-
tively. It's a financial axiom: the markets *will* always test your patience.

But if you have the right blend of risk exposure and asset diversification for your unique financial goals, this kind of fluctuation
shouldn't be a matter of serious concern. A good financial manager
will meet with his clients regularly and advise any needed changes
based on factors that include the realities of the financial marketplace.

Training my clients not to focus on day-by-day performance is
typically the most difficult part of the relationship.

It's hard to pick up the phone and hear a frantic voice ask,
"David—what happened? My account was down last month! What
are you doing about it?"

They are usually a little dismayed at my normal answer: "Let's
do . . . nothing, at least at present." I'll repeat my oft-heard mantra:
"Markets fluctuate over time; here's why it is happening *this* time."

Most are satisfied with the answer. They elect to wait until their
annual review for a full discussion of any possible changes—that is,

changes based on their lives and desires, not the markets' monthly swings.

But others can never relax. They'll call back several times each month—at least, until they learn the lesson of trust.

And trust comes hard to most of us. It is the result of experience, both good and not so good: of surviving the peaks-and-valleys of several investment cycles; of riding out the not-infrequent tempests that blow in for no apparent reason, and blow themselves out in the same way. Only then can we discount the frantic tone of the talking heads on TV, the screaming headlines in the financial publications, and even the frantic chatter of our occasionally doom-speaking friends and families.

It's called "perspective," and for that, time is indeed the best teacher.

NOTE ON SOURCES

The Internet is a wonderful tool for research, as well as a seductive temptress for procrastinators everywhere. During the course of preparing this book, I procrastinated at every opportunity; most writers, faced with the terror of having to fill the day's quota of blank pages, do.

But I also have freely availed myself of the wealth of information that, like a virtual Mississippi, flows across (and, much like the actual Mississippi, occasionally *over*flows) the Net.

Among the most valuable information I found were verbatim transcripts of congressional hearings and the meeting minutes of federal and state agencies, as well as media coverage of those same sessions; the former often served as eye-popping revelations of how much information does *not* make it into the latter, proving time and again the adage "The devil is in the details."

I also data-mined dozens of Internet discussion forums, hundreds of Web blogs, and thousands of Web sites, frequently finding myself alternately impressed, skeptical, or appalled at the scope and accuracy—or lack thereof—of the statements published.

As with every venture into the extractive industries, I came up with far more pyrite—alas, the generic term is *fool's gold*—than pure gold. What nuggets I could confirm occasionally contributed to content in this book.

Not surprisingly, the information that I could *not* verify was often the most colorful or provocative stuff, and it pained me greatly to rule it out of bounds. It's hard when the facts (or the elusiveness of same) get in the way of a good story—but when they did, I left that particular story out.

When needed, I've also interviewed experts to fill the gaps in my own expertise. Occasionally I disputed their opinion—and when, after sober reflection, I still *do,* I say so in this book. But I am also aware that my personal point of view might be skewed by circumstance or personal prejudice, so I've striven mightily to present the occasional opposing view fairly and accurately.

But the overwhelming majority of the material I've covered in this book comes from my own personal experiences and from the stories of thousands of people with whom I've worked as advisor—and more often than not, as a friend—for more than a quarter of a century.

These people often amaze me with their resilience in the face of personal distress, and I've felt their strength of character like the heat from a bonfire as they've fought their way back from adversity that would have left lesser souls crushed to dust.

It is for each of them—and for each of you who have turned to these pages for guidance—that I wrote this book. Thank you for the lessons you have taught me, and God bless each of you.

—David W. Latko
January 2006

INDEX